# Criminal Justice
## Recent Scholarship

Edited by
Marilyn McShane and Frank P. Williams III

A Series from LFB Scholarly

# Feeding the Fear of Crime
## Crime-related Media and Support for Three Strikes

Valerie J. Callanan

LFB Scholarly Publishing LLC
New York 2005

**Library of Congress Cataloging-in-Publication Data**

Callanan, Valerie J., 1956-
  Feeding the fear of crime : crime-related media and support for three
strikes / Valerie J. Callanan.
      p. cm. -- (Criminal justice)
  Includes bibliographical references and index.
  ISBN 1-59332-062-0 (alk. paper)
  1. Fear of crime--United States. 2. Crime--United States--Public
opinion. 3. Criminal justice, Administration of--United States--Public
opinion. 4. Mass media and crime--United States. I. Title. II. Series:
Criminal justice (LFB Scholarly Publishing LLC)
  HV6789.C35 2005
  364.973--dc22

                                        2004019391

ISBN 1-59332-062-0

Printed on acid-free 250-year-life paper.

Manufactured in the United States of America.

# Table of Contents

# Acknowledgements

Many individuals deserve thanks and recognition for the completion of this book, and there are many more than just those listed below. I am fortunate to have worked with many critical scholars and these individuals have helped developed my thinking about crime and justice. Professor Robert Nash Parker at the University of California Riverside encouraged the development of this manuscript, for which I am very grateful, and provided funding for the project through the Presley Institute of Crime and Justice Studies. I also thank him for his helpful guidance and feedback on earlier drafts of this manuscript. Working with Rob was a real pleasure and I am thankful for the opportunity. I also thank Professor Austin Turk of the University of California Riverside for his careful reading of the manuscript as it was being developed, and for helping me shape the research framework. Austin's intellectual approach is the reason I chose a career in criminology.

The research staff at the Social and Behavioral Research Institute at California State University San Marcos was of great assistance in drafting the questionnaire, and they did an excellent job in collecting the data. A special thanks to Director Richard Serpe, Allen Risley, and Lori Large.

The final manuscript could not have been completed without the help of three individuals. I am very grateful to Susan Cratty. She was more of a help than I had a right to expect. She read proofread multiple drafts, procured reference material and worked long hours into the night. I am also grateful to Tammy Booth for helping me put the manuscript together. I could not have done this without her. Thanks also to Patty Cratty, for carefully proofreading.

Finally, I wish to thank my husband, Professor Richard Serpe, for his endless encouragement, patience and support. He read multiple drafts, helped me with technical aspects of this manuscript, and did whatever he could to help me see this project through. Thank you Richard.

This book is dedicated to my parents, Dorothy and Howard.

# Introduction

On June 29, 1992, Kimber Reynolds was shot in the head when two men tried to steal her purse as she exited a California restaurant. She died two days later. Shortly thereafter, the alleged shooter was killed in a gun battle with police. The other assailant pled guilty to robbery and was sentenced to nine years in the state prison, with the possibility of parole after fifty percent of his sentence was served. When Kimber's father, Mike Reynolds, learned of the short sentence he became outraged and vowed to change the sentencing structure.

Within weeks, he had met with members of the criminal justice system and the local media to see if he might be able to craft a new law that would not only significantly increase the sentencing received for habitual violent offenders, but *any* serious repeat offender. He was able to garner support from his state assembly representative and in March 1993, they put forth Assembly Bill 971, which tripled the usual sentence received for any third felony conviction. Assigned to the Public Safety Committee of the Assembly, the bill failed in committee.

Disheartened by the Democratic-controlled legislature, Reynolds decided to attempt to get his proposal on the state ballot for the election in Fall 1993.[1] With his own financing, some funding from the National Rifle Association and the California Correctional Police Officer's Association (more commonly known as the prison guard union), and a direct mailing effort by the Christian Coalition, the process of signature gathering began. After three weeks, he had only collected 15,000 signatures - less than five percent of the minimum required. Then the unimaginable happened.

On October 1, 1993, Polly Klaas, a twelve-year old girl in Petaluma, California, disappeared from her bedroom during a sleep-over at her home. Her grandfather, a former radio disc jockey in San Francisco, immediately took the story to the media. Within hours, Polly's photogenic image was broadcast over the local and national news and regular programming was interrupted with numerous appearances of her grief-stricken family tearfully begging for Polly's safe return. Within days, her disappearance was known internationally. Hundreds of community members and people from all over the country volunteered in the effort to find Polly. The media barrage that followed her disappearance was unprecedented, as was the public outcry that ensued when it was learned that she had been kidnapped and subsequently murdered by a repeat violent offender.

On the day that her murderer, Richard Allen Davis, led police to her body, a media firestorm erupted. A radio station identified Davis as a repeat violent offender and asked listeners to avenge Polly's murder by doing something to change the lax sentencing laws in California – namely, to call Mike Reynolds' office and register support for his proposed three strikes law. Numerous newspapers, radio stations, and television news channels quickly followed suit. Within days, Reynolds' proposition had gathered hundreds of thousands of signatures. The public outrage quickly jelled into the passage of the three strikes proposition by an overwhelming majority of voters, particularly since it was 'spun' as a bill to incapacitate extremely violent repeat offenders.

## NOTES

1. Under California law, citizens can propose legislative changes, which can be placed on a ballot with the requisite number of signatures (5% of all the votes for governor in the previous gubernatorial election. Reynolds needed 385,000 valid signatures).

# CHAPTER 1

# Understanding American Punitive Attitudes

## TRENDS IN PUBLIC OPINION OF CRIME AND CRIME POLICY

Over the last 25 years, public opinion polls have recorded an enormous increase in concern about crime; among Americans, this concern skyrocketed to unprecedented levels in the mid 1990's. For example, only 3% of Americans cited crime and violence as the number one problem in the country in a Gallup poll in 1982. Over the next decade, concern for crime crept upward, reaching 9% in 1993, and jumping to 37% in 1994. Although this unprecedented level of concern was anomalous, and abated somewhat the following years, 20% or more of Americans still cited crime and violence as the number one problem in the country through 1998, in spite of the fact that crime rates dropped dramatically during the mid to late 1990's. Public opinion about drugs and drug abuse has followed a similar trend as public concern about crime. For example, only 2% of Americans listed drugs and drug abuse as the number one problem in a 1982 Gallup poll, but that number shot up to 27% in 1989, declined somewhat in the early 1990's, increased again in the late 1990's, and now stands at 7% in the early 2000's.

As concern about crime and drugs increased over the last 25 years so did a corresponding increase in the fear of crime. Most polls and surveys recorded a dramatic increase in fear of crime, which continued to rise or at best, remained high, even as crime rates began to fall in the early 1990's. During the same time period, these same polls and surveys also reported a growing dissatisfaction with the American criminal justice system, and a rise in the belief that criminals were treated too leniently. For example, in 1994, the year that three strikes was enacted, more than 40% of surveyed respondents stated they had "very little" or "no confidence" in the criminal justice system (Maguire and Pastore, 1995).

In this climate, many politicians, policymakers, and even criminologists began to suggest that fear of crime was driving Americans' punitiveness. Politicians in particular, cited this increase in fear to justify an escalation of punitive crime control legislation that swept the nation in the late 1980's and early 1990's - mandatory sentencing, truth-in-sentencing, sentence enhancements, and three strikes laws, to name but a few (Irwin, Austin and Baird, 1998). Lead by sweeping changes in federal drug laws that stipulated minimum (and often draconian) mandatory sentences for numerous drug offenses, by the beginning of the 1990's almost every state had also implemented some form of mandatory sentencing; about one-third had truth-in-sentencing laws, which stipulate that offenders serve most (usually 85%) of their sentence (Austin, 1996; Cullen, Fisher and Applegate, 2000).

These changes set the tenor for the enormous political and public support for get-tough laws for habitual offenders. Most states adopted some form of minimum mandatory sentencing that disproportionately attached additional years (usually life) to the sentence if the offender had been convicted for at least two prior specified crimes.[1] The political gains from promoting 'three strikes and you're out' were enormous. State politician after state politician proposed these legislative changes - each one attempting to demonstrate they were "tougher on crime" than their political opponents. The wave of this change cannot be minimized. Within a two-year time period (between 1993 and 1995) twenty-four states and the federal government had passed some form of three strikes (Austin et al., 1999; Shichor and Sechrest, 1996).

The rush to sponsor increasingly punitive sentencing is exemplified by the wave of crime control legislation that California legislators sponsored the same year that the three strikes mandatory sentencing was enacted. In 1994, over one hundred crime control bills, such as sentencing enhancements, and more mandatory sentencing laws, were passed by the California legislature. The same year, not one, but two, three strikes laws were approved in California (Kieso, 2003). The first, passed with a nearly unanimous vote of the state legislature in

March 1994, was the most broadly defined three strikes law enacted by any state. Under the law, any offender convicted of *any* type of felony offense automatically receives a minimum of 25 years to life imprisonment if he or she has two prior convictions for violent or *serious* felonies. Unlike other states that had limited the three strikes laws to violent offenders, California's three strikes law was to engender a host of questionable convictions almost from its inception (such as the Santa Monica man whose third serious felony conviction was for stealing a slice of pizza), and the broad contours of the statute are still debated.

Although many view California's three strikes law as 'overkill,' the possibility of overturning the law remains slim because of the second three strikes legislation passed by the voters in November 1994. Mike Reynolds, fearing that future legislators would dismantle or weaken the three strikes bill, continued his push for a ballot proposition even after the legislature had passed the law. Continuing to capitalize on the public outrage that still smoldered about Polly Klaas' murder, her ever-present media image and Reynolds' impassioned pleas mobilized voters. He also collected more campaign money from politicians and gubernatorial candidates, as well as endorsements from the governor, the attorney general, scores of district attorneys and police officials. Virtually everyone running for political office in California in 1994 - whether statewide or local - pledged support for three strikes. By May, Reynolds had collected more than 800,000 voter signatures to have his proposition placed on the November ballot - the most any proposition had ever received, and a record that still stands. Not surprisingly, sold as a law that would eradicate violent offenders from California communities, and as a way to avenge Polly's brutal murder, voters approved the proposition by an overwhelming 78 percent. Consequently, any changes to three strikes legislation now must be approved by two-thirds vote of California legislators, or two-thirds of the voting public - an unlikely prospect at this junction.

## THE POLITICS OF CRIME CONTROL

Although crime control issues were first used in presidential campaigns in the 1960's, Nixon's administration is usually credited with manipulating crime issues to achieve political success[2] (e.g., Beckett,

1997). Since then, politicians have continued to use 'tough on crime' campaigns to their advantage. As politicians discovered the utility of punitive campaign slogans and promises, measured and rational public debate on the issue waned considerably, and all but disappeared during the 1990's. No matter which side of the political spectrum, candidates have discovered that to win the office, and be re-elected, they must stay the course with punitive crime control measures. The specter of the Willie Horton ad campaign, credited with derailing Dukakis' lead in the 1988 presidential campaign (Mendelberg, 1997), cast a pall over any attempts at rational public debate on the issue of crime control. In short, over the last ten to fifteen years, as politicians have discovered both the benefits of using crime policy, and the pitfalls if they do not, a ratchet effect has occurred - politicians race to pass increasingly punitive legislation, and each time they do, it ups the ante for the next politician. The net result is a barrage of legislation over the last two decades that caused the American jail and prison populations to balloon from approximately 200,000 in 1980 to almost 2.2 million in 2003 - prompting one criminologist to state that we seem to be in the grip of a moral panic akin to that of the McCarthy era. As he states, "...then we were convinced there was a communist spy behind every door, now we fear the 'predatory criminal' who has just been released from prison" (Krisberg, 1994:3).

Although there are differences in the crime control promises made dependent on the political office; presidential, senatorial, and gubernatorial candidates appear to use crime issues most often. As Scheingold (1995) notes, promises about crime control delivered to a national audience are largely abstract and symbolic, as crime control is usually handled at the state level. He notes that statewide political candidates also use crime control issues very effectively, as governors and other statewide politicians can push for state legislation, but are not held accountable for crime to the same degree as local politicians, who, as a result of being held accountable, tend to use the issue much more judiciously.

The disproportionate use of crime issues in state and national campaigns means that these messages are more likely to be covered by the mass media. However, as is the case with television campaign advertisements, they are usually presented or examined in a relatively short and superficial manner. The campaign messages that politicians use are usually delivered in quick, snappy sound bites or headlines -

which are more likely to get press coverage (Adatto, 1993). Hence, such slogans as 'three strikes and you're out,' become widely used and quoted. These simple campaign slogans also mesh nicely with the presentation of crime in the mass media. As we will see, both the news media and fictional programming disproportionately attend to crime, and both present distorted images (Dixon and Linz, 2000; Dorfman and Schiraldi, 2001; Graber, 1980; Kooistra, Mahoney and Westervelt, 1998; Randall, Lee-Simmons and Hagner, 1988). Crime is typically one of the leading topics in local television news, radio programming, and newspapers; and is even more likely to lead if the crime is particularly gruesome, involves a celebrity, or is unusual in some other aspect. Violent crimes, especially heinous murders, are the most likely story to lead - particularly if it is a random act of senseless violence perpetrated against a helpless and innocent victim. Hence, stories about grandmothers being raped and strangled in their homes are more likely to capture the headlines than other types of 'everyday' murders, such as an argument between friends that escalated out of control. Yet, elderly women are least at risk of being murdered than any other age/gender group. Moreover, of all the crimes committed annually, murder is by far the least likely Index crime to occur. Currently, the chances of being murdered are approximately 5.6 out of 100,000 - a very low number. Moreover, this risk is not distributed evenly across the population, but varies significantly by gender, age, race/ethnicity, social class, and location. In reality, middle-class, middle-aged or older Americans have a greater chance of being struck by lightening than of being murdered in their homes by strangers.

But this only demonstrates one small problem with crime news coverage. Even if the media were to present a more realistic picture of homicide, it would still distort the reality of crime in America. Homicide represents less than one-half of one percent of all the Index crimes committed in 2002 as reported in the Uniform Crime Reports; and only one percent of the Violent Crimes index. Yet, it is the most likely crime to be presented in the news media.

The sheer amount of news coverage devoted to crime far outstrips most other types of issues, and grew significantly during the 1990's. According to the Center for Media and Public Affairs, a non-partisan non-profit organization that monitors the media, the number of crime stories on national television news broadcasts nearly quadrupled from

1990 to 1995 - from 757 to 2,574. Research has found that the public believes that crime levels are the same *or worse* than what is presented in the media (Parisi et al., 1979). Not surprisingly, surveys conducted in 1993 and 1994 found that almost 90% of respondents thought crime was rising and at an all time high, even though crime, particularly violent crime, had already started to decline (Maguire and Pastore, 1995; 1996).

Clearly, what the public sees on the television news are the least likely types of crimes to be committed. The nature of these crime stories engenders public outrage about criminals and criminal punishment. After all, random acts of violence that happen to completely innocent victims *is* frightening - and apt to make individuals demand that *something* be done about the crime problem.

Consequently, the simplistic political messages used by politicians resonate with their audiences because the messages correspond with the depiction of crime and crime control presented in the news media and entertainment programming. Simply put, crime issues capture the attention of the American public because of the sensational nature of crime presented in the media. This sensationalism elevates fear of crime, especially of violent and predatory strangers, and increases demand that something be done about the problem. Politicians respond to the outcry, as it is an uncontroversial campaign platform. After all, being 'tough on crime' is a vague promise. Any crime control legislation or increased funding for law enforcement and other criminal justice agencies can be used as evidence of being responsive to public concern about crime. Moreover, there is little, if any, political opposition to a tough on crime stance. Those who dare to suggest that the crime control policies are flawed are quickly branded 'soft on crime' or as champions of criminals by their political opponents, a tactic used by Governor Pete Wilson when he successfully pushed for three strikes legislation in early 1994 (Kieso, 2003).

Because most people are ill informed about crime and crime control issues, these messages become part of the public's understanding about crime, and form the foundation for a deceptively simple approach to the problem - hence 'do the crime, do the time.' The problem is on relying on the general public's understanding of crime and crime policy. Studies find that the vast majority of Americans are unaware of changes in crime trends, overestimate the prevalence of violent crime, do not understand most alternatives to imprisonment, are unaware of recent changes or additions to crime legislation, and greatly underestimate the amount of sentencing lengths convicted felons receive.[3,4] Many in the public also appear to have a very narrow image of criminals – that of physically unattractive, unemployed gang members.[5] They are also pessimistic about rehabilitation,[6] grossly overestimate recidivism rates, and believe that judges are too lenient on offenders.

Nevertheless, numerous polls and surveys ask relatively simple questions to a generally unaware public - and then find that the public is 'punitive.' The irony in these findings is this so-called punitiveness is often used by politicians and government officials to justify increasingly harsh crime control legislation.[7] Yet, these polls suffer from a number of conceptual and methodological issues that make this punitive stance questionable.

## PROBLEMS WITH PRIOR RESEARCH ON PUBLIC OPINION OF CRIME AND CRIME POLICY

The numerous polls and surveys which have followed public opinion about crime and the criminal justice system for decades,[8] have narrowly focused on a handful of issues - fear of crime, the police, the criminal courts, and punishment of criminal offenders. Although sentencing and parole issues have generated the largest number of studies and polls in public opinion research of crime-related issues, many have failed to examine attitudes about criminal punishment with much detail or specificity. As noted, most Americans know little about the criminal justice system; moreover, their opinions about sentencing and correctional policies are much less informed than their views about other components of the justice system, such as law enforcement or the courts (Flanagan and Caulfield, 1984). Consequently, past surveys of criminal sentencing have asked questions about policies for which Americans have very little knowledge.

Nevertheless, because crime often engenders an emotive response, most respondents readily offer an opinion (Durham, 1993). Not only are they much more likely to render an opinion about correctional policy than other issues about crime (Roberts and Stalans, 1997), but they are also much more confident about these opinions (Roberts and Doob, 1990). But these responses are suspect, considering that what the public 'knows' about crime and crime policy is thought to be heavily influenced by the mass media (Roberts and Doob, 1990; Roberts and Stalans, 1997). Research on public opinion of crime policy is also flawed by the superficial methods in which opinions are gathered. As Cullen et al. note, "complex opinions cannot be measured if complex questions are not used" (2000:7). Typically, simple single-item close-ended questions are used to assess public support for various criminal sentences; worse, in many cases, only one or two questions are asked. As research on public opinion methodology finds, this type of question format tends to evoke off-the-cuff responses that do not capture the full range of attitudes and beliefs about the issue at hand (Durham, 1989; Innes, 1993). This is particularly important if we are to accurately assess public opinion of crime and crime policies. Simple global assessments of support for various crime policies tend to evoke very punitive responses, which may be more reflective of malaise with societal changes, alienation, or disappointment with government rather than real opinions about specific criminal sentencing (Innes, 1993; Thomson and Ragona, 1987). As such, many respondents are quick to agree with statements such as "criminals get off too easy." Yet, when individuals are given more information about the issues at hand, such as costs of imprisonment and long-term societal consequences, and when individuals are allowed to consider a full range of alternatives to incarceration (such as probation, restitution, or electronic monitoring), they tend to provide more reasoned and less punitive responses (Applegate and Cullen, 1996; Doble, 1987; Hough and Roberts, 1999; Keil and Vito, 1991; Roberts and Doob, 1990; Thomson and Ragona, 1987; Warr, Meier, and Erickson, 1983).

Many surveys use rather crude measures, such as questions that present the issue in simple dichotomies. For example, most public opinion polls and surveys have focused on the purpose of prisons by posing correctional policy as a dichotomy between rehabilitation and punishment. This dual theme of punishment and reform has been widely surveyed for many years, and has led to the oft-cited belief that Americans favor punishment over rehabilitation. However, when respondents are asked to choose from a longer list of reasons to imprison, most support rehabilitation as well as other reasons, such as deterrence or incapacitation; far less support for retribution and punishment is found (Gerber and Engelhardt-Greer, 1996; Thomson and Ragona, 1987), particularly when prison is juxtaposed against early intervention as an effective crime reduction measure (Cullen et al., 1998). Moreover, when incarceration costs are provided, support for incarceration drops even further, especially for lengthy prison terms (Roberts and Stalans, 1997). Research has also found that the terminology used in questioning can make a large difference. For example, when offenders are referred to as "criminals" the public responds more punitively than when they are referred to as "prisoners." Thus, support for in-prison programs increase when it is clear to the respondent that the alleged offender is behind bars (e.g., Cullen et al., 1990; McCorkle, 1993). Similarly, polls that find the greatest support for rehabilitation, do not use the actual word "rehabilitation," but instead, use something akin to "teaching people how to be law-abiding citizens" (Innes, 1993).

Public opinion research on specific mandatory sentencing policies also suffers from lack of detail in survey questions. Typically, respondents are asked whether they agree that a specific policy, such as three strikes sentencing, should be mandated for repeat criminals, without giving much (if any) information about the crime and/or the offender's history. This can also skew respondents' punitive responses - research shows that without specific information, respondents envision the worst type of crime and the worst type of offender (e.g., Brillon, 1988; Roberts and Doob, 1990; Sprott, 1998; Stalans and Diamond, 1990). Consequently, their responses make them appear more punitive than they would be with a more 'typical' offender. Not surprisingly, surveys that ask about sentencing severity that fail to address offender and offense specifics document an overwhelmingly and increasingly punitive response to offenders (Durham, 1993; Roberts, 1992; Zimmerman, Alstyne and Dunn, 1988).

Not much information is known about the determinants of punitiveness. In general, with the notable exception of public opinion regarding the death penalty, which has been widely surveyed, the literature on public punitiveness and its determinants have been largely contained to crime seriousness, offender history, and sociodemographic characteristics of the respondents (including religiosity and political ideology).

Research on public opinion of criminal sentencing has consistently found that crime seriousness and criminal record are the two most important variables determining sentence severity. Crime seriousness speaks to the idea of proportionality in punishment - the more serious the offense, the lengthier the sentence deserved. Numerous studies have found that the single most important predictor of public opinion of punishment is the seriousness of the alleged crime (Blumstein and Cohen, 1980; Samuel and Moulds, 1986; Thomas, Cage and Foster, 1976).

The alleged offender's past criminal history also has a large influence on punitiveness. For example, research has documented that support for rehabilitation falls dramatically and sentencing severity and/or length of prison sentence increases if the offender is a repeat offender (e.g., Applegate and Cullen, 1996; Blumstein and Cohen, 1980; Finkel et al., 1996). The public simply does not believe that rehabilitation is a viable alternative for recidivists. Nevertheless, as Roberts and Stalans (1997) note, this does not mean that public support for increasingly harsh penalties is without limit. For example, in one study respondents were asked to suggest prison terms for a repeat offender with six priors, in which information about the alleged offender and the 'trial' were manipulated (Finkel et al., 1996). In all but one scenario, the sentencing length suggested was lower than that required by law. The only condition under which respondents suggested dramatically longer terms was when subjects were told that under the state recidivist statute, the offender was eligible for "life without the possibility of parole," *and* the prosecution labeled the offender as a recidivist the state had a right to punish severely (with no counter-argument from the defense). Even with these conditions, less than five percent of the subjects suggested that the offender receive life imprisonment. It appears that the public does desire lengthier sentences for repeat offenders. But clearly, the extent of their punitive response is conditional on numerous factors.

Those that study public opinion of crime policy have spoken of the importance of media in influencing punitiveness. Yet, the research of media impact on public opinion of crime policy has been rather limited. Only a handful of studies have empirically tested the impact of media on public opinion of crime sentencing, and these were relatively simple tests that did not adequately control for a variety of other factors known to influence public opinion of sentencing.

Most research on crime-related media focuses on content and the distortion of crime. Such studies typically compare the amount of actual crime (usually reported crime), or specific types of crime, to that which is portrayed by the various media (e.g., Dominick, 1973). Other content analyses compare the reality of the criminal justice system to that which is shown on television (e.g., Crew, 1990). These content analyses consistently document the distortion of crime and crime control presented in the media. Depiction of sentencing is similarly unrealistic. For example, a study of newspapers found that the vast majority of stories covered violent offenders who were sentenced to prison, although the majority of offenders are not violent and receive other forms of penalties, such as probation or fines (Doob and Roberts, 1988). As Hough and Roberts note, the media present a "steady stream of stories about sentencing *mal*practices...when lenient sentences are passed, the attention given to them, and the editorial comment on them, tend to be shrill" (1999:23).

Because the media distortion is so extreme, many researchers suggest that heavy consumption of crime-related media must affect individuals' attitudes and beliefs about crime, specifically fear of crime. Although the research has been sharply criticized on a number of grounds - primarily methodological - most studies do find that crime-related media consumption is related to fear of crime. However, in spite of the oft-made claim that fear of crime is driving Americans' punitiveness, only a handful of studies have theoretically examined the role that fear of crime plays in public opinion of criminal justice policies. Those that do suggest the relationship between fear of crime and punitiveness are not so simplistic. For example, recent studies of aggregate level data suggest that other factors, such as political manipulation, propel crime issues to the fore of public opinion. The ensuing law and order legislation that is passed, in turn, elevates fear of crime among the general public and a corresponding demand for increased punitiveness (Beckett, 1997; Irwin et al., 1998).

This book examines support for a specific penalty - California's three strikes law that mandates 25 years to life in prison for an offender convicted of any felony following two prior convictions for serious crimes. Unlike prior research of public opinion of three strikes laws and other similar forms of mandatory sentencing for repeat offenders (e.g., Tyler and Boeckmann, 1997), the study design allows for a close examination of support for three strikes along two dimensions - the severity of the crime and the type of crime committed - to ascertain where majority support for three strikes begins to erode. The focus of the study, however, is not to determine where support for three strikes sentencing wanes, but to examine in detail, the determinants of support for three strikes. In general, this study aims to understand the relative importance of determinants of punitiveness - and specifically, the influence of different forms of crime-related media. This research provides an important test of the assumptions that fear of crime and crime-related media consumption increase punitiveness. It also examines the impact of media consumption on the constellation of other beliefs and attitudes about crime largely thought important to punitiveness. Also, this study is unique because it compares the relative influence of specific forms of crime-related media on punitiveness and it also compares these effects between Whites, Latinos, and African Americans, which has never been done before in this context.

This study, however, is not a detailed examination of the process of mediated reality about crime and crime policy - for example, how people process information about crime, how people construct images of criminals, or even how the media construct these images. Nor is it a detailed examination of California's three strikes law - for example, its political history, its effects, its criticisms, and so forth.[9] Instead, this study uses support for three strikes as a means to understand the determinants of punitiveness - that is, what increases the probability that a given respondent will support harsher punishment. We start with an overview of prior research on public opinion of criminal sentencing, and review the literatures on fear of crime, and crime-related media.

## NOTES

1. Most states also have provisions in the statute that allow for sentence enhancements for 'second strikers.'
2. A growing body of literature suggests three 'wedge issues' were used by Nixon's campaign: crime control, welfare reform, and affirmative action. Critics charge these issues were used to appeal to racist Southern White Democrats disenchanted with the changes issued in with the Civil Rights movement (Beckett, 1997; Tonry, 1998).
3. Ignorance about crime control policy is not limited to the American public. Studies find that the public in many Western industrialized countries are similarly unaware of crime and crime policy (e.g., Hough and Roberts, 1999).

4. See Roberts, 1992; Roberts and Stalans, 1997; Roberts et al., 2003 for a review of the research.

5. There is often a racial undertone to this stereotype. For example, one-third of respondents in a 1993 Gallup poll believed that African Americans were more likely to commit crimes than any other race/ethnic group, and other surveys show similar results (Roberts and Stalans, 1998). Surveys also document that Whites have much higher fear of Black strangers than they do White; this fear may be exacerbated by racial prejudice (St. John and Heald-Moore, 1995).

6. The general public does have more optimistic views about the potential of juvenile offenders to desist from criminal behavior (e.g., Applegate, Cullen and Fisher, 1997).

7. Recent work focusing on the political manipulation of crime suggests politicians create or exacerbate the public's fear, not merely respond to it (Beckett, 1997). Others question whether public opinions really matter in policy decision-making (e.g., Durham, 1993).

8. According to Roberts and Stalans, (1997) the first empirical study of public opinion of sentencing was conducted almost one hundred years ago.

9. For a comprehensive overview of the political history of California's three strikes law see *California's Three Strikes Law: The Undemocratic Production of Injustice* (Kieso, 2003), available on-line at www.facts1.com.

CHAPTER 2

# Public Opinion of Criminal Sentencing

This chapter reviews the research on public opinion of criminal sentencing. It begins with a brief overview of the research that is followed by theoretical explanations for punitiveness. This chapter highlights the research on the relationship between beliefs about crime and experiences with crime, including fear of crime, on punitive attitudes. s theoretical arguments are reviewed, the hypotheses to be tested will be presented.

## PRIOR RESEARCH ON PUBLIC OPINION OF CRIMINAL SENTENCING

The early literature on public opinion of criminal justice punishments focused largely on capital punishment. Death penalty attitudes are the most researched issue of public opinion of criminal justice policy, and have been widely surveyed for decades.[1] Many studies of death penalty opinions find that attitudes are based more on emotions and symbolism than on reason (Ellsworth and Gross, 1994; Ellsworth and Ross, 1983; Tyler and Weber, 1982); see Haddock and Zanna's modification, (1998). This is not surprising given the moral and/or religious foundation that individuals often invoke to either justify or condemn the taking of human life, whether state sanctioned or not. Consequently, those who may be strong supporters of three strikes, even for less serious offenses, may not uphold the taking of another's life. It is erroneous, therefore, to assume that the correlates and determinants of death penalty support would be the same for sentencing preferences.

In the 1970's and 1980's, research on public opinion of crime and crime policy expanded in many ways. First, more attention was paid to assessing the extent and magnitude of public punitiveness and correlating these attitudes with other factors such as fear of crime or criminal victimization (e.g., Cullen et al., 1985; Seltzer and McCormick, 1987; Taylor, Scheppele and Stinchcombe, 1979; Thomas and Foster, 1975). Second, the research widened to include other issues such as assessment of law enforcement and judicial effectiveness, the support for rehabilitation, and support for other sentencing policies and laws (e.g., Thomas et al., 1976; Warr, 1982; Zimmerman et al., 1988). Third, studies also became more sophisticated in their design. For example, rather than using simple global measures (e.g., "do you support the death penalty for murderers?"), many researchers used a series of vignettes that manipulated offender and offense characteristics (e.g., Rossi, Simpson and Miller, 1985; Rossi and Berk, 1997). Ellsworth and Ross (1983) examined how support for capital punishment changed with more specific wording and information, and asked why respondents supported or opposed the punishment. In general, these studies began to find that the public is punitive, but selectively so. For example, death penalty researchers found that many respondents were willing to endorse absolute incapacitation (life without the possibility of parole) as an acceptable alternative to capital punishment, as long as the offender was guaranteed to remain behind bars (see Cullen, et al., 2000 for review).

Research in the late 1980's and 1990's continued to investigate methodological issues, but also turned to examining the importance of public opinion on the behavior of criminal justice system officials and politicians (Beckett, 1997; Cullen et al., 1985; Ouimet and Coyle, 1991). Studies of this nature find that politicians use concern and fear of crime in an effort to gain public support and in doing so, fuel concern and fear among the public. They also suggest that criminal justice officials seem to respond to what they think the public desires. Some suggest however, that policymakers overestimate the public's degree of punitiveness (e.g., Gottfredson, Warner and Taylor, 1988; Whitehead, Blankenship and Wright, 1999).

As seen, research on public opinion of crime and crime sentencing has expanded in many directions. Currently, work continues on developing more sophisticated methods and surveys to better capture the nuances of public punitiveness; and the development of more complex models to ascertain the determinants of punitiveness. However, no one has yet conducted a study of the relative influence of crime-related media consumption on punitive attitudes at the individual level, especially with a complex model that controls for a large number of other factors believed to influence punitiveness. The following section outlines these factors.

## THEORETICAL VIEWS OF PUBLIC OPINION OF CRIMINAL SENTENCING

There are several theoretical viewpoints in the literature to explain public attitudes toward sentencing and punishment. One line of argumentation links punitive attitudes to fear of crime. Increased fear is hypothesized to increase punitive attitudes toward criminal offenders. In turn, fear of crime, is influenced by personal victimization, neighborhood levels of crime, vicarious victimization (received primarily through mass media), political exploitation of criminal justice issues, and the presentation of crime news in the media.

The second body of inquiry focuses on the attribution of criminal behavior or what people believe about crime causation. As Cullen et al (1985:310) note, "how people explain crime will affect what they want done about it." They found that explanations about criminal behavior were strongly related to preferences for criminal sentencing. Most of this type of research has largely centered on the political, moral, and religious beliefs of individuals because explanations for criminality appear rooted in these beliefs. For example, political conservatives are thought to be more punitive in their responses toward criminal offenders because they believe that individuals have free will to choose their course of action. Consequently, they believe punishment is both deserved and serves as a deterrent against future offending. In contrast, political liberals are less punitive because they tend to view crime as a manifestation of underlying social problems, which are not addressed by punishing individual offenders (Scheingold, 1984).

A third area of explanation focuses on beliefs about crime control, specifically, the efficacy of the criminal justice system. For example, if people believe the courts are too lenient or that rehabilitation efforts do not work, they are more likely to support mandatory sentencing, and longer prison sentences (Hough and Roberts, 1999). In turn, people's beliefs about the criminal justice system are influenced by a variety of factors, most notably the mass media, as some hypothesize.

A fourth area of inquiry focuses on the sociodemographic correlates and socio-psychological attributes related to punitive attitudes. For example, research on death penalty support has been linked to race prejudice (Barkan and Cohn, 1994; Borg, 1997; Soss, Langbein and Metelko, 2003), religiosity (Moran and Comfort, 1986), political ideology (Tyler and Weber, 1982) and authoritarianism (Vidmar, 1974), and to other sociodemographic variables such as gender and race. Most of these studies find significant race and gender differences - Whites and men are more likely to support the death penalty - and the relationship to social class is curvilinear. Those with very low levels and very high levels of educational attainment are the most opposed to capital punishment (e.g., Longmire, 1996). However, research on support for other types of criminal punishment is not so consistent about the effects of gender and social class, although studies repeatedly find that other race/ethnic groups are significantly less punitive than Whites.

The following section explores these four areas of inquiry in more detail. Relevant hypotheses are presented after each section. The model used in this analysis is very complex, and can be viewed in figure 4.1. While the model displays unidirectional causation, it is highly probable that most effects are circular, particularly the effects of media. For example, media affects what people believe about crime, and what people believe about crime in turn, has impact on the specific media they attend to. But given the complexity of the model, we could not test for feedback loops.

## *Sociodemographic Correlates*

With the exception of capital punishment attitudes, research on demographic correlates of punitiveness has usually produced weak and inconsistent results (Cullen et al., 1985; Langworthy and Whitehead, 1986; McCorkle, 1993; Stinchcombe et al., 1980; Tyler and Weber, 1982).[2] Two consistent themes appear in the literature: 1) consistent sociodemographic differences in death penalty opinions and 2) sociodemographic correlates of criminal punishment other than capital punishment vary depending on the specific penalty (or criminal justice

justice policy), type of criminal activity, or type of offender respondents are asked to judge.

For example, while most studies of death penalty attitudes consistently find less support among women (Blumstein and Cohen, 1980; Cullen et al., 1985; Ellsworth and Gross, 1994; Keil and Vito, 1991, Longmire, 1996), studies of attitudes toward other criminal sentencing policies find weaker gender effects (Stinchcombe et al., 1980). It appears the effects of gender on sentencing length opinions vary according to the specific crime. For example, one survey of six crimes that ranged from petty theft to homicide found that men and women only differed with respect to punishment for murderers; women supported longer sentences (Samuel and Moulds, 1986). Similarly, other studies have found that women support longer sentences for sex offenders, and person offenses (Newman and Trilling, 1975); others find that men endorse longer sentences for violent offenders than do women (Blumstein and Cohen, 1980).

More recent research suggests that women are significantly more punitive than men. For example, they are more likely to think that adult sentencing is too lenient (Sprott, 1999), less likely to support parole for serious offenders, and half as likely than men to think prisoners' sentences should be reduced (Flanagan, 1996b; Haghighi and Lopez, 1998). However, women appear to believe more strongly in the potential of rehabilitation than do men (Cullen et al., 1985; Haghighi and Lopez, 1998), especially if the intervention efforts start early, or if the offender is a juvenile (Sprott, 1999).

Other sociodemographic factors such as education, income, and age also have varying results. Some find strong evidence that higher levels of education are associated with lower sentencing lengths (e.g., Rossi and Berk, 1997), although some find education has no effect (Cullen et al., 1985; Flanagan, 1996b; Gerber and Engelhardt-Greer, 1996). Some studies find the influence of education varies depending on the type of crime a respondent is being asked to judge. For example, Samuel and Moulds (1986) found a positive relationship between respondents' education and suggested sentencing length for armed robbery, but educational attainment made no difference in suggested sentencing for the other five crimes respondents were asked to assess.

The effects of income on punitiveness also differ by types of offenses. Some studies find that on average, those with higher income support lengthier penalties for property crimes, but income appears to make little difference in sentencing preferences for violent crimes (e.g., Flanagan, 1996b). Yet, Samuel and Moulds (1986) found the exact opposite - income made little difference in preferred sentencing lengths for property offenders, but those with higher incomes supported lengthier sentences for armed robbers. Others find that income has no impact on respondents' sentencing opinions (Cullen et al., 1985; Rossi and Berk, 1997).

Some studies find older respondents are less punitive toward street criminals compared to middle-aged respondents (Blumstein and Cohen, 1980; Rossi and Berk, 1997), although others find the relationship between age and punitiveness is positive (Cullen et al., 1985; Haghighi and Lopez, 1998). In general, it appears that older respondents are more punitive of drug-related crimes than are younger respondents (Rossi and Berk, 1997).

Taken together, these studies suggest that the type of crime is most salient in public punitiveness. This resonates with Boydell and Grindstaff's (1974) study that found no effects of gender, income, education, and age differences on preferred sentencing lengths for serious violent offenders. They suggested that punitive attitudes toward violent offenders are so strong across all segments of society they render the effects of sociodemographic correlates inconsequential.

Most public opinion research on sentencing that examines the differences between race/ethnic groups has focused on the death penalty, primarily differences between African Americans and Whites. Studies of this nature have consistently documented that Blacks are far less likely to support the death penalty (e.g., Bohm 1991; Hindelang, 1973; Longmire, 1996; Taylor et al., 1979). The few studies that have examined race differences in support for other types of criminal sanctions have found no clear pattern of consensus or disagreement for various types and lengths of criminal sentencing, although African Americans and Whites tend to agree on the relative seriousness of offenses (Blumstein and Cohen, 1980). Some find that Blacks are less punitive compared to Whites (Blumstein and Cohen, 1980; Browning and Cao, 1992; Stinchcombe et al., 1980; Surette, 1985); yet others find that race does not have much of an impact (Flanagan, 1996b; Rossi and Berk, 1997). For example, Samuel and Moulds (1986) found race differences for only one crime out of six - Whites and Latinos suggested longer sentences for armed robbers than did Blacks.

There is some evidence of a growing convergence between Black and White attitudes (Secret and Johnson, 1989). It appears that Blacks have grown more punitive over time, while Whites' punitiveness has declined slightly or remained relatively stable. Secret and Johnson analyzed NORC data from 1980 to 1986 and found that, in 1985 and 1986, African Americans were more likely to support increased government spending to combat drugs than they were in the early 1980's. Moreover, in 1986, more Blacks (5%) agreed with the statement that courts were not harsh enough on criminals compared to 1980, but Whites were less likely to agree that courts were not harsh enough, although the percentage decrease was small (2%). Nevertheless, even though African Americans appeared to be growing more punitive, they are still much less likely to support the death penalty than Whites (Ellsworth and Gross, 1994).

African Americans are also more likely to perceive the criminal justice system as discriminatory and unjust (Hagan and Albonetti, 1982; Macmillan, Wortley and Hagan, 1997; Wortley, 1996), and have more negative ratings of the police (Maguire and Pastore, 2000). This may explain why African Americans are not as punitive as Whites, even though they have significantly higher levels of fear and direct victimization. Since they are more likely to live in high crime areas than are Whites, they may be less likely to hold punitive attitudes, regardless of levels of fear and direct criminal victimization, because they are more likely to be the recipients of suppressive crime control policies (Stinchcombe et al., 1980).[3] Thus, one would also expect to find that African Americans are more supportive of rehabilitation, as some studies have found (McCorkle, 1993). Nevertheless, as with Whites, punitive attitudes among Blacks appear to have increased over the last two decades, although the effects appear mediated by class and gender (Macmillan et al., 1997; Sasson, 1995).

While the above studies have focused on differences between Blacks and Whites, few academic studies have examined Latino attitudes of sentencing policies. Rossi and Berk (1997) compared public preferences with the federal sentencing guidelines, using a nationally representative sample of households in which respondents were weighted to mirror the most recent census data. Although they found Latinos tended to prefer shorter sentences for street crimes and were less likely to support life sentences than Whites, these statistically significant differences did not hold when they added political views and respondents' experiences with the criminal justice system into the model (as was the case for Black respondents).

Most information about Latino attitudes toward crime and the criminal justice system come from public opinion polls; a large portion has focused on perceptions of the police. Harris and Gallup polls conducted in the early 1990's found that Latinos sometimes hold views similar to Whites, sometimes their views are similar to that of Blacks, and sometimes their views lie between the two (Roberts and Stalans, 1997). In general, Latinos were more negative than Whites in their perceptions of police honesty, integrity, fairness and respect for community members, as were Blacks. However, Latinos were more likely than Blacks to rate the police positively, as did Whites, when asked about law enforcement's ability to prevent or solve crimes, their overall helpfulness (Roberts and Stalans, 1997), or their ability to protect the community's people and property (Davis, 1990). A recent comparison of White, Latino and Black assessment of police performance in Texas found similar results: compared to Blacks, Latinos and Whites hold similarly positive views of police quality of service, honesty, friendliness, professional knowledge and conduct, and ability to prevent or fight crime. Latino ratings of police fairness and politeness were between those of White and Black assessments (Cheurprakobkit, 2000).

Given their social structural position, their perception of unfairness among the police, and other assessments of police performance that lie between Whites and African Americans, it seems reasonable to hypothesize that Latinos will hold attitudes about criminal sentencing more similar to Blacks than Whites. Thus, in terms of support for three strikes, Blacks should be the least supportive, Latinos moderately supportive, and Whites the most supportive of all.

Prior research suggests that the relationship between sociodemographic correlates and attitudes toward criminal punishment is not straightforward, but dependent on the interaction of factors such as gender, race/ethnicity, social class, education, income, and the like (e.g., Blumstein and Cohen, 1980). For example, Hindelang (1973) found that White, male Republicans with only a grade school education were the most punitive group in his study. More than two decades later, Longmire's (1996) study of death penalty attitudes using a nationally representative sample found similar results (the level of education was different). However, because they are not the theoretical focus of this study, formal hypotheses about sociodemographic correlates are not included, except for race. Given the paucity of research on Latino opinions of the criminal justice system, this study is uniquely positioned to examine Latino views on a number of opinions about crime and criminal justice policies. In short, as presented below, Latinos are hypothesized to be less punitive than Whites, but more punitive than Blacks.

| | |
|---|---|
| *Hypothesis 1:* | *Whites are more supportive of three strikes than African Americans and Latinos.* |
| *Hypothesis 2:* | *Latinos are less supportive of three strikes compared to Whites, but more supportive than African Americans, who are the least likely to support three strikes.* |

## Beliefs about Crime and the Criminal Justice System

Many studies of beliefs about crime focus on how individuals rate the seriousness of specific crimes, usually in terms of their harmful effects. Others focus their attention on public opinion of the efficacy of the criminal justice system and how this influences punitiveness; some examine beliefs about overall crime rates and how these beliefs are correlated with support for sentencing policies. This section reviews the literature on beliefs about the seriousness of crime, beliefs about crime trends, and the purpose of imprisonment on punitiveness.

### Crime Seriousness

Studies have consistently found that crime seriousness is the most important predictor of punitiveness (Blumstein and Cohen, 1980; Gebotys and Roberts, 1987; Hamilton and Rytina, 1980; Newman and Trilling, 1975; Rossi et al., 1985). Public ratings of crime seriousness have been widely surveyed for decades, although earlier work was primarily centered on methodological issues (e.g., Coombs, 1967) such as constructing and using indices of offense seriousness. The classic work by Sellin and Wolfgang (1964) is widely noted for its development of a reliable index measure of offense seriousness. The work stimulated a spate of replications that tested crime seriousness measures as well as research into substantive issues, such as the meaning of crime seriousness opinions, their relationship to other criminal justice issues, and how such judgments are made.

Most studies of public opinion of crime seriousness use brief vignettes that describe a particular crime (often devoid of victim and offender characteristics, intent and culpability). Respondents are then asked to rate the seriousness of the behavior described. Seriousness is undefined, as these studies assume people have a common and simple understanding - seriousness is the amount of harm inflicted, (although many argue that the relative consensus found across sociodemographic groups is evidence of normative consensus).

Warr (1989) argues there are two dimensions of importance to crime seriousness ratings - harmfulness or wrongfulness. Harmfulness is usually thought of as the amount of harm done to the victim, whether physical, monetary, or psychological. But harm can also be construed as the harm done to a community or society. Wrongfulness is a judgment about how much the behavior is seen as a disruption, or affront to the moral code. The salience of each dimension is dependent on the features of the criminal event being assessed.

Interestingly, Warr found that about one-quarter of his sample did not distinguish degrees of 'wrongfulness' by crime types. For this group, all crime was morally wrong, consequently, the seriousness of the crime varied only by the amount of harm inflicted. The others in the sample differed in their assessment of 'wrongfulness' dependent on the criminal act. The more serious crimes (violent crimes) were seen as both wrong and harmful.

Intention is another dimension of wrongfulness that researchers believe impacts assessments of the seriousness of a given behavior. If an individual does not intend to do harm, then respondents are probably more likely to perceive the behavior as less serious, regardless of the harm inflicted. Interestingly, some have found that the offender's intent to commit harm does not appear to influence the assessment of seriousness. For example, Riedel (1975) found that only the consequences of the action mattered to respondents. However, subsequent research has found modest correlations between intent and seriousness (Gebotys and Dasgupta, 1987), especially when the respondent is free to impute intent. Studies of this ilk find that respondents are more likely to assume violent offenders intended to do harm; consequently, these actions are also ranked as much more serious relative to other offenses (Roberts and Stalans, 1997). This is important because it hints at another possible influence of media. Since news media reports of violent crimes are usually decontextualized, viewers are more likely to believe the crime was intentional. Over time, more exposure to this type of information should escalate an individual's assessment of the seriousness of crime.

A review of crime seriousness studies shows that while absolute seriousness ratings of specific crimes may fluctuate over time, the ranking of these crimes relative to others does not.[4] Cross-sectional studies find fairly consistent agreement about the relative ranking of crime severity across various race, gender, social class, age and occupation groups (Rossi, Bose, and Berk, 1974; Sellin and Wolfgang, 1964; Warr, 1989), and between victims and non-victims of crime (Rossi et al., 1974), but there are slight differences between subgroups. For example, Rossi et al. (1974), found that women were more likely to rank rape as the most serious crime (followed by homicide), whereas men ranked homicide as most serious (followed by rape). Moreover, while there is local consensus across most groups regarding the seriousness of person offenses, there is some disagreement concerning property crimes, victimless crimes, and white-collar/corporate crimes; although again, most research suggests these differences are not large (Carlson and Williams, 1993; Cullen, Link and Polanzi, 1982; Rauma, 1991; Rossi et al., 1974; Thomas et al., 1976).

This apparent consensus may be due, in part, to measurement problems. For example, Gottfredson et al. (1988) argue that crime seriousness has many dimensions reflective of both type of crime and the harm inflicted from the crime - and groups vary significantly in their assessments of these dimensions. In their comparison of six groups (lawyers and judges, students, police, prison guards, parole officers and inmates) they found large differences between groups - students rated all crimes as more serious than any other group, and inmates rated property crimes, major drug offenses, and offenses involving physical injury as much less serious than any other group.

Similarly, Miethe (1984) found that scales that sum items of different crime types tend to mask differences structured by sociodemographic factors. He found a high degree of consensus on perceived seriousness of violent crimes (rated most serious) and for public order crimes (rated least serious), but more disagreement for property and white-collar crimes, which fell in the middle range of seriousness ratings. Because the extreme ends of seriousness scales are the areas with the highest degree of consensus, real differences between African Americans and Whites are diminished.

While the relative ranking and rating of specific crime types is fairly consistent between various sociodemographic groups, overall assessments of crime seriousness find some evidence of slight disagreement. For example, in studies that use the mean scores across all crime types surveyed, crime seriousness ratings are higher for African Americans than Whites (Miethe, 1984; Rossi et al., 1974; Rauma, 1991), for those with less formal education (Miethe, 1984; Rossi et al., 1974), and for political conservatives (Rossi et al., 1974); although again, these differences are not large.

Despite different methodologies and different samples, prior research reveals not only consistency on the ranking of global assessments of crime seriousness, but also a strong positive correlation with sentencing severity (Blumstein and Cohen, 1980; Hamilton and Rytina, 1980; Warr et al., 1983). In short, the crime committed appears to be the most significant predictor of sentencing severity, (although the relationship appears less strong for the specific *length* of sentence).

However, as some have cautioned, the scales typically used to measure crime seriousness are heavily skewed with violent crime categories, thus elevating the importance of crime seriousness ratings to punitive attitudes (Miethe, 1982; O'Connell and Whelan, 1996). If scales were to include more measures of relatively harmless crimes, the relationship between crime seriousness and punishment severity may be attenuated. Nonetheless, in this analysis, the items used for crime seriousness scale are all street crimes, and many are violent crimes. Consequently, there should be a significant relationship between crime seriousness and support for three strikes.

*Hypothesis 3:*    *The higher the rating of crime seriousness, the greater the support for three strikes.*

## The Purpose of Punishment

One of the most explored areas of public attitudes about crime is the purpose of punishment. There are several purposes of punishments: retribution, incapacitation, rehabilitation, and deterrence, both general and specific. While this line of inquiry is vast, the findings are inconsistent. Much of this is due to the diverse questions used by the various polls and studies that tap into different dimensions of punishment principles. Still, as Warr notes, "There is no single dominant ideology of punishment...individuals commonly invoke or support more than one theory of punishment" (1994:52).

Studies that examine criteria that the public uses to anchor preferred punishments often infer the underlying rationale for punishment from the data patterns found. For example, Hamilton and Rytina (1980) found that perceptions of crime seriousness were proportionately correlated with preferred punishments. They interpreted this as evidence of support for a retributive 'just deserts' sentencing philosophy. Yet, as noted in a commentary of their work, the idea of proportionality underpins not only retributive theories of punishment, but deterrence principles as well (Warr, 1981). This idea was buttressed by work that found that the most important predictor of sentence severity was the seriousness of the crime, and not the perceived frequency of the crime in society; which the authors argued is evidence of both retributive and utilitarian (deterrence) rationale (Warr et al., 1983).

Although there are many problems in interpreting the trend data due to the changes in wording and question ordering, overall, polls have shown a significant decline in support for rehabilitation since the late 1970's and early 1980's, and the public appear to have become more punitive (Flanagan and Caulfield, 1984; Maguire and Pastore, 1995). For example, 59% of American respondents in a Gallup poll supported rehabilitation in 1982, compared to 48% in 1989, and only 23% in 1993. Whereas less than half of respondents in 1989 supported some form of punishment of offenders (38%) instead of rehabilitation, almost 70% did in the late 1990's. Surveys have also documented a negative correlation between support for rehabilitation and punitive attitudes (Flanagan, 1996a).

The claim that the public is becoming more punitive however, (as evidenced by the decline in support for rehabilitation) is often derived from polls that ask respondents to name the most important reason for imprisonment. More detailed surveys have questioned this so-called punitive stance. Studies that ask respondents to rate the importance of imprisonment find that respondents often endorse several purposes; and rehabilitation remains important for a significant number of Americans (McCorkle, 1993). Moreover, while many Americans cite retribution and deterrence as the most important reasons to imprison offenders, they fully endorse rehabilitative efforts once the offender is behind bars

(Gerber and Engelhardt-Greer, 1996). This suggests support for rehabilitation does not preclude support for deterrence, incapacitation, or retribution. That view may be changing however. Cullen et al. (2000) suggest that the growing number of Americans who endorse long prison sentences for violent offenders yet want alternatives to prison for non-violent offenders is evidence of public disenchantment with the rehabilitative capacity of our modern prisons. Clearly, punishment preferences are multidimensional and complex, and not easily captured by a global statement, or delimited options.

The purpose of punishment also varies by specifics of the offense and/or the offender, and is conditioned by sociodemographic characteristics of the respondent (Rossi et al., 1985). When asked to rate the purpose of punishment for specific offenses and/or offenders, factorial surveys find that the responses given by an individual vary widely across the hypothetical vignettes presented (Durham, 1993). For example, surveys indicate the public still desires rehabilitation for juvenile offenders (Applegate et al., 1997; Baron and Hartnagel, 1996: Moon et al., 2000), although that support erodes if the crimes committed are serious and/or violent in nature, particularly if the juvenile is described as a repeat violent offender (Roberts, 1992). Likewise, support for rehabilitation declines significantly when an adult offender is described as a repeat offender (Finkel et al., 1996). Support for rehabilitation also varies across sociodemographic groups: it appears highest among women, nonwhites, and younger respondents (Haghighi and Lopez, 1998). Although political liberals used to be far more supportive of rehabilitation efforts, recent work suggests that political liberals are no longer different from the general public - they too, are less likely to believe that rehabilitation is a viable alternative for offenders, particularly repeat offenders (Cesaroni and Doob, 2003; Garland, 2000).

Studies that ask respondents to choose the most important reason for imprisonment find that retribution, deterrence and incapacitation operate similarly in their relation to other attitudes about crime and criminal justice, such as crime seriousness (Hamilton and Rytina, 1980), and preferred length of imprisonment. Moreover, all three reasons are negatively related to rehabilitation as the *primary* purpose of imprisonment. The explanation for this may be that unlike a just deserts orientation that hinges on proportionately, (no matter what the underlying purpose); rehabilitation is geared more to the offender, rather than the offense. This suggests that an interdependency of punishment purposes is found among retributive, deterrence and incapacitation orientations; a rehabilitation orientation should follow a different dynamic. Last, because it appears support for rehabilitation is predicated upon the belief that offenders are amenable to rehabilitative efforts, the logical derivative is that those who are more likely to endorse lengthy prison sentences are assuming offenders are not likely to rehabilitate. Thus, support for rehabilitation is most likely at odds with endorsement of three strikes.

> *Hypothesis 4:*     *Support for rehabilitation is negatively related to support for three strikes.*

## Direct Experiences with Crime - Victims and Offenders

Although the research evidence is slight, logic suggests that direct experience with crime and the criminal justice system, either as a crime victim or as an offender, may influence punitive attitudes. Most of the research has focused on the effects of criminal victimization on punitive attitudes.

### *Prior Criminal Victimization*

Studies of the direct relationship between criminal victimization and attitudes about criminal sentencing have produced mixed results. Although it is intuitive to believe that those who suffer from criminal victimization would be more inclined to adopt 'get-tough' attitudes, such as support for lengthier prison sentences, mandatory sentencing, and the use of the death penalty, the evidence reveals only weak relationships, if any at all. For example, Rossi et al. (1985) found that prior criminal victimization was not related to punitiveness, as did Cullen et al. (1985) and Hough and Roberts (1999). But Dull and Wint found that crime victims rated the police and courts less positively, and were less likely to agree the courts were sentencing properly. They suggested "...victims of crime see themselves additionally victimized by a court that is too easy in its sentencing" (1997:752).

The studies that do find a relationship between victimization and punitiveness typically find them for only a limited number of crimes. For example, Ouimet and Coyle (1991) asked respondents to give preferred sentence lengths for a number of different crimes, and found only one type of crime - homicide - for which crime victims were more punitive than those that had not been victimized. A similarly constructed study found that, compared to non-victims, victims only desired lengthier prison sentences for murderers and burglars (Rich and Sampson, 1990). Sprott and Doob (1997) examined Canadians' opinions of court sentencing and found that even victims of violent crimes differed in their punitive responses. They found that robbery victims and those whose houses were broken into while they were at home were more punitive than non-victims, but victims of assault and sexual assault were less punitive than non-victims. Other studies also find modest relationships between violent criminal victimization and *decreased* punitiveness (Seltzer and McCormick, 1987; Taylor et al., 1979). Studies of death penalty attitudes also do not find a relationship, or only small correlations, between prior victimization and punitiveness (Dull and Wint, 1997; Sprott and Doob, 1997; Tyler and Weber, 1982).

These mixed findings may be due to a number of methodological problems. To begin with, several of the studies employed very low sample sizes (e.g., Ouimet and Coyle, 1991), had low response rates (e.g., Dull and Wint, 1997), or were confined to one small and non-representative geographical area (e.g., Cullen et al., 1985). Those that did have larger samples often used secondary data sets such as the General Social Survey (GSS) that use global statements, most often measured dichotomously. For example, Taylor et al.'s (1979) examination of punitiveness and prior victimization relied on two global statements for punitiveness: "Do you favor or oppose the death penalty for persons convicted of murder" and "In general, do you think the courts in this area deal too harshly or not harshly enough with criminals?" Moreover, victimization was limited to being a victim of burglary in the prior year. Studies that employ more specific measures of attitudes toward criminal sentencing often use vignettes or offer detailed information about the crime event and the offender (such as their personal background and motivation) that differ from study to study. Together, these differences in methodology and measurement are apt to produce inconsistent findings.

Some studies suggest that the effects of victimization on punitiveness work indirectly through fear of crime (e.g., Langworthy and Whitehead, 1986; Sprott and Doob, 1997). However, the direct relationship between victimization and fear of crime is also not definitive. Many studies indicate that criminal victimization increases fear of crime (Gomme, 1988; Giles-Sims, 1984; Lawton and Yaffe, 1980; Lee, 1983; Liska, Sanchirico and Reed, 1988; Miethe and Lee, 1984; Parker and Ray, 1990; Skogan, 1987); but some work suggests the relationship is not very strong (Braungart, Braungart and Hoyer, 1980; Garofalo, 1979; Skogan and Maxfield, 1981; Stafford and Galle, 1984; Van Der Wurff and Stringer, 1989) or nonexistent (Hartnagel, 1979).

Recent work indicates that fear of crime is dependent on the type of prior criminal victimization and/or the number of prior victimizations within a given time period. For example, Smith and Hill (1991b) found that victims of property crimes, and victims of both property and violent crimes were more fearful than victims of person crime only; but most research that examines the type of criminal victimization finds fear levels are higher for victims of violent crime (Denkers and Winkel, 1998; Skogan and Maxfield, 1981; Thompson and Norris, 1992). Longitudinal studies find that fear levels are higher for victims than non-victims, victims of violent crime exhibit fear longer than victims of property crime (Skogan, 1987; Norris and Kaniasty, 1994), and those that had multiple victimizations were more fearful than those that had been criminally victimized only once (Kury and Ferdinand, 1998). Thompson, Bankston and Pierre (1992) found that fear of property crimes increased significantly among respondents who lived in households in which someone had experienced a violent victimization, but property victimization had no effect on fear.

Research also suggests interactive effects between age, gender, race and prior victimization on fear of crime, although these differ from study to study. For example, some find the effects are stronger for older, Black and female victims (e.g., Parker and Ray, 1990; Thompson and Norris, 1992; Vitelli and Ender, 1993), yet others find that older men and women are less afraid after an assaultive offense (Weinrath and Gartrell, 1996).

Much of the confusion may be related to measurement problems in the fear of crime, but there are also other concerns. For example, the inability to recall past victimizations may lead to the conclusion that there is no relationship between criminal victimization and fear of crime. Another problem is that many victims take protective and active stances against crime, which may actually *reduce* their fear of crime. Third, research on the psychological effects of victimization argues that victims often employ various attitudinal defense mechanisms to convince themselves that their victimization was not harmful (Agnew, 1985; Weinrath and Gartrell, 1996). Finally, it may be that only specific types of criminal victimization lead to increased fear of crime, notably, serious violent personal attacks, as Baumer's (1978) earlier review of the literature suggests.

One overarching concern is the limited value of criminal victimization to explain fear of crime. Given the relatively low probability of criminal victimization, particularly serious violent criminal victimization, the explanatory utility of the phenomenon is very limited. As Langworthy and Whitehead note, "fear is much more prevalent than either real or vicarious victimization; a rare event cannot explain a much more frequent event" (1986:577). Nevertheless, given the importance of criminal victimization to fear of crime, and the intuitive appeal of its link to punitiveness, prior criminal victimization will be included in the model. Moreover, because serious victimization appears to be more closely linked to increased fear of crime, prior criminal victimization will be measured ordinally to capture the severity of victimization.

| | |
|---|---|
| *Hypothesis 5:* | *The more serious the prior criminal victimization, the higher the increase in fear of crime.* |
| *Hypothesis 6:* | *The more serious the prior criminal victimization, the greater support for three strikes sentencing.* |

## *Household Arrest*

Few studies have examined the punitiveness of offenders, although it seems logical to think that offenders are less punitive than the general public. One study that compared interview data from 53 offenders (40 were incarcerated) to the general public (over 400 respondents) found that offenders were more likely to endorse rehabilitative efforts for serious violent offenders than the general public (Indermaur, 1994). Yet, both groups were similarly supportive of rehabilitation efforts for young property offenders. Offenders were much more likely to perceive sentencing as unfair; almost all stated the courts were not consistent in meting out punishment. Another study compared the responses of 106 sociology college students and 52 prisoners to a vignette about a robbery that varied the blameworthiness of the victim and the sentencing of the offender (O'Quin and Vogler, 1989). The study found no group differences in the perception of sentencing justness, or in victim blaming. But the generalizability of these results is questionable. Sociology college students are more likely to be critical of the criminal justice system than the general public, and they probably have more empathy toward offenders. Moreover, as O'Quin and Vogler caution, the inmates in the study were atypical offenders. They were selected by the prison officials to be in the college courses because of their exemplary behavior.

A third study used the Sellin-Wolfgang Delinquency Scale to compare assessments of crime seriousness between two groups of prisoners and undergraduates in a sociology class (Figlio, 1975). Inmates in the state prison (who were generally convicted for violent offenses) rated crimes less seriously than inmates at the juvenile detention center (who were generally convicted of property crimes), as did the college students. Again, the generalizability of the results is problematic given the unique features of the samples. Gottfredson et al. (1988) also compared inmates to other groups, such as lawyers and judges, students and other criminal justice personnel and also found that inmates rated all crimes as much less serious as the other groups.

Although there are too few studies to draw upon, it seems logical to suggest that those who have been arrested would be less supportive of three strikes sentencing, as would members of their household, because sentencing policies are more likely to affect them.

*Hypothesis 7:*    *Respondents with a household member that has been arrested will be less supportive of three strikes compared to respondents that have not had a household member arrested.*

## Beliefs about Crime Causation

The research on public opinion of criminal sentencing that has focused on individuals' values and beliefs suggests that the role of ideology - especially political and religious - is far more important in determining attitudes toward punishment of criminal offenders than are other factors such as prior experience with crime - particularly for explaining support for the death penalty. The research also suggests that political and moral beliefs influence the perception of harm to society caused by crime. The following section reviews the extant literature of political and moral beliefs, and how these influence beliefs about crime causation as well as punitive attitudes.

## *Just World Beliefs*

In an important early work, Stinchcombe et al. (1980) argued that future research of attitudes toward criminal sanctioning might profit from exploring the relevancy of attribution - or how people define cause and effect of various social phenomena. Examinations of the relationship between moral beliefs and attitudes toward criminal sentencing have largely focused on the reasons people regard crime as harmful. For example, people who believe crime represents a threat to the moral order believe people who violate the moral order should be punished. This line of inquiry finds very strong links between religiosity and punitiveness.[5]

Other lines of inquiry have focused on the beliefs individuals have about what causes crime because these beliefs determine what to do with people that break the law. The classical explanation of criminality rests on the assumption that humans freely choose criminal behavior, after reasoning through the possible consequences of the action. Since the perspective also assumes humans are naturally hedonistic, punishment must be proportionate to the pleasure or rewards derived from the offense. In order to reduce crime in society, laws must be transparent; punishment must be fair, not overly harsh, and delivered with certainty for all those convicted of criminal behavior. In stark contrast, the positivist position views crime as behavior that is somewhat determined by factors outside of an individual's control. This orientation promotes the use of individualized sanctions; and in more modern applications, with an eye to correcting or ameliorating the conditions that caused the behavior.

Cullen et al. (1985) found that belief about crime causation was the strongest correlate of punitive attitudes toward offenders. Those who attributed crime to free will were much more punitive than those who believed that crime was largely determined. While some studies support this finding (Nettler, 1959; Tygart, 1996), other work suggests the relationship is more complex. For example, Viney, Waldman, and Barchilon (1982) found that college students who scored higher on a 'determinism' scale (purported to measure free will versus deterministic explanations for criminal behavior) had consistently higher punitive attitudes than those who scored lower. They suggested this might indicate that attitudes toward criminal sanctioning were conditioned by concern that punishment be administered fairly, (interestingly, one of the tenets of punishment administration under classical criminology).

Although punishment principles inherently rest on the idea of fairness, researchers have used the concept narrowly and usually only gauge if respondents deem various types (and lengths) of punishment as just. An area of inquiry seldom explored in the literature on public opinion of crime policy is of individuals' beliefs in a just world - the idea that merit and fate are closely aligned and that people get what they deserve. People who believe in a just world think the world operates fairly and that those who abide by the 'rules' will eventually rise to the top, while those who break the rules deserve the punishment they get (Rubin and Peplau, 1975). Research in this area has found that those who believe in a just world are less likely to perceive social inequality, and that which they do perceive is justified as fair and inevitable (Smith, 1985; Smith and Green, 1984). They are also more likely to admire the wealthy and societal elites and believe them deserving of their position; conversely, they are also more likely to blame the poor for their misfortune (Furham and Gunter, 1984; Smith, 1985).

Although very little research has examined the relationship between just world beliefs and public sentencing preferences, Finamore and Carlson (1987) suggest that higher belief in a just world should be associated with a 'crime-control' attitude, including a lack of sympathy for offenders, but they found the relationship held only for Protestants. Moran and Comfort (1986) found that support for the death penalty was higher among men with high just world views, but this relationship did not hold for women.

However, belief in a just world is a complicated process, not perfectly correspondent with punitiveness. Those who view the world as just are also more likely to attribute blame to victims (Finamore and Carlson, 1987; Lerner, 1980; O'Quin and Vogler, 1989), particularly if the victimization is random or if the victim appears blameless. People with a strong belief in a just world have to reconcile 'bad' things that randomly happen to 'good' people, because such scenarios violate their sense of justice.[6] Consequently, they attribute blame to the victim in order to explain why these events occurred. (Interestingly, people are more likely to derogate the victim's actions rather than find fault with their character if the victim is of high status). If they are more likely to derogate the victim, they may be less punitive toward the offender. Similarly, those who believe in a just world may be less likely to support punitive measures that seem unjust, such as a three strikes conviction for property offenses.

In an experimental research design in which subjects read a description of a robbery which varied the blameworthiness of the victim and the length of the perpetrator's sentence, O'Quin and Vogler (1989) found that those with high just world beliefs were much more likely to blame offenders and perceive the sentences given as appropriate than those with lower just world beliefs - but only up to a point. When the punishment was perceived as too lengthy and/or unjust, those with high just world beliefs were more likely to derogate the victim, and perceive the offender as a victim of the criminal justice system. This suggests the relationship between just world beliefs and three strikes sentencing for non-violent crimes may not be linear.

Belief in a just world should be related with belief in free will. Individuals who believe that people get what they deserve - that is, their actions will be justly rewarded or punished - have to assume that individuals have the ability to freely choose their actions, as well as control their fate. Consequently, the logical derivation is that those who are more apt to view the world as just are more apt to prefer punishment proportionate to the crime. The only variable then, would be how an individual ranks the severity of a given offense since the perception of crime severity (assessment of harm to the victim and/or society) is the assumed foundation of the principle of just deserts. Since this study employs a summative index of support for three strikes that includes both the dimensions of crime severity and type of crime, crime severity should be captured (by implication) in the measure. Thus, the higher an individual's belief in a just world, the higher their ratings of crime seriousness should be.

The effects of belief in a just world should be correlated with increased support for three strikes, at least for serious violent offenders. However, if respondents with high beliefs in a just world perceive three strikes as unduly harsh punishment for non-violent offenders, this may diminish the effects of just world beliefs in the model. Additionally, if those who believe in a just world are more likely to believe that people get what they deserve, and that free will determines our actions, they should be less likely to support rehabilitation compared to those that are less likely to view the world as just.

*Hypothesis 8:* *The higher the belief in a just world, the higher the ratings of crime seriousness.*

*Hypothesis 9:* *The higher the belief in a just world, the less likely the support for rehabilitation.*

*Hypothesis 10:* *The higher the belief in a just world, the higher the support for three strikes.*

## *Political Ideology*

Political conservatism is one of the largest determinants of punitiveness. Studies have consistently found political conservatives are far more supportive of the death penalty, incarceration, and lengthy sentences; and are less likely to support rehabilitation (Flanagan, 1996b; Gerber and Engelhardt-Greer, 1996; Longmire, 1996; Stinchcombe et al. 1980). However, recent evidence suggests that as crime becomes an increasingly salient feature of our culture, support for alternatives to incarceration has declined among liberal elites (Cesaroni and Doob, 2003; Garland, 2000). Some suggest that political ideology is not nearly as important as experiential factors and other ideological beliefs (e.g., Thomas and Foster, 1975). But most multivariate analyses that include political ideology, fear of crime and other factors such as prior criminal victimization, find political conservatives are more punitive than liberals, independent of fear of crime, or personal criminal victimization (Cullen et al., 1985; Langworthy and Whitehead, 1986; Stinchcombe et al., 1980; Taylor et al., 1979; Tyler and Weber, 1982).

Republicans tend to view criminality as a matter of choice. Consequently, they are more likely to endorse punishment, whether for retributive or deterrence reasons. In contrast, political liberals are more likely to view criminality as a product of social problems; consequently, they are more likely to view imprisonment as ineffective in changing what engenders crime. Moreover, political liberals are probably more likely to perceive injustice within the criminal justice system; as such, they would probably be less likely to support increases in sentencing that may cause even more unjustified harm.

Political party differences are found in the research on just world beliefs. This area of research finds that Republicans have very high belief in a just world, and are much more likely to attribute poverty to poor choices such as drug addiction, laziness, and lack of moral values (Furnham and Gunter, 1984; Smith and Green, 1984). Consequently, Republicans should also be less likely to support rehabilitation as the most important reason to imprison, because they would be more likely to view offenders as people who have low moral standards, thus, not amenable to change.

> *Hypothesis 11:*    *Republicans will be less likely to support rehabilitation compared to political Independents or Democrats.*
>
> *Hypothesis 12:*    *Republicans will be more supportive of three strikes compared to political Independents or Democrats.*

## *Fear of Crime and Attitudes toward Criminal Sentencing*

Although a very small percentage of Americans actually experience a serious personal crime, fear of criminal victimization has increased significantly over the last three decades. For example, less than one-third of respondents surveyed expressed fear of their immediate environment in the 1960's, compared to almost one-half of those surveyed in the 1980's and 1990's (Donnelly, 1988; Smith et al., 1999). Some of this increase may be attributed to actual increases in crime, particularly as crime rates shot up during the late 1960's and early 1970's. Some have suggested that the 'fear' increase may have been due to a number of other social changes. The late 1960's and early 1970's were a time of large social upheaval compared to the relatively quiescent 1950's. Beginning with the Civil Rights Movement, the 1960's were characterized by scores of social movements, much of which turned violent. About this time, middle-class White fears were further exacerbated when images of Black civil unrest were televised nightly; 'inner city' became synonymous with 'poor, lazy, morally irresponsible Black'; imagery that was quickly used as political capital. Nixon is credited with successfully using the political concept of 'crime' as 'code' for anti-Black sentiment. The problem crimes to quell were mugging, robbery and in the mid-1980's - crack cocaine.

Fear of crime remained relatively stable, albeit at high levels, during the late 1970's and into the mid-1990's (Warr, 1995). For certain segments of the population, especially women, reported fear of crime was even higher (Ferraro, 1996).

But why did crime fears remain high, even after crime rates decreased precipitously in the early 1990's? Some criminologists have suggested that the government sponsored crime victim surveys developed in the 1970's in many Western countries, were central to the construction of 'fear of crime' as a social problem in the 1980's (Sparks, 1992; Walklate, 1998). The public's fear of crime uncovered in these surveys were reported by the media, and among many criminologists, became a social fact to be explained, not questioned.

Criminologists have critiqued the fear of crime research for over two decades, including the overuse of quantitative methodological approaches that dominate the field and how the 'knowledge' gained from these methods is used to facilitate the reproduction of class relations and hegemonic social control (Walklate, 1997). For example, one issue raised by critical criminologists is the politicization of 'fear.' Mainstream criminologists have primarily focused on fear of street crime rather than the public's reactions to corporate or white-collar crime. As Shirlow and Pain (2003) argue, attending to fear of street crime legitimizes the fears of the more powerful social classes, which are then acted upon by governments to control marginalized groups. Hence, the enormous increase in incarceration rates of the poor and nonwhites over the last two decades in Western countries can be explained, in part, as a 'legitimate' response of governments to this fear - even though the dominant classes are, in reality, less vulnerable to street crime, and actually report lower levels of fear.

A growing number of criminologists are questioning the many assumptions of the research. For example, Farrall and Gadd (2004) question if fear of crime is really as prevalent as the research suggests, particularly given the lack of studies on the frequency and intensity of fear. Their study asked respondents to quantify the number of times during the prior year they had been fearful of becoming a victim, and found that 37% of respondents had been fearful at least once. However, only half of those respondents felt fearful more than five times in that year. Thus, Farrall and Gadd argue that Western governments' reliance on crime victimization surveys to assess crime prevention programs is seriously flawed, as fear of crime is a relatively unlikely event.[7]

Another issue is the reification of 'fear of crime,' most apparent in the debate of the so-called victim-fear-paradox; namely that women and the elderly reportedly have higher levels of fear, but lower levels of criminal victimization. In the 1970's, surveys claimed that the elderly were so fearful of crime they became 'prisoners in their own homes;' a claim that was widely reported by the mass media (Ziegler and Mitchell, 2003). Yet, as Ferraro and LaGrange (1988) observed early on, these claims were very questionable, given the conceptual and methodological problems with the research. As research into fear of crime has developed better measures of fear and grappled with disentangling the many dimensions of the concept, more recent work that employs these measures tend to find that the elderly have *lower* levels of fear than other age groups (e.g., Chadee and Ditton, 2003), but they feel more 'vulnerable' to crime – that is, unable to defend themselves if they were physically attacked (Warr, 1984; 1987).

The claim that the fears of women and the elderly are irrational has been disputed on other grounds. For example, many argue that women's fear of crime *is* a rational response to the high levels of violence perpetrated by men against women. This line of argumentation observes that in the public realm, women are regularly subjected to sexual harassment and other forms of degradation, in addition to the very real danger of sexual violence (Junger, 1987; Stanko, 1990; 1995). In the private realm, women are much more likely to be victimized by their intimate partners. Indeed, studies using more sensitive surveys and/or qualitative techniques uncover these real victimizations and document that women are victimized with great frequency (e.g., Bilsky and Wetzels, 1997), although some suggest these assaults are relatively minor (Smith, 1988).

Some find that women's fears stem from knowing they face high risk of sexual and physical violence; this knowledge of potential sexual violence heightens their fear of other types of criminal victimization (Ferraro, 1996; Stanko, 1990). Yet, as Pain notes, "harassment and violence are very different experiences, and most women draw a distinct division between them" (1997:300). She asked women to identify their perceptions of the most likely rapist 'in general,' and the most likely rapist if they were the victims of rape. She found that although a large percentage of women correctly identified the most likely rapist 'in general' as a friend/acquaintance, fewer than 10% believed a friend/acquaintance or family member could rape them. Pain argued that women's fear of crime is associated with certain public spaces and with fear of strangers as a means to distance themselves from potential dangers. Women can *control* fear of public spaces and strangers - by avoiding dangerous public places, or people they perceive as dangerous. Women feel less fearful of potential non-stranger victimization because they don't associate with men of 'that' class, or they feel confident in their ability to quickly assess the potential danger from new men they meet.

A third critique of the apparent fear-victimization paradox centers on assumptions criminologists have made about gender: man as offender, woman as victim; that men are reticent to disclose fear (Newburn and Stanko, 1994); and that boys learn to internalize fear "...in order to retain some semblance of control and power in relation to others" (Goodey, 1997). For example, a recent qualitative analysis of both men and women found that men *were* willing to discuss their fear of victimization. The interviews revealed that men and women could be either fearful or fearless; moreover, fearful men and women were much more similar than dissimilar (Gilchrist et al., 1998).

Perhaps the most damning criticism of the number of studies that have been devoted to explaining the victim-fear-paradox, is as Sparks notes, the assumption that an "appropriate level of fear was empirically decidable, when in fact it involves moral and political choices" (1992: 126). Similarly, the criticism that researchers treat fear as a debilitating state, by failing to distinguish between 'fear' and 'caution' can also be framed in terms of Spark's question: Are there an 'acceptable' number of precautionary behaviors? How many protective behaviors signify debilitating fear, and moreover, who decides?

The most numerous critiques of the research on fear of crime are centered on how poorly the concept is defined and operationalized. Yet, in spite of years of debate, the issues remain unresolved. Moreover, as Bilsky and Wetzels note, "although the shortcomings...have been evident and discussed in the literature for years, research practice has hardly benefited from these debates" (1997:310).

One of the largest complaints about the earlier fear of crime literature was the propensity to use a single-item indicator of fear (usually dichotomous), that seriously under- or overestimated the extent of fear of crime (although it is impossible to know in which direction the data were skewed). For example, most of the earlier research used either the GSS question "Is there any area right around here - that is, within a mile - where you would be afraid to walk alone at night?" or the National Crime Survey (NCS), "How safe do you feel or would you feel being out alone in your neighborhood at night" (with a parallel question for day). Neither question distinguishes between *perceptions of risk* and actual *fear* of crime, nor explicitly asks the respondent about being afraid of being a victim of crime. The questions also suggest a situation - walking alone at night - that may be an unlikely event for many, thus leading respondents to assess a situation they rarely experience. Although many people may avoid this activity because of the perception of danger, such a question measures perception of risk or vulnerability, not actual fear (Ferraro and LaGrange, 1987).

In a review of earlier research on fear of crime, Ferraro and LaGrange (1987) found that many of the measures of fear employed were capturing worry about crime, or the perception of crime risk in one's neighborhood, or feelings of vulnerability to crime; but not *fear*. Ferraro and LaGrange suggested that there are three different facets of *crime salience* - general concerns about crime, cognitive judgments about the risk of victimization and emotive fear of crime. They argued that concerns about crime reflect political issues such as 'law and order' policies, or concerns about rising crime rates. Judgments about crime risk are assessments about the likelihood of crime victimization in one's environment, and/or perceptions of what would happen if one were victimized; what many researchers have termed vulnerability. Neither concerns about crime nor do judgments about crime risk capture fear, which is really the emotional, anxious response to potential victimization.

Over the last ten to fifteen years, quantitative researchers have explored the interrelationships of various dimensions of fear and how these dimensions engender fear. In general, research has moved away from global single-item indicators of fear, and most agree that, at a minimum, researchers need to distinguish between general fear (or concern about crime) and fears tied directly to a specific type of crime (Ferraro, 1995; Ferraro and LaGrange, 1987; Weinrath and Gartrell, 1996); and distinguish these cognitive and affective processes from behavioral responses (Gabriel and Greve, 2003; Ferraro and LaGrange, 1987; Skogan, 1993).

Research on fear of crime lends support to the argument that there are conceptual distinctions of the dimensions of fear. For example, Rountree and Land's (1996) study of different Seattle neighborhoods found that the perception of neighborhood risk to crime had a different distribution than the fear of home burglary. Distinguishing between fear of crime, worries about crime, and perceptions of local problems with crime, Walker (1994) found significant differences between Whites, Asians, and Blacks, but differences between groups varied by the concept being examined (although she relied upon a single-item to measure fear).

Recently, Williams, McShane and Akers (2000) argued that researchers should work toward creating more reliable and unidimensional scales to tap into worry about criminal victimization. Citing criticism that much of the research has arbitrarily transposed dimensions of fear of crime as predictors of other dimensions of fear of crime, they factor analyzed nine measurements of the concept, including single-item measures and scales that assessed worry about crime, perception of risk, concern about crime in general, and behavioral precautions. They were able to establish a unidimensional scale that was both factorial invariant and highly reliable, which included both measures of worry about specific victimizations and perceptions of specific forms of victimizations; behavioral precautions and measures that assessed worries about walking in the neighborhood at night did not load on the factor.

Skogan (1993) suggests that researchers should not worry about the lack of agreement on what is meant by the term 'fear of crime.' He argues that because the concept is multi-faceted there is no correct or incorrect definition; rather the purpose of the research should drive the definition(s) used in the study. Following his reasoning, we employ several dimensions of 'fear of crime' in our research model, and refer to this constellation of 'fear' dimensions as 'crime salience.' Based on prior research, crime salience can easily be categorized into affective and cognitive components. The affective component is the emotional, anxious response to potential victimization - fear of crime. The cognitive components of crime salience are the perception of crime risk in one's neighborhood, concerns for one's personal safety and ability to defend oneself against criminals, and the perception of society in general - crime 'out there.'

There is considerable overlap between affective and cognitive dimensions of crime salience. Studies find that perception of neighborhood risk, feelings of vulnerability, and the perception of general crime rates are correlated, yet distinct from, the emotive fear of crime. For example, many studies find that those who perceive higher crime risks in their neighborhood have higher fear of crime, independent of other sociodemographic and experiential variables (Baumer, 1985; Box, Hale and Andrews, 1988; Chiricos, Eschholz and Gertz, 1997; Smith and Hill, 1991a; Taylor and Hale, 1986).

Nevertheless, the perception that crime risk is high in the neighborhood and even prior criminal victimization does not preclude an increase of fear of crime across all potential crime victimizations. Studies have found that fear of home burglary and potential harm to one's family is usually viewed as the most fear producing (Ferraro, 1995; Skogan and Maxfield, 1981), even for individuals who were victims of violent crimes (Smith and Hill, 1991b). Some have suggested this is a 'rational' fear because the likelihood of home burglary is greater than personal victimization, especially for those who live in higher income neighborhoods (Rountree and Land, 1996; Skogan, 1987).

Most studies find only a weak relationship between fear of crime, or perceived vulnerability to crime, to official data on criminal activity in the community (Lewis and Maxfield, 1980; Rucker, 1990; Skogan and Maxfield, 1981). Part of this discrepancy may be due to the inaccuracy in individuals' assessment of crime. For example, individuals tend to believe that crime rates are higher in other neighborhoods than they are in their own (Rucker, 1990). Individuals are also less accurate in assessing property versus violent crime risk (Hindelang, Gottfredson, and Garofalo, 1978; Lewis and Salem, 1986; Warr, 1982).

This does not mean that criminal activity has no effect on people's perceptions or feelings about their local community. Residents of high crime areas do report greater fear than people in low crime areas (Clemente and Kleiman, 1977). The stronger effect, however, appears to be between the perception of neighborhood crime and fear of crime. Skogan and Maxfield (1981) argue that fear is greatest among those who live in areas in which environmental cues - what they term physical incivilities - trigger a sense of danger and vulnerability to crime. Thus, those who live with the daily reminders of crime - graffiti, abandoned cars, vacant lots, abandoned houses, and so forth - will perceive that crime is high in their neighborhood (LaGrange, Ferraro and Supancic, 1992). When people perceive crime risks are higher, they become more fearful. Thus, even in low crime areas, people will become more fearful of crime when they hear reports of neighborhood break-ins (Rountree and Land, 1996).

Perceptions of risk to crime are conditioned by both individual and neighborhood level factors, such as social integration (Hartnagel, 1979; Riger, Le Bailly and Gordon, 1981; Rucker, 1990). People in high crime areas report less satisfaction with their neighbors and a greater sense of social isolation, both of which are correlated with increased fear of crime (Lewis and Salem, 1986). In higher income (and hence, low crime) communities social integration also produces greater fear, but in a different manner. In highly cohesive neighborhoods in which neighbors communicate with regular frequency, research finds that news of local crime is disseminated throughout the neighborhood, thus increasing fear (Rountree and Land, 1996). More recently, research has also hinted at the importance of neighborhood integration in reducing fear of crime (Reid, Roberts, and Hilliard, 1998). Individuals who are fearful rely on their neighbors and the community in order to reduce these feelings. Although the research suggests that fear is not reduced, the stress associated with increased fear is, thus allowing individuals to continue their daily routines, even in high crime areas.

On an individual level, social isolation and loneliness appear to impact fear of crime, but the effects are conditioned by age and gender (Braungart, Braungart, and Hoyer, 1980; Silverman and Kennedy, 1985). For example, among women, fear appears linked to the number of people living in the household. Among men, fewer people in the household increased loneliness, but this loneliness was not related to fear. Much of the recent work examining fear of crime among women and the elderly suggests that the notion of their 'irrational' fear is exaggerated. They find substantial variation of fear of crime within gender and age groups: in fact, within-group variation is much greater than between-group variation (Gilchrist et al., 1998; Pain, 1995).

Some suggest that fear of crime is really reaction to unwanted social change, such as racial integration, racial change in composition of neighborhoods, loosening of morals, or economic decline (Donnelly, 1988; Taylor and Covington, 1993; Taylor et al., 1979). For example, Donnelly (1988) found that rising fear of crime in Cincinnati was more linked to unease about the failing economy, rather than neighborhood levels of crime, as factories closed, and unemployment grew.

Structural changes appear to have differential impact by race. For example, one study found that the fear of White respondents was most affected by the percent of nonwhite population, the proportion of local crime that was interracial, and property crime rates. In contrast, only the racial composition of the population and the level of racial segregation affected the fear of nonwhite respondents (Liska, Lawrence, and Sanchirico, 1982).

As is the case with perceptions of neighborhood crime risk, feelings of vulnerability or personal safety are also correlated with the emotive fear of crime. Perceived vulnerability is defined as a person's perception of their "openness to attack, powerlessness to resist attack, and exposure to traumatic physical consequences if attacked" (Skogan and Maxfield, 1981). Feelings of vulnerability result from the perception that one would suffer serious consequences if criminally victimized (Garofalo, 1979; Killias, 1990). The logical derivation is that one who feels vulnerable to personal victimization should have higher fear of crime than someone who feels less vulnerable, all else being equal. For example, the elderly and women may not feel as capable of physically defending themselves from violent criminal attack, as do younger individuals or men. Warr (1984) finds evidence of this 'differential sensitivity to risk' of victimization. In his study, women and elderly respondents had much higher fear of crime than male or younger respondents, even when controlling for perceptions of risk.

But feeling vulnerable may not elevate one's fear of crime if one employs strategies to reduce the risk of victimization (Greve, 1998). For example, Skogan (1993) found that the elderly are not necessarily more afraid than younger individuals; they are only more worried about personal attack after dark, but avoided these areas anyway, rendering the worry and fear inconsequential. Moreover, feelings of vulnerability are also conditioned by perceptions of environmental risk, usually perceptions of neighborhood crime (Warr, 1987). Thus, the elderly may not be fearful of crime when they live in low crime areas, even if they feel vulnerable to attack (Baumer, 1985).

Fear of crime, then, captures people's emotional reactions to perceived dangers in their local community. In contrast, perceived vulnerability captures people's cognitive assessments of how they would handle possible criminal victimization. Although these two responses to crime are related, it is possible for people to fear crime, yet not see themselves as vulnerable. Conversely, people may also see themselves as vulnerable to criminal activity, yet not feel fearful.

Last, another cognitive dimension of crime salience is the belief about societal crime rates. Intuitively, it would seem that worry about increasing crime in society should also lead to an increase in the emotional fear of crime. A belief that crime is increasing may produce anxious feelings and perhaps even a sense of helplessness about the phenomenon. However, research has suggested the relationship is not so direct. For example, research has found that even if respondents believe crime in society is increasing, they are less likely to perceive that crime in their own communities is increasing, and far less likely to believe that crime in their neighborhood is increasing. In fact, some studies suggest that newspaper reports of nonlocal crime make people feel safer in their own neighborhoods, regardless of actual crime risk (e.g., Liska and Baccaglini, 1990). It appears that the accuracy of estimates of crime risk is dependent on the type of crime, the time period and the geographical location under question. For example, research has shown that there is considerable public accuracy in judging *general* crime risk for one point in time; that accuracy decreases when crime trends are considered.

This brief review of the fear of crime literature serves to emphasize the difficulties associated with measuring 'fear of crime,' and of the numerous ways in which fear is conditioned. Clearly, fear is a very complicated process not easily captured in cross-sectional quantitative analysis. This study will employ more detailed measures of fear than most other studies, and use a large number of control variables, thus, interpreting the results will be even more complicated given the inherent problems in measuring punitiveness outlined earlier.

## *Prior Research on Crime Salience and Punitiveness*

The few studies that examine fear of crime and attitudes toward punishment utilizing individual level data have produced mixed results. Most of the research finds evidence of a weak relationship between fear of crime and punitiveness (Hough, Lewis and Walker, 1988; Rankin, 1979; Stinchcombe et al., 1980; Taylor et al., 1979; Tyler and Weber, 1982), or none at all (Barkan and Cohn, 1994; Baron and Hartnagel, 1996; Cullen et al., 1985; McCorkle, 1993; Ouimet and Coyle, 1991; Seltzer and McCormick, 1987; Tygart, 1996). Others find evidence of strong positive effects - higher fear drives punitiveness (Hough and

Moxon, 1988; Keil and Vito, 1991; Langworthy and Whitehead, 1986; Sprott and Doob, 1997; Thomas and Foster, 1975).

The inconsistencies are due to a number of factors. To begin with, few studies focus on the theoretical implications of fear of crime and punishment; most include fear of crime in their models as statistical controls, not as theoretical variables of interest. Additionally, fewer still have focused specifically on the effects of fear of crime on punitiveness as defined and measured by sentencing lengths. Instead, much of this research uses support for capital punishment as the dependent variable (e.g., Keil and Vito, 1991). These studies find that crime salience is a much less important determinant than political and/or moral beliefs and attitudes, and is often rendered inconsequential by these beliefs and attitudes (Tyler and Weber, 1982).

Few studies have examined the impact of the perception of rising societal crime rates on punitiveness. Rising crime rates may not lead to increased fear of crime if the perception of individual risk remains low. But rising crime rates may lead individuals to respond with increasing severity of sentencing, no matter what their level of fear.

As Ferraro and LaGrange (1987) note, one of the dimensions of fear of crime is the behavioral response to that fear. Although little research has been done that explicitly examines the different responses to the different types of crime salience, it seems logical to suggest that responses would differ depending upon two different dimensions: whether the salience of crime is emotive versus cognitive in nature, and whether the crime source is geographically near or distant. For example, a cognitive worry about the rising crime rates in society is apt to produce a much different response than worry that stems from a perceived increase of crime in one's neighborhood. More immediate concerns are much more likely to produce changes in one's environment and/or daily routines as these actions are more likely to directly result in decreasing the probability of victimization. For example, a rash of neighborhood burglaries would probably cause many residents to take precautions such as locking doors, buying a security alarm system, forming a Neighborhood Watch program, and so forth. Although some residents may respond to the increase in burglaries with more punitive attitudes, this type of response is probably not as prevalent because it does nothing to change the probability of risk in the neighborhood. On the other hand, worries about rising societal crime rates might lead to more concerns and corresponding demands for punitive laws and policies, rather than changing one's immediate environment and/or daily routine because these responses have little impact on crime rates.

In spite of the inconsistent findings in the literature on fear of crime and punitiveness, given the points discussed above, crime salience is probably an important determinant of punitiveness. But the type of crime salience is key. Concerns about rising crime rates in society are probably more likely to lead to demand for criminal justice policy changes than is feeling vulnerable when walking the street at night. If so, those who believe crime is increasing in the state will be more likely to support lengthier prison sentences than those who do not. Those who have an emotional fear of crime may also be more likely to support lengthier prison sentences, as they get criminals off the streets. On the other hand, a decline in feeling safe or the perception that crime in the neighborhood is increasing are probably not as strongly related to support for lengthier sentencing, because individuals will alleviate these conditions with actions that modify their immediate environment and/or daily routine.

| | |
|---|---|
| *Hypothesis 13:* | *The higher the emotional fear of crime, the greater the support for three strikes* |
| *Hypothesis 14:* | *Belief that crime in the state has risen increases support for three strikes* |
| *Hypothesis 15:* | *Feeling safe is not related to support for three strikes* |
| *Hypothesis 16:* | *Perceptions of neighborhood crime risk are not related to support for three strikes* |

## NOTES

1. Gallup polls have tracked American death penalty attitudes since 1936 and reveal that although support fluctuates slightly over time, there has been a steady upward trend in support for the death penalty since the early 1970's. Approximately three-fourths of the American public supported the death penalty in the late 1990's; a relatively stable estimate for the last twenty years, (Bohm, 1991; Longmire, 1996).

2. The research on death penalty support usually finds very strong effects of gender, race, and political party, and somewhat weaker effects of religiosity, education, income and age (Barkan and Cohn, 1994; Blumstein and Cohen,

1980; Bohm, 1991; Ellsworth and Gross, 1994; Keil and Vito, 1991; Longmire, 1996)

3. Research documents that police practices unfairly target Blacks, regardless of social class. 'Driving while Black' studies find African Americans are much more likely than Whites to be pulled over for non-moving traffic violations. Blacks also are the targets of racial hoaxes – deliberately averting attention to an alleged Black offender in order to escape police scrutiny (Russell, 1998).

4. Drug crimes are the exception. Public opinion surveys have documented large increases in seriousness ratings over the last two decades (Roberts and Stalans, 1997).

5. See Newman and Trilling, 1975 for an earlier review of the literature.

6. See Lerner, 1980; Lerner and Miller, 1978 for reviews of the literature.

7. Another concern is tendency to treat fear of crime as a stable trait. Psychology studies argue that fear of criminal victimization can also be a transitory reaction to a threatening stimulus that dissipates once the stimulus disappears (Gabriel and Greve, 2003). The disposition of being fearful fluctuates over time, and is mediated by other personal dispositions and situational and social influences.

# CHAPTER 3

# Media and Public Opinion of Crime

The mass media have generally been credited with raising the public's fear of being victimized, heightening a sense of anxiety about crime, and propelling crime onto the top of the public agenda. Although mass media are often posited as very important influences on American attitudes and beliefs about crime policy, these ideas have not been tested to any large degree, with the exception of media impact on fear of crime.

The shortage of studies that examine effects of crime-related media on attitudes and beliefs about crime may be due to the many difficulties researchers face. The ubiquitous nature of the mass media, especially television, makes it impossible to use control groups in longitudinal research designs. Experimental designs that manipulate media content can only speak to the short-term effects of media and cannot address the long-term cumulative effects. Thus, most of the studies that examine the effects of crime-related media employ longitudinal or cross-sectional survey designs and infer causality from correlated results.

Much of this work has centered on fear of crime. Earlier studies of the influence of media on fear of crime did find modest correlations between media consumption and increased fear (Gerbner and Gross, 1976; Gerbner et al., 1980), but these findings were widely questioned (Doob and Macdonald, 1979; Heath and Petraitis, 1987; Hirsch, 1980; 1981). More recent studies continue to find modest effects of media, but the effects are variable depending on audience characteristics, media format, media content, local crime rates, racial composition of the neighborhood, and a host of other social and individual factors (Chiricos et al., 1997; Chiricos, Padgett, and Gertz, 2000; Eschholz,

Chiricos and Gertz, 2003; Gordon and Heath, 1981; Gou, Zhu and Chen, 2001; Tyler and Cook, 1984; Weaver and Wakshlag, 1986).

Very few studies have examined the influence of media on individuals' opinions of criminal punishment. Surveys that do, generally limit their questions to one specific form of media such as newspapers (Roberts and Doob, 1990), use superficial measures such as the number of hours spent watching television to capture crime-related media intake (Barrile, 1984), or employ relatively small samples (Sotirovic, 2001). Nevertheless, since numerous media studies have documented the importance of both media content and form on attitudes and perceptions of other social phenomena,[1] it is not unreasonable to suspect that crime-related media influence attitudes about crime, criminals and criminal sentencing.

This idea is based on a number of reasons. First, crime coverage is ubiquitous. It saturates news media, and accounts for a large percentage of prime-time entertainment programming. Although crime has long been a staple of American news and entertainment (Einstadter, 1994; Rafter, 2000), it appears that the percentage of mass media devoted to crime has been increasing, particularly on television (Cavender and Fishman, 1998; Dorfman and Schiraldi, 2001; Fox and Van Sickel, 2001; Surette, 1998). For example, the number of television news magazines such as *48 Hours* and *20/20* expanded both in number and in the number of broadcasts aired weekly during the 1990's. Over the same time period, their percentage of crime coverage more than doubled, from 20% to over 40% (Fox and Van Sickel, 2001). In the 1980's, sensational crime stories were featured on daytime talk shows and soap operas and became the staple of a new form of entertainment - 'reality' programming (Cavender and Fishman, 1998); also known as 'info-tainment' because it blends news with entertainment. Shows such as *Cops, America's Most Wanted,* and *Unsolved Mysteries* are indicative of crime-based reality programs. In the 1990's, American's penchant for titillating crime trials was so great that cable channels emerged dedicated solely to crime coverage, such as *Court TV* (Howitt, 1998).

Second, media is thought to have an important influence on punitiveness because most people do not have direct experience with criminal victimization, or the criminal justice system. Therefore, the media provide an important source of information about crime and criminals not otherwise available. Surveys show that as many as 75%

to 95% of Americans and Canadians cite the mass media as their primary source of information about crime (Dorfman and Schiraldi, 2001; Graber, 1980; Roberts and Doob, 1990). As such, it probably has a great deal of influence in shaping attitudes and beliefs about crime and crime policy.

A third reason why media is thought to influence punitiveness is related to the distortion so prevalent in crime-related media content. Numerous studies have consistently documented the over-representation of street crimes, rather than white-collar and corporate crimes, although there is variation in this distribution depending on the medium (Chermak, 1995; Entman, 1989; Garofalo, 1981; Graber, 1980; Jerin and Fields, 1994; Schlesinger, Tumber and Murdock, 1991; Sheley and Ashkins, 1981). But even the coverage of street crimes is narrowly focused on serious violent crimes, especially robbery and murder (Chermak, 1994; Estep and Macdonald, 1984; O'Keefe and Reid-Nash, 1987; Sheley and Ashkins, 1981). For example, three surveys of local television crime news conducted in the mid-1990's found that homicide comprised one-fourth of crime coverage (Dorfman and Schiraldi, 2001).

The portrayal of crime victims and offenders is also misleading. For example, White victims are represented in the media far more frequently than their rates of victimization would suggest (Carlson, 1985; Chermak, 1995; Estep and Macdonald, 1984; Pritchard and Hughes, 1997). In contrast, Black males are much more likely to be portrayed as offenders, and less likely to be portrayed as victims, even though their rates of criminal victimization are the highest (Chermak, 1995; Entman, 1992; Gilliam and Iyengar, 2000). The media also distort the reality of crime control by their narrow focus on the front end of the criminal justice system; particularly, the police and the courts (Carlson, 1985; Graber, 1980; Sherizen, 1978). One of the most striking distortions is the focus on celebrity trials, which really ramped up in the 1990's (Fox and Van Sickel, 2001). Media seldom report on plea negotiations, which is how the vast majority of criminal cases are settled. When media do report on case dispositions, they overwhelmingly report on cases in which the convicted are sentenced to prison (Graber, 1980; Roberts and Doob, 1990).

A fourth reason why media may influence punitive attitudes is that media discourse about crime is dominated by messages that promulgate a narrow and simplistic ideological viewpoint, usually presented in simple black and white terms. Criminals are portrayed as evil, predatory strangers who viciously attack unwary innocent victims (Surette, 1994). Although the image of the predatory criminal has been a part of entertainment for centuries, "...the modern mass media have raised the specter of the predatory criminal from a minor character to a common, ever-present image" (Surette, 1994:132). Moreover, explanations for criminal behavior focus on individual problems, rather than broader structural and societal factors. Even worse, media often imply that nothing that can be done about crime (Bortner, 1984; Donovan, 1998).

As many suggest, when the media is awash with images of senseless, inexplicable violence, or when criminal behavior is explained as individual pathology, then the only rational means of dealing with crime is to execute or incapacitate those that threaten our safety, (once of course, their culpability has been established in a long drawn-out court trial). These media depictions mesh nicely with the cherished values and beliefs held by a majority of the American public - namely, the emphasis on individual responsibility, and a sacrosanct belief in the fairness of the American justice system.

The presentation of crime and criminals in the news media is fairly conservative, in that it does not upset the prevailing dominant ideology of individualism, and support for 'law and order.' This is not to suggest that the media are controlled by a monolithic group of elites. Rather, in capitalist society, the imperative to produce profit creates pressures that almost ensure a conservative outlook. In part, this is due to the unequal access of organizations and individuals to news media. State agencies provide easy access to information that the media needs, and the agencies' spokespersons are viewed as more knowledgeable and credible (Schlesinger and Tumber, 1994). Less organized groups and individuals are seldom heard unless they are victims (Altheide, 2002); alternative viewpoints are often relegated to opinion pieces that are less visible and less likely to be perceived as credible (Entman, 1989). Additionally, unlike other specialized media that target specific groups, mass media work to garner large audiences for their sponsors. As such, the messages they produce have to appeal to the large middle-class, primarily White audience. Consequently, the messages delivered tend to support the status quo, rather than challenge it.

Clearly, there are numerous reasons to suspect that media influence public opinion about crime and crime policy. Yet, prior empirical research on the effects of mass media on public opinion of crime and crime policy is scant and inconclusive. Moreover, exactly how media influence public opinion is still very much debated.

## MASS MEDIA EFFECTS ON PUBLIC KNOWLEDGE AND ATTITUDES

There are three main theoretical approaches that guide current academic research on the effects of mass media (Fox and Van Sickel, 2001). The first and earliest approach, assumes that mass media greatly influence people's attitudes and beliefs about the world. Dubbed the hypodermic model, it assumes individuals rely on the mass media for information about the world and they unquestioningly adopt the beliefs and perspectives promoted by the media.

The second approach, known as the limited effects model, suggests that the influence of media is a reciprocal process complicated by both media form and audience characteristics. As numerous communication studies have documented, media news consumers are not passive receptors of information. In fact, some studies suggest that in spite of the distortion of crime presented in the media, viewers receive the information with a healthy dose of skepticism, particularly so for sensationalistic news or entertainment programs (Sacco, 1995). Moreover, although people turn to the media for information about crime issues, they do not accept the information at face value. They imbue meaning framed by knowledge and prior experiences, other media stories, local gossip and rumor, perception of the credibility of the story and/or storyteller, and so forth (Eschholz et al., 2003; Gomme, 1988; O'Keefe, 1984; Williams and Dickinson, 1993).

The third approach argues that the effects of media do not influence individuals' attitudes and beliefs, per se, but that the media shape the level of importance people attach to various national issues (Iyengar, Peters and Kinder, 1982). Research in this vein has primarily focused on political attitudes and behaviors of the general public, and of policymakers. Earlier studies suggested, paraphrasing a common quote, media tell us not what to think, but what to think about.[2] These 'agenda-setting' studies found that individuals' concern about various issues was positively related to television news coverage of these issues, at least among uncommitted voters (e.g., McCombs and Shaw,

1972). For example, Iyengar et al. (1982) found that television news coverage of specific issues such as unemployment or education significantly influenced viewers' evaluations of presidential performance. Moreover, the more prominent the story was in the broadcast, the more influence it appeared to have. For the politically uninformed, media presentations were much more influential in shaping their attitudes. Among the more politically knowledgeable, media accounts triggered critical deliberations of the information. They concluded that viewers do actually use television to understand their social reality, especially to determine which national issues to consider as most serious.

Research on agenda-setting also finds that individuals use media information differently, depending on the salience of the information. Individuals pay more attention to new information when it meshes with prior interests, experiences, and existing beliefs. Although research suggests that individuals attempt to ignore information that challenges fundamental values, individuals do process most new information, and then either cognitively store the information or discard it. Some researchers argue that for most matters of national interest, Americans have little prior knowledge or experience, consequently, the media messages, no matter how repetitive, have little salience, and therefore, little influence on attitudes and beliefs. But others argue that when individuals have little knowledge, they tend to have weakly anchored beliefs, which are more likely to be influenced by media messages (Entman, 1989). Additionally, weakly anchored beliefs are probably more susceptible to media influence if the issue becomes salient to the viewer.

Criminal victimization is less likely to be of interest to viewers if it is perceived as an event that is unlikely to happen to them. However, when violent crime is presented as a random event that could happen to anyone at any time, viewers are more likely to believe that they too could be victimized. When repetitive images of unusual, random, and serious violence saturate media, viewers are apt to become more fearful and more vengeful, for such crimes represent the ultimate breakdown in moral and social order. Thus, understanding how crime is constructed in the media is important to understanding how crime issues become salient to viewers.

Much media research examines how stories are 'framed,' or how the information that is disseminated is organized. Media interpret events for their audiences, thus as Gamson and Wolfsfeld state, "story lines and events take on their meaning from the frame in which they are embedded" (1993:117). For example, illicit drug abuse could be framed as a health issue, or a criminal justice issue; criminality could be framed as a failure of the economic labor market, or as a problem of individual pathology and greed. When story lines about crime are embedded in frames designed to titillate, excite, disgust or sadden the viewer, research suggests the issues become more salient for audiences.

Research finds that television news, in particular, makes heavy use of symbolism and emotionally laden frames in order to capture audience interest. Crime stories, in particular, are stories that are likely to capture audience interest because of the compelling human drama usually found in the story line. For example, a typical crime story: yellow tape around the crime scene, flashing lights of the police cars, the murder victim in a body bag being lifted into the coroner's van, and a brief snippet from a confused and grieving relative; are dramatic and emotional scenarios. Moreover, this script is repeated night after night on the evening news, creating the perception that crime is unpredictable, on the increase, and inevitable. Because of these typical crime scripts, viewers are probably more likely to think about crime issues than they would otherwise.

## THE EXTENT OF CRIME-RELATED MEDIA

As many have suggested, crime-related media influences public opinion about crime because of its pervasive presence in American society. It is well documented that crime content is a pronounced feature of mass media; moreover, the coverage of both crime news and crime drama has steadily increased over the past few decades. For example, a survey of fictional prime-time programs on the three major networks from 1953 to 1996, reported that the percentage of coverage about crime and law enforcement climbed from 4% in 1953 to 16% in 1960, to 33% in 1975, peaked at 37% in 1987, and stood at 20% in 1996 (Surette, 1998). Similarly, others have found that approximately one-third of prime-time television programming from the late 1950's through the mid-1970's was about law enforcement and crime (Dominick, 1973); as was the case in the 1990's (Kasinsky, 1994).

Crime is also a major component of television, newspaper, and radio news. Within newspapers, the percentage of coverage devoted to crime ranges from 4% to 28%, averaging about 7% (Surette, 1992). When news about the criminal justice system is included, coverage ranges from 22% to 28%, and constitutes the third largest subject area. Graber (1980) studied the content of three Chicago newspapers and found that the coverage of individual crime stories surpassed the coverage devoted to Congress and the presidency. Besides making up a sizeable portion of the total news, crime news is consistently read and remembered by a larger percent of subscribers (approximately 25%) than any other type of news (Graber, 1980; Sherizen, 1978).

The percentage of television devoted to crime news is even higher than newspapers, and more prominent. In the early 1990's, Surette (1992) reported that crime news accounted for about 15% of national television news and anywhere from one-fifth to one-third of local television news. The percentage of coverage devoted to crime climbed even higher in the following decade. According to the Center for Media and Public Affairs, throughout the 1990's, the three major television networks covered crime more often than any other topic in their national news broadcasts, and the percentage devoted to crime far surpassed any other topic, including politics and world affairs. (Although crime coverage on the national news broadcasts dropped almost 40% in 2000, it still remains the third largest topic). A survey conducted in the late 1990's of one hundred local television stations found that stories about violent crime comprised about one-third of all news coverage, outstripping coverage of government (approximately 10%) and health (approximately 7%) topics (Klite et al., 1997, in Chiricos et al., 2000). Moreover, crime is often the lead story, especially on local stations (Gerbner, 1996; Romer, Jamieson and Coteau, 1998). Klite et al. (1997) reviewed television news programs over a one-day period and found that 72% of the stations began their evening news broadcasts with a story on crime.

In the late 1980's, crime-related info-tainment programs such as *Cops*, *America's Most Wanted*, and *Unsolved Mysteries*, created a new genre by mixing news and entertainment. This form of crime-related media is important because it deliberately targets lower-income, lower-educated people (Fishman, 1998); heavy viewers tend not to read newspapers, or watch much news on television. Thus, individuals who would not normally get much information about crime from mainstream news are receiving some media information about crime. Although market share from crime-related info-tainment programs is relatively low compared to other prime-time programs, they continue to be a staple of television programming, as they are much less expensive to produce (Fishman, 1998).

## THE DISTORTION OF CRIME IN THE MEDIA

Because most people rely on the mass media for information about crime, realistic presentations of crime and crime distribution are important. This is particularly imperative for news media, since individuals are much more likely to believe the depiction of crime and criminals in the news media than that which is presented in entertainment media.[3] But, it is well documented that the news media distorts the true picture of crime in America. Briefly stated, news media focus on the most atypical crimes, and present distorted images of victims and offenders. News media also paint an unrealistic picture of the criminal justice system by focusing on specific components - such as the police - to the exclusion of others. The reliance of news media on law enforcement as the primary source of information about crime means that only law and order views about crime are presented to the general public on a regular basis.

### *News Media and the Process of Newsmaking*

The process of news creation is important to understanding how information about crime gets distorted. Early research in communications was based on two theoretical models (Surette, 1998). Both hinge on the concept of newsworthiness - what elevates the likelihood that a given story from a pool of potential stories will be important enough to be broadcast or printed. The first model, known as the market model, suggests that reporters gather factual information and objectively report on the issues the public wants to know more about; in other words, public interest drives news media content. In contrast, the manipulative model suggests that what is disseminated to the public is driven by the interests of the news organizations' owners, not the general public. This model assumes that owners are politically conservative, thus, the information that is chosen as news reflects this inherent bias. Most have argued, however, that the process of news dissemination is not quite so simple. As Ericson notes, "mass media economics...work against tight ideological control because mass media texts must articulate with the concerns of a broad array of organizations and institutions in order to obtain a sufficiently broad share of the market" (Ericson, 1991:223).

Organization theories eschew both the market model and the manipulative model by focusing on the demands news organizations face in a market economy. These studies suggest that the daily pressure of producing the news in a profit driven environment creates organizational processes that routinize the reporting system, and in doing so, privilege particular sources and types of information (Chermak, 1994; Ericson, Baranek and Chan, 1989).

News agencies, like other business organizations, must plan and schedule resources. Yet, as Surette notes, the "...central organizational task [of news agencies] is to routinize the processing of nonroutine events" (1998:61). One of the ways news agencies maximize resources is by developing working relationships with organizations that are likely to feed stories of interest to reporters. Journalists are typically assigned to particular 'beats' or specialties, such as local politics, the state department, and local crime. While this may increase a given reporter's understanding of the larger issues, it also has the consequence of delimiting the sources of information about the issues, since reporters assigned to a beat typically develop a small cadre of expert sources to whom they turn, depending on the issue at hand.

With respect to crime stories, numerous studies have documented that reporters typically rely on personnel from criminal justice agencies, (predominantly law enforcement and the courts), for information about crime (Ericson et al., 1989; Fishman, 1980; Sherizen, 1978). These sources provide an easy means of obtaining information, and the public perceives their officials as credible spokespersons. Nonetheless, criminal justice agencies have their own claims about crime; suggesting they are objective sources of information is to ignore the political and economic pressures they face. This is underscored by Schlesinger and Tumber's (1994) work that documents the explosive growth of public relations personnel within law enforcement from the 1970's to the 1990's. During this time period, numerous anti-crime grass-roots organizations (usually victims' rights groups, such as *MADD*) sprang up; these organizations initially competed with law enforcement agencies for media access to promote their messages, many of which denounced ineffective and impersonal police and court treatment.[4] Schlesinger and Tumber believe the large increase in public relations personnel within law enforcement was due, in part, to competing with victims' rights organizations for news media access, as both sides sought to legitimize their claims.

The development of formal linkages to criminal justice organizations facilitates access to crime information for news media, but in doing so, increases both the percentage of crime news that comes from law enforcement and positive images of the police (Kasinsky, 1994). The importance of these criminal justice agencies to the development of crime news is underscored by a recent study that found over 50% of the primary sources cited in crime news stories were from either police or court personnel; almost 30% were from law enforcement alone (Chermak, 1994).

Criminal justice agencies benefit because they determine the pool of available crime stories, and the information that is presented about them. In such a manner, the police and court personnel can focus on certain types of crime events (e.g., rape) or focus on certain types of offenders (e.g., gang members), and in doing so promote their own objectives (Ericson et al., 1989). For example, at press conferences, police departments can preempt potential public criticism of crime control policies by dispassionately presenting reasons why these activities are in the public's best interest. On the other hand, residents whose neighborhoods are targeted may cry police brutality to the press, but their comments come across as emotional and unprofessional.

The courts also have professional spokespersons, thus information about criminal defendants is more apt to come from the prosecution's point of view. During election years, district attorneys often use the media to convey to the public they are 'tough on crime' (Haynie and Dover, 1994). One common strategy is to try high profile cases that are easily winnable, as media coverage of these trials is unusually intense.

This is not to suggest that the mass media unquestioningly accept the official viewpoints of criminal justice agencies. News media regularly criticize criminal justice agencies, particularly the police. Many exposés have uncovered police corruption, management problems, and the inability of police to solve crimes (Ericson et al., 1989; Reiner, 1997). Yet, even negative portrayals are ultimately beneficial to both institutions. By exposing problems within law enforcement, media outlets legitimate their own claims to independent and impartial newsmaking. As Reiner states, "the process of legitimization could never be effective if the media were seen as mere propaganda machines" (1985:139). In turn, the perception of law as an impartial and just system is underscored when corrupt officers are rooted out of the organization, or when unfair policies are modified. Moreover, when police corruption is framed as a 'one bad apple' problem, structural critiques of the institution are averted, as are attacks to its legitimacy (Ericson, 1991; Reiner, 1997). On a more mundane level, police agencies can use their inability to solve crimes to buttress claims for more equipment and personnel.

Although negative evaluations of police or court performance may be found frequently in the news media (particularly newspapers) they usually involve a specific incident; thus problems are perceived as isolated, not ongoing or systematic (Kasinsky, 1994; Reiner, 1997). Moreover, they are more than offset by the enormous amount of favorable media coverage, particularly of the police. For example, Graber's (1980) analysis of newspaper coverage found that the police were portrayed in a positive light six times more frequently than the courts. Of all crime stories, over 21% of them cast the courts in a negative light, compared to only 12% involving police.

Some communications researchers suggest that the news media are hesitant to report on systemic miscarriages of justice within law enforcement agencies because of their heavy reliance on them for information. For example, police officials appear to favor reporters who protect the reputation of law enforcement agencies, and are less likely to help those who have published unfavorable stories about them (Ericson, Baranek and Chan, 1991). Additionally, tabloid reporters appear to be more privy to information about crimes than journalists from more reputable papers because they tend to offer uncritical accounts of the police. In a similar vein, Doyle (1998) found that producers of police info-tainment programs also tend to depict the police in a positive light because of their dependence on them for film footage.

This discussion about newsmaking has focused on how access to information structures the available pool of crime stories. But there are many qualitative dimensions that determine the newsworthiness of a given story. Although there is some difference by type of news media, in general, newsworthiness is also driven by periodicity, consonance, drama, and seriousness of the event, among other factors.

## *Periodicity*

Events more closely tied to a news organization's scheduling needs are more likely to be reported. In general, news organizations prefer day-length events, or longer scenarios that can be compartmentalized into day-length events. One of the reasons crime is so prevalent in the news is because it fits nicely with the requirement of day-length periodicity. This is imperative for television news, which typically uses two minutes at most to deliver a story (Hans and Dee, 1991). Crimes, especially street crimes, are events that occur in the span of minutes, and thus, can be easily compressed into short texts. Thus, the heavy use of the 'perp walk,' in which handcuffed criminal suspects are walked in front of the awaiting press, as they are lead into the police station Ruiz and Treadwell, 2002). Longer, more drawn-out criminal events, such as the taking of hostages, or fleeing from the police down the freeway, can be accommodated with 'special reports' that interrupt regular scheduled television programming.

The requirement of periodicity also impacts how stories are framed. For example, Iyengar (1989) argues there are two types of frames related to timing: 'thematic' coverage that discusses general trends and contextualizes stories within a broader structural perspective, and 'episodic' coverage that uses stories of individuals and individual events divorced from social and historical context. Since thematic coverage requires more information, it cannot be compressed into the short time allowed for television news coverage, and thus is more likely to be found in print media.

How stories are framed contributes to attributions of responsibility about the causes of, and remedies for, social problems. For example, television news media tends to frame the causes of crime as a failure of personal responsibility. Thus, Iyengar found that individuals in his study were more apt to attribute criminal behavior to character flaws (34%) than to societal level causes such as poverty (22%) or cultural norms (14%). Moreover, fully one-half of the respondents believed the solution for crime was strengthened punishment, rather than rehabilitation (16%), a reduction in poverty (9%), or an improved economy (7%). These findings correspond with Sasson's (1995) observation that the dominant media theme used in the 1990's to explain crime was the failure of the criminal justice system; particularly lenient judges and lack of punitive laws.

Most often, crime stories are presented without much information. Studies have documented that the news media seldom examine the causes or motives of a crime. For example, an analysis of six newspapers and three television stations found the causes of crime were mentioned in only 2-4% of all crime stories, and the motives in 20% (Graber, 1980).

## Drama

Drama, excitement, sentiment, and seriousness of the event are easily found in stories about crimes, especially those involving serious violent offenses. Crime news tends to focus on violent personal street crimes; the more common actual offenses such as burglary and theft are usually ignored (Antunes and Hurley, 1977; Ditton and Duffy, 1983). Murder, the rarest type of crime, is the most reported (Surette, 1998). In actuality, murders account for less than one-half of one percent of all crimes known to the police, but they comprise the largest percentage of crime coverage. For example, Graber (1980) found that 25% of crime news is devoted to homicide, and Antunes and Hurley (1977) found coverage ranged between 40% and 50% in the newspapers they studied.

Yet, news media coverage of homicide is misleading as well. Multivariate analyses of homicide coverage in newspapers find that the largest predictor of the length of a story and the prominence of its placement within the newspaper is the number of victims; coverage increases with multiple victims (Chermak; 1998; Johnstone, Hawkins and Michener, 1994). Moreover, a single homicide event often receives multiple stories, especially if the homicide is unusual in some regard (e.g., involves a celebrity or a child victim). For example, one analysis of homicide coverage in *The Los Angeles Times* found that 75% of the homicides reported in the newspaper had at least one follow-up story (Sorenson, Manz and Berk, 1998).

## Consonance

A news story is considered more newsworthy if it ties in with prior coverage. When a new story is presented, themes enable audiences to easily connect it to past stories to situate their understanding of the current information. Thus, criminal events are more likely to become news if they piggyback on themes already familiar to the public. This is a principle known as consonance, for it is believed that stories become more salient to their audiences when they are organized thematically, and when stories make reference to information that has already been presented. However, when reporters employ these reference themes, the information they present about crime becomes horribly skewed and distorted. In meeting the demands of consonance, news media often create crime waves, or moral panics - the perception that particular types of crimes are increasing in number, when in reality, they are not.

Longitudinal studies of news media find that crime coverage is seldom related to actual crime rates (Beckett, 1997; Davis, 1952; Dorfman and Schiraldi, 2001; Graber, 1980; Sheley and Ashkins, 1981). The coverage of crime in the news has steadily increased since the 1950's, whereas crime rates fluctuated up and down over this period.[5] In the 1990's, when crime rates were falling, the number of crime stories in the media exploded. For example, from 1992 to 1995 the national news broadcasts more than quadrupled their crime coverage; from 830 to 2,574 stories. A content analysis of the *Los Angeles Times* newspaper from 1990 to 1994 found that the number of homicide stories increased by 473%, although homicide rates in Los Angeles County had decreased by one-third during that time period (Dorfman and Schiraldi, 2001). When actual crime rates do increase, the media often use hyperbolic terms to describe them. Increases in crime are frequently described as a 'mushrooming cloud,' or 'spreading cancer' (Sacco, 1995).

Similarly, when media focus on specific types of crime, the trends they describe are seldom based on any significant actual increase in these crimes. As Fishman (1978) noted in his influential work on media-created crime waves, it is the *perception* that crime is increasing, rather than crime itself that rises. In his study of the wave of crimes against the elderly in New York City, Fishman found that it began from the efforts of one television news editor to organize individual crime stories into a compelling news theme during a particularly slow news day one summer. When scanning the police dispatches, the news editor discovered two elderly citizens had been mugged near where the police were hosting a crime prevention meeting for senior citizens. Both stories were relevant to a series the station had been airing about a new in the police department to handle senior victims of crime. Thus, the theme - crimes against the elderly - was created for the evening broadcast.

Over the ensuing days, other news organizations quickly picked up the theme, and also reported on crimes against the elderly. In turn, local police agencies responded by providing more stories about crimes against the elderly from their available pool of reported crimes. The police and other city officials also used the media to demonstrate to the public what they were doing to combat the problem. As Fishman notes, one-third of the news coverage of the crime wave was generated from covering the responses of politicians, law enforcement and other officials to the 'threat.' But the actual number of crimes against the elderly never did increase during this time, just the number of media reports about it. Other studies in this vein have repeatedly documented this process of creating crime waves and 'moral panics' over the last twenty years, for cocaine use (Orcutt and Turner, 1993), crack cocaine epidemics (Reeves and Campbell, 1994; Reinarman and Levine, 1997), drug-related violence (Brownstein, 1995), serial murder (Jenkins, 1994), and gangs (Zatz, 1987).

During the process of crime waves, institutions of social control and media both gain legitimacy. Media is perceived to be a legitimate institution working in the best interests of the public by 'discovering' a potential threat, by alerting citizens to the issue, and by demanding government action. In responding to the crime wave, institutions of social control are legitimized as a necessary force to combat such menacing threats to public safety.

Barak argues that during the 1990's, increased competition from other media outlets drove mass media news organizations to develop more and more dramatic themes during times when crime waves could not be exploited. Three dominant crime themes emerged during the 1990's: criminal predators, sexual victims, and police-citizen encounters. He argues the theme of the violent, depraved criminal predator, "a euphemism for young, Black male" has so saturated the news media that it needs no contextualization: crime is serious violence "committed by unpredictable strangers" (1994a:137, 144). Thus, "only the state and its agents of control are capable of confronting a crime problem that is out of control" (145).

## *Media Depictions of Offenders and Victims*

The news media have long distorted the image of the typical criminal (Graber, 1980) - if an image is given. However, crimes are most often reported without any description of the perpetrator, leaving the viewer to draw their own conclusions (Sheley and Ashkins, 1981). Yet research has shown that public perceptions of offenders are extremely narrow and biased. For example, in one study respondents read descriptions about violent crimes but were given no information about the offenders. When asked to identify the alleged offender, the majority of respondents described a lower class, uneducated male (Roberts and Gebotys, 1989).

When the news media does present information about offenders, it is also unrepresentative. Most studies find only slight differences in the percentage of Black offenders compared to White offenders, for all crimes reported in the news media (Chermak, 1995; Dixon and Linz, 2000; see Gilliam and Iyengar, 2000 for larger difference). Some research finds Blacks are disproportionately portrayed as offenders in the news media relative to their proportion of actual crime offenders; either overrepresented as offenders (Dixon and Linz, 2000), or underrepresented (Chiricos and Eschholz, 2002). More importantly, most research finds that Blacks are far more likely to be portrayed as violent offenders than are Whites (Dixon and Linz, 2000; Dorfman and Schiraldi, 2001; Entman, 1992; Gilliam and Iyengar, 2000; Romer et al. 1998; Sheley and Ashkins, 1981); Whites are much more likely to be depicted as non-violent and white-collar offenders. Moreover, Black offenders are portrayed as more troublesome than Whites - they are much more likely to be shown resisting arrest and/or assaulting police officers compared to Whites (Oliver, 1994) - and police use of force is much more likely to involve Black offenders (Entman, 1992). This tends to promote the concept that African Americans are dangerous, and may serve to underscore prejudice against them. In fact, one study found that respondents actually perceived *greater* involvement of Blacks in street crime that what was reflected in media accounts (Graber, 1980).

Entman (1992) analyzed approximately 2500 minutes of footage from local news broadcasts in Chicago, and found that one-half of all the stories about African Americans were either stories about politics (the largest category) or crime (the second largest category). Of all crime offenders covered in the news, 84% of Blacks were involved in violent crime, compared to 71% of White offenders. There were also significant differences in the visual presentations of African Americans and Whites accused of violent crimes. For example, 65% of Whites were named when their mug shot was televised; in contrast, only 49% of Blacks were named. Entman argues that "the anonymous individual portrait exemplifies the stereotype" of Black as offender (350). Similarly, Chiricos and Eschholz (2002) found that Blacks were twice as likely as Whites to have their mug shot shown on the news.

Entman also found that African Americans were twice as likely to be shown in the "grip of a restraining officer" than Whites (38% versus 18%); and they were much more likely to have a White officer speak about them. In contrast, no Black officers were ever shown speaking about a White offender. Another study found that 85% of Blacks were identified as the offender when the victim was of another race, compared to only 62% of White offenders that had victimized someone of another race. Although relatively few content analyses have specifically examined the portrayal of Latinos in television crime news, recent studies find they are much more likely to be shown as offenders than as victims (Chiricos and Eschholz, 2002; Dixon and Linz, 2000).

Communication researchers suggest that this race/ethnicity distortion in crime news adds to an ethnic-blame discourse in which nonwhites are blamed for the problems of Whites (Van Dijk, 1993). Entman argues that the typical crime scripts found on television news increases the tendency of "some Whites to lump...most Blacks into categories with negative characteristics" (1992:345). Many believe that when the media sends the message that young Black men are predacious, eventually we believe the message.

Scheingold (1995) refers to this message as the "myth of crime and punishment." If we are led to believe that criminals are fundamentally different in character and appearance - predatory strangers waiting to attack unsuspecting victims - then the morally justifiable and effective response to street crime is harsh punishment. Moreover, if criminals are easily identifiable and punishment is promoted as an effective solution, then crime is not so complex - it becomes a morality play between good and evil. In this manner, the myth not only offers scapegoats for the complex problems of economic decline and racial injustice, but easy solutions as well.

In an interesting experiment (Gilliam and Iyengar, 2000), subjects (n=1675) watched a fifteen-minute selection of local news reports; the middle of the clip contained a crime story with a five-second snapshot of the suspect. Only the race of the suspect was manipulated in the experiment (Black, White or none). Subjects were then asked to answer a series of questions on race and crime issues. Subjects were more likely to recall the offender as Black, even when no offender had been shown. Most importantly, among White respondents, watching the video of the Black offender heightened negative attitudes toward African Americans and punitiveness (as measured by dichotomous responses to support for the death penalty, three strikes legislation, and more police). The researchers concluded that the racial narrative of crime that dominates television news "does not go unnoticed" and "...has made race an even more central component of American life" (571-572).

The presentation of victims is also distorted by the news media. To begin with, criminal victims are usually ignored (Chermak, 1995), and if portrayed, are misrepresented. Women, the very young or old, and those of higher status are disproportionately overrepresented as victims (Chermak, 1995). Whites are much more likely to be presented as victims; and the race of an offender is usually identified when the victim of a violent crime is White (Pritchard and Hughes, 1997). An analysis of crime coverage in *The Los Angeles Times* found that inter-racial homicide and those involving strangers were the most likely murders to be covered, particularly if they happened to affluent victims (Sorenson et al., 1998); an analysis of Chicago newspapers also found similar results (Johnstone et al., 1994).

## COMPARISON OF CRIME-RELATED MEDIA

### *Crime News: Television and Print Media*

While both television news and newspapers present a distorted construction of crime, criminals, and the criminal justice system, there are some differences in the type of information presented. In general, newspaper coverage of crime is much more substantive than television news, understandable given the short time frame in which television stories have to be presented (Graber, 1980: Stroman and Seltzer, 1985).

Newspaper accounts usually present more detailed information about criminal events and cases. This level of detail is important because some studies find that the more information presented about specific criminal cases, the lower the punitive response (Doob and Roberts, 1984; Roberts and Gebotys, 1989). Newspapers are more likely to report on crime trends, often accompanied with a number of visual aids, such as charts and graphs.

Research suggests that the processes that govern newsmaking do not operate equally for print and television news. In particular, television news programs face more competition than do newspapers, and they are more expensive to produce. Such pressure creates the need for stories that are more visually interesting, dramatic and exciting (Sheley and Ashkins, 1984). Consequently, most research finds television news programs place an even heavier emphasis on violent crimes than do newspapers. For example, although the percentage of total news coverage devoted to crime was slightly higher in newspapers than television, Sheley and Ashkins (1981) found that homicide coverage accounted for 45% of newspaper crime news but 80% of television crime news.

Newspaper coverage of crime also presents more information about the criminal justice system than does television news, although the relative amount of news coverage on the criminal justice system, especially the courts and corrections, is slight overall (Surette, 1998). For both forms of media, seldom is any glimpse into the court process given, except for the sentencing phase, which is most likely to be reported, particularly for more serious offenses (Graber, 1980). Thus, people are more aware of problems (or perceived shortcomings) with judges and sentencing than they are of earlier and less publicized stages such as plea negotiating.

The exceptions are the media blizzards that swirl around celebrity court trials, or the trials of those accused of the most egregious crimes; in the last twenty years American's have developed an insatiable appetite for coverage of these types of trials, particularly on television (Fox and Van Sickel, 2001). As Surette notes, these trials may comprise a small portion of total crime coverage, but an important one, for these depictions are taken as representative of typical court processes (1998).

Fox and Van Sickel (2001) analyzed how coverage of sensational criminal trials (such as the O.J. Simpson and JonBenet Ramsey cases) influenced viewers' understanding and opinions of the criminal justice system. One group of respondents was 'primed' (that is, they were asked about specific criminal trials before they were asked to give their opinions of the criminal justice system); the other group was not primed before they were asked about the criminal justice system. Fox and Van Sickel found that respondents had significantly less confidence in the system if they were primed, than respondents that were not primed. Moreover, respondents with knowledge of media trials were much less confident that they would be treated fairly by the criminal justice system if they were accused of a crime. Fox and Van Sickel concluded, "Such increased cynicism may be the most damaging effect of tabloid-style legal coverage. This overall decrease in legitimacy...is what concerns us most of all" (2001:143), especially given changes in news media consumption of the American public.

Trends in mainstream news media consumption patterns document a steady erosion of consumers over the last three decades. GSS data reveals that the percentage of people who read a newspaper daily has significantly decreased, from 75% in 1970 to 43% in 1998. Similarly, Nielsen Media Research finds that the percent of households that view network news broadcasts on any given evening of the week has decreased from 75% in 1970 to 49% in 1998. Fox and Van Sickel (2001) argue that faced with declining public consumption, coupled with stiff competition from alternative sources, such as cable television and the Internet, mainstream media have had to repackage the way news is presented. In the 1990's, both respectable print media and national network television news programs changed to more 'tabloid' style of reporting: heavy emphasis on the sensational, personal and unusual; and more emphasis on entertainment rather than educative components.

Research on the effects of reading crime coverage in tabloid journals suggests similarities to research on the effects of television news. Both tabloid journals and television news present decontextualized short stories that focus on sensational, violent crimes. They both make heavy use of visuals of the crime scene, or grieving victims, and mug shots of the offender (if any information is given about the offender). Studies which compare the effects of crime presentations in tabloid journals compared to the mainstream press find that readers of tabloid journals have higher fear of crime than those that read more respected newspapers and they greatly overestimate the amount of local crime risk (Schlesinger et al., 1991; Williams and Dickinson, 1993).

In short, crime news takes the relatively rare event and presents it as a more common occurrence. However, because white-collar crimes or convoluted corporate schemes are too complex for television news they are more likely to be covered in newspapers. In contrast, television news is more likely to have sensational coverage of violent crime. Since television crime news presents much less information and detail compared to the print media, it is likely that the effect of newspapers on punitiveness will be far less influential than television news viewing. The few studies that have compared the effects of newspaper to television news consumption find that viewers of television report more fear of crime than do readers of newspapers (Chiricos et al., 1997; O'Keefe and Reid-Nash, 1987; Stroman and Seltzer, 1985). Television viewers are also more likely to attribute crime to a lenient justice system, or to the character flaws and lifestyles of individuals, suggesting that the tendency of television news to frame crime as individual pathology does seem to effect individual's perceptions. In contrast, newspaper readers were more likely to cite poverty as the primary cause of crime (Stroman and Seltzer, 1985).

## *Crime-Related Television Entertainment*

### *Crime Info-tainment*

Crime info-tainment programs are a hybrid of entertainment and news programming. The presentations usually take one of two approaches: a documentary style format in which the details of the crime are given, often through re-enactments; or actual coverage of the event, most often centering on the apprehension of the criminal suspect by the police. Some shows, such as *America's Most Wanted*, increase ratings through audience participation in which viewers are asked to call in if they have information about the alleged offender.[6]

As with television crime news, crime info-tainment programs also present a much distorted picture of crime, but place an even greater emphasis on violent crime (Doyle, 1998; Oliver, 1994). For example, 33% of the stories about crimes committed against women on *America's Most Wanted* were about homicide and 17% were about sexual molestation of girls (Cavender and Bond-Maupin, 1999).

Similar to television news, portrayals of offenders and victims are also race biased. Blacks and Latinos are much more likely to be depicted as offenders than Whites. In contrast, Whites are far more likely to be portrayed as victims or as police officers (Cavender and Bond-Maupin, 1999; Oliver, 1994).

Crime info-tainment programs also devote little time to the complexity of the criminal justice process. Instead, these programs usually focus on the crime event, or the criminal offender. Reality programming emphasizes the apprehension of criminals as the most expeditious way to curb crime (Donovan, 1998); on *Cops*, 75% of the events police respond to end in an arrest (Kooistra et al., 1998). They also tend to present the police as more effective in their work than arrest data would suggest they are (Oliver, 1994).

As Surette (1998) outlines, the troubling aspect of crime info-tainment programs is that they appear to discuss the crime issue from all angles and viewpoints, as if the portrayal were factual, objective, and comprehensive. Recent studies suggest that viewers of crime info-tainment perceive these shows as much more realistic than crime dramas (Doyle, 1998). But content analyses demonstrate a different reality: as with crime news, the focus is on sensational, atypical crime events or the apprehension and arrest of criminal suspects. The 'crime-stopper' shows such as *Unsolved Mysteries* focus on homicides, kidnapping, and other serious violent crimes (Doyle, 1998; Surette, 1994). While *Cops* tends to focus on more common street crimes such as domestic violence, public order disturbances, or public drunkenness than do the crime-stopper programs, it still contains a disproportionate amount of violent crimes. Moreover, while glimpses into the futility of offenders' lives are occasionally shown on *Cops*, seldom is any sympathetic portrayal of the alleged offender given, nor is any structural explanation to account for the crime.

Crime control issues focus primarily on law enforcement efforts, most often by depicting the actual chase and capture of the criminal(s), or by documenting the painstaking efforts of the police investigation. This implicitly justifies the portrayal of police use of force so often shown on *Cops*. Content analyses that compare reality-based crime shows find that law enforcement programs, such as *Cops*, contain the most violence, usually directed against the alleged offender (Oliver, 1994). For example, Oliver found that 51% of the police officers on *Cops* used at least one form of aggression against an offender during arrest; officers acted much more violently than did the suspects in all situations.

Other aspects of the criminal justice system are seldom mentioned; if they are, the reference is often indirect, fleeting, and implicitly negative. This is particularly true for certain aspects of the courts (such as judges and defense attorneys), and corrections (such as parole boards). Although seldom depicted, when shown, the courts are usually presented as soft on criminals, and the court system as privileging the civil rights of offenders over the rights of the innocent. Corrections are also usually cast in a negative light - prisons are portrayed as ineffectual systems that do not rehabilitate offenders but instead operate a revolving door through which violent offenders pass again and again. In contrast, the police are portrayed as effective soldiers who struggle daily to keep their communities safe from the rising tide of crime. Not surprisingly, research finds that increased viewing of reality-based crime shows is associated with increased race prejudice, authoritarianism, and punitiveness among Whites (Oliver and Armstrong, 1995).

## *Crime Dramas*

The effects of crime dramas are probably not as strong as other forms of crime-related media because they are fictional entertainment. The narrative in crime dramas typically follows a relatively simple and straightforward presentation. Crime is perpetrated by bad or evil people and represents a threat to the moral fabric of a community. Whether it is a police chase, an investigation, or a trial that is dramatized, the resolution almost inevitably involves a restoration of law and order. When it does not, it is often attributed to the system's inexplicable allegiance to the due process and civil rights of defendants.

Analyses of crime dramas find that coverage of law enforcement predominates, followed by the courts, which tend to focus on the efforts of prosecutors. Yet, as Stark (1987) outlines, judges and prosecutors spend as much time solving crimes as they do practicing law. As Surette (1998:39) suggests, the most common depiction of lawyers and judges is that they "secretly want to be police officers." The offenders they do represent are usually dangerous and violent; and unlike the reality of plea-bargaining, compromises, and assembly-line justice, most cases go to trial (Hans and Dee, 1991; Stark, 1987). Again, this is more likely to make viewers believe that most criminals, even vicious predators, receive a more than adequate defense, and free of charge if necessary. Therefore, if criminals are found guilty, it is because they *are* guilty, not because of some miscarriage of justice.

In general, police are portrayed in a much more positive light than are the courts, but they are more likely to be engaged in vigilante justice. Courts are more likely to be portrayed as offender friendly. Criminals are set free on 'technicalities' and judges seem to care more about the rights of defendants than they do about victims (Crew, 1990). Similarly, criminal defense attorneys are often presented as unscrupulous characters that would do anything to get their clients acquitted, or as individuals morally torn about having to defend guilty clients.

In contrast, police heroes often appear wary of the criminal courts. Disgusted with their ineffectiveness, police have to turn to other methods to deal with criminals. Often portrayed as lone individuals working outside of the system, they sometimes have to violate the law in order to catch criminals. This is all justified when the criminal is finally removed from society by either being killed or captured by the rogue cop. The message delivered is that heroes often have to resort to unlawful and unethical modes of conduct when fighting crime. If they break a few laws, or step on an individual's rights, these are portrayed as infrequent and necessary. Consequently, the criminal justice system's moral and philosophical foundation is never challenged - only the unnecessary bureaucracy that impedes its effectiveness (Crew, 1990; Surette, 1998).

Unlike television news and crime info-tainment programs, crime dramas present a more racially balanced view of offenders and victims. Content analyses of crime fictional programming find that African Americans are not as likely to be portrayed as criminal, or aggressive (Dominick, 1973; Estep and Macdonald, 1984; Potter et al., 1995). But one recent content analysis of crime dramas found that police use of force was more common when the offender was a young, ethnic minority (Mastro and Robinson, 2000).

Nevertheless, "the repeated message in the entertainment media is that crime is perpetrated by predatory individuals who are basically different from the rest of us and that criminality stems from individual problems. Crime is behavior criminals choose freely, and media criminals are not bound or restrained by normal social rules and values"

(Surette, 1994:134). If crime is perceived as increasingly violent and random; committed by increasingly animalistic, predatory, and irrational criminals on a helpless and innocent public, this is apt to produce an increase in a punitive response toward offenders, if media has any influence on public opinion of crime and crime policy.

In fact, Zillman and Wakshlag (1985) suggest that heavy viewers of crime drama should not only have a greater dislike of criminal offenders and higher esteem for "those who restore justice and safety," but also greater acceptance of violence to combat crime. A recent test of this hypothesis found that the association was mediated by gender. Heavy male viewers of crime drama were more accepting of aggression against criminals than males that viewed less crime drama, but this relationship was not found among women (Reith, 1999).

In short, the influence of crime dramas on punitiveness and fear of crime should be relatively slight or non-existent, given that most people will perceive the programs as fictional, and not truly reflective of social reality. However, heavy viewers of crime drama should have higher just world beliefs, as there is always a resolution to unlawful behavior that upholds the law and order perspective.

# MEDIA EFFECTS ON PUBLIC OPINION OF CRIME

## *Crime-related Media and Fear of Crime*

Research into the effects of media on fear of crime began in the 1970's with the work of George Gerbner and associates who developed the 'cultivation hypothesis.' According to this view, the media communicates a very narrow and homogenous view of the world. Over time, with repeated exposure to television, individuals' beliefs about the world more closely mirror television reality, no matter how inaccurate television portrayals might be. In particular, heavy viewers develop what Gerbner has termed a 'mean-world view': they become cynical, distrustful, and fearful (Gerbner and Gross, 1976; Gerbner et al., 1986; 1994). Early empirical tests found some evidence that heavy television viewers were more likely to view the world as 'mean,' violent, and crime-ridden. They were also more distrustful, cynical, fearful, alienated, and suspicious of others (Gerbner and Gross, 1976; Gerbner et al, 1980; 1986). Yet, subsequent studies found no effects, or very small effects when controlling for sociodemographic variables or when redefining the measurement of 'heavy viewing' (e.g., Hirsch, 1980; 1981; Hughes, 1980). For example, Hughes found that when controlling for local crime rates, size of town of residence, and sociodemographic factors, the effect of television viewing on fear of crime was nonexistent. Further studies indicated the effects of media are not uniform, but vary according to local crime rates (Doob and Macdonald, 1979), crime media format (O'Keefe and Reid-Nash, 1987), the type of crime depicted (Schlesinger et al., 1991; Williams and Dickinson, 1993), the location of the criminal event (Heath, 1984; Gunter, 1987; Winkel and Vrij, 1990), and whether the crime is presented as random (Heath, 1984; Liska and Baccaglini, 1990).

For example, Doob and Macdonald (1979) found no relationship between television watching and fear of crime when actual neighborhood crime levels, sex and age were controlled. However, within high crime areas they found a significantly higher level of fear for those that watched the most television, and a significantly lower level of fear for those who read newspapers. In low crime areas there were no such patterns. In fact, Doob and Macdonald concluded that the relationship between media exposure and fear of crime is completely spurious - those who live in high crime areas stay inside and watch more television *because* they are fearful of local crime. Similarly, Zillman and Wakshlag (1985) argued that fear of victimization was antecedent to television viewing. Fearful people watch crime dramas because the restoration of law and order at the end of each episode provide some sense of security. One study did find that viewing crime dramas cultivated perceptions of a just world, but not fear (Gunter and Wober, 1983).

In reply to Doob and Macdonald and others, Gerbner et al. (1980) hypothesized that variable responses to crime-related media are indicative of the 'resonance' of the media message with the consumer's experiences: media effects are stronger when they reflect real life experiences. When mediated reality reflects lived reality, media messages are more salient to the viewer, for they resonate with personal experiences. Nevertheless, they argued this does not negate the 'mainstreaming' effects of television. That is, heavy viewers of television will develop social perceptions of the world that are reflective of media reality; moreover, these perceptions will be homogenous across viewers, regardless of demographic characteristics.

Subsequent tests find evidence of resonance; people that live in high crime areas are more fearful (e.g., Chiricos et al., 2000; Heath and Petraitis, 1987). Recent research also suggests that fear is further amplified when residents perceive they live in neighborhoods with a high percentage of Black residents; again providing support for the resonance hypothesis given the media' inordinate attention to Black offenders (Eschholz et al., 2003).

Others have tested for the effects of media while controlling for direct personal experiences, such as prior criminal victimization (Gomme, 1988; Weaver and Wakshlag, 1986). Some studies report the effect of mass media on fear of crime is mediated by prior personal victimization, but not in the direction indicative of resonance. For example, Weaver and Wakshlag (1986) found a significant positive correlation between exposure to crime-related television programming and fear of crime for individuals who had never experienced direct victimization. Conversely, the effects of media were negatively correlated with those who had been victimized, leading them to conclude that crime-related television programs allow for a 'safe,' accessible, and acceptable means of relieving anxiety about possible future victimizations, because the portrayals are dissimilar to their own lives and/or prior victimization experience. Gomme (1988) compared the direct and indirect effects of media exposure and direct personal victimization and found that direct victimization has a larger effect on fear of crime than does media. Because of these conflicting results many continued to argue the effects of media are spurious (Gunter, 1987).

Analogous to evidence from agenda-setting research, some have suggested that the effects of mass media on fear of crime are strongest for those that have no direct experience with crime; thus media depictions serve as a substitute for reality. Without real experiences to counterbalance the media messages, people more removed from crime, namely, higher social class individuals, are more susceptible to the fear engendering aspects of crime-related media. Empirical tests of this perspective have shown that media effects are more significant for people who have no direct experience with crime, are more significant for new issues, and are more significant for those who are socially isolated (Gunter, 1987; Liska and Baccaglini, 1990; Weaver and Wakshlag, 1986).

Research also suggests that an important dimension to the resonating effects of mass media on fear of crime is proximity of the media depicted criminal activity. For example, Heath (1984) found that the impact of crime news in newspapers is dependent on whether the reported crime is local or distant. Not surprisingly, news about local crime was found to significantly increase fear of crime. Moreover, when local criminal activity was presented as sensational or random, the increase in fear of crime was even greater. Conversely, sensational acts of distant random violence tended to decrease reported levels of fear. Heath explained this paradox by suggesting that news of distant crime allows people to compare their situation with others who are worse off, thus alleviating anxiety about crime in their own communities. Similarly, in a series of experimental designs, Tyler and Cook (1984) found that exposure to media influences the judgments an individual makes about the larger community and social phenomena (societal level judgments), but does not impact an individual's assessment of their own lives (personal level judgments). Thus, media influences attitudes and perceptions about the 'crime problem,' but does not influence an individual's fear of crime, or assessment of potential victimization (see also Sacco, 1982; Skogan and Maxfield, 1981). As Heath and Petraitis conclude, television appears to increase fear of "distant urban settings," but not one's neighborhood unless "those neighborhoods look like the crime-ridden neighborhoods depicted on TV" (1987:122).

One of the problems with disentangling the effects of media on fear is the variation in their content. Although earlier work suggested the level of violence was the important factor in developing mean-world syndrome and elevating fear, subsequent research suggests that the perceived realism of the content is the most important factor (Potter, 1986).

More recently, Chiricos et al. (1997) found that the specific content of the news is key to elevating fear of crime. In their study of television news and fear of crime, the only respondents whose fear of crime was strongly related to television news consumption were those most likely to be portrayed as victims - White women. Similarly, Winkel and Vrij (1990) found that women who read newspaper stories about rape became more fearful of possible rape victimization, but not of other types of criminal victimization. The effects were even larger if the media stories were of local rapes.

However, crime stories typically do not provide much detail about the victim(s), the setting in which the crime occurred, and the circumstances surrounding the event. Consequently, these presentations may be irrelevant to most of the audience; they simply do not use the stories to assess their own risk of victimization. Likewise, because most crime news is comprised of non-local events, these presentations probably do not influence assessments of one's immediate neighborhood.

In contrast, reports of crimes spread by family, co-workers and neighbors are more likely to include victims that are known to either the storyteller or the audience. Consequently, these portrayals are far less easy to dismiss, and much more likely to impact one's assessment of personal risk. In fact, many studies of fear of crime find that media coverage of crime is not as important as gossip or rumor about crime, especially for local crime stories (Smith, 1984; Tyler, 1984), although Guo et al. (2001) find that media exaggerations about crime in other areas arc amplified by informal communication with members of one's community, thus increasing fear of other environments.

As outlined, media impact on fear of crime is certainly a very complicated process. Moreover, as with the general literature on fear of crime, studies of media effects on fear of crime have also suffered from a number of the methodological problems noted earlier: very small sample sizes, use of single-item indicators to measure fear of crime, and too few control variables in the models. Television viewing is often measured only in number of hours, not specific content. Although the large body of research does strongly suggest a relationship between crime-related media consumption and fear of crime, much more work remains to be done. In particular, various forms of crime-related media need to be examined in a multivariate model to ascertain their relative effects on fear of crime.

## Crime-related Media and Crime Seriousness

A relatively unexplored area of research is media influence on public perceptions of crime seriousness. Roberts and Stalans note "public perceptions of crime seriousness reflect stereotypical conceptions of crimes and their consequences, just as perceptions of individual offenders are influenced by what the public think a typical offender is like" (1997:59). Consequently, media may not only influence our emotional response to crime, but also how we view crime relative to other harmful or wrongful acts.

As noted earlier, if the presentation of crime is distorted by the overrepresentation of violent crime, it seems reasonable to assume that this will create the perception among the public that most crime is violent in nature. Moreover, since little information about the details of the crime, offender, or motive is given, people fill in the missing information from their repository of information about crime (most likely gleaned from media presentations). Since most depicted crime is serious and/or violent, and criminals presented as abnormal, respondents are likely to perceive crime as more similar to that in the media, namely, more severe in its perceived harm than in its actual harm. Given that research on crime seriousness finds consistently high absolute and relative rankings of violent crime, and given that research finds intent is often imputed for violent offenses, it seems reasonable to assume that heavy crime-related media intake will be positively related to the rating of crime seriousness. In fact, both survey (Gebotys, Roberts, and Dasgupta, 1988) and experimental (Roberts and Edwards, 1989) research finds this relationship.

In a survey of news media consumption and ratings of crime seriousness for nine offenses, Gebotys et al. (1988) hypothesized that heavy crime-related media consumption could result in one of two outcomes. First, heavy viewers of crime-related media could become desensitized to the seriousness of most crimes because they pale in comparison to the gory and brutal acts frequently shown on television. If so, the relationship between crime-related media consumption and crime seriousness ratings would be negative. On the other hand, the manner in which crime is portrayed could provide a contextual judgment that bleeds over into other judgments about subsequent unrelated criminal events; what they term an 'anchoring effect.' If so, consumption of violent crime-ridden media may make other crimes seem more serious as well, suggesting a positive relationship. The researchers found support for anchoring effects as did an experimental design in which subjects that had read about a series of brutal crimes before rating the seriousness of other crimes viewed the other crimes as more serious than did subjects who had not read the stories (Roberts and Edwards, 1989).

## *Crime-related Media and Punitiveness*

While the widespread belief is that heavy crime-based media consumption engenders support for punitive criminal justice policies, in reality, very few studies have actually attempted to measure the relationship. Moreover, most of the supporting evidence is based on simple correlations, fails to account for numerous other important factors known to influence attitudes about criminal punishment, and often uses non-representative samples. The few studies that surveyed public opinion of sentencing policies have found consistent evidence of a positive correlation between media consumption and punitiveness (Barrile, 1984; Carlson, 1985; Surette, 1985). However, these studies have primarily used correlated data with few control variables. For example, Barille's work examined only simple (from zero-order to fifth-order) partial correlations and used a very small sample (n=187) of residents in one Connecticut city. He found that increases in the number of hours spent watching television were correlated with stereotypical views of offenders (as immoral individuals who commit crimes because of selfish desires or evil tendencies) and support for more punitive prison sentences, controlling for the effects of income, occupation and social class background. Moreover, heavy viewers of television were also more likely to support the death penalty and believe that the courts coddle criminals. Similarly, Carlson's (1985) work also employed simple correlations, and while his sample was considerably larger (over 1200), it was of adolescents. Nevertheless, he also found a strong correlation between television viewing and support for more punitive criminal justice policies. He also found that heavy viewers had less knowledge of the criminal justice system and processes, and were more likely to favor crime control.

One quasi-experimental study compared the reactions to a criminal case covered by both a tabloid journal and a mainstream newspaper. The researchers found that respondents who had read the shorter (and more sensational) tabloid version supported a lengthier prison sentence than those who had read the longer and more detailed coverage presented by the mainstream press (Roberts and Doob, 1990).

## *Crime-Related Media Hypotheses*

A number of hypotheses can be derived from the above discussion. To begin with, given the disproportionate presentation of violent crime in the media, increases in crime-related media should increase fear of crime, although these effects will be conditioned by other sociodemographic factors. For example, given their structural position relative to Whites, Latinos and African Americans are probably more likely to have experience with crime; therefore, crime-related media should have more impact on their fear if the resonance hypothesis is correct. If the affinity hypothesis is correct, heavy news consumption should engender more fear among Whites since they are more likely to be depicted as victims.

Second, because there are differences in the type of information about crime presented in the various media, they should have variable effects, especially on fear of crime. Specifically, because newspapers present more information about the details of a criminal event, they should have less effect on fear of crime compared to the more sensational and hyperbolic presentation of crime found in local television news, crime info-tainment, and crime dramas.

Third, given that media present a world that is increasingly crime-ridden (and often at odds with actual crime trends) increases in crime-related media content should increase perceptions that state crime is increasing. Moreover, because newspapers present more information about crime, and are the most likely media form to show graphs and other detailed information about crime trends, those that read newspapers more frequently should have more accurate perceptions of actual statewide crime rates. Because crime rates had already been declining for many years prior to this study's survey administration, we should find that those who read newspapers more frequently are less inclined to believe crime rates had increased than those that do not read as often.

Fourth, the consumption of crime-related media should also influence cognitive perceptions of local crime, dependent on the type of media. Specifically, local television news and newspapers will have an impact on the perception of crime in one's neighborhood, because they are more likely to feature stories about crime that involve one's local environment compared to crime info-tainment or crime dramas. Therefore, increases in both local television news and newspaper consumption should lead to perceptions of greater neighborhood crime risk. Moreover, as specified above, these effects should be greater for Latinos or African Americans, since they are more likely to live in neighborhoods presented in crime news.

Fifth, if feelings of safety are actually measuring physical vulnerability to crime, crime related media should not influence assessments of one's ability to fend off a criminal victimization. Therefore, crime-related media consumption should not be related to feeling safe.

Sixth, because of the nature of crimes presented in the media, those who are bigger consumers of crime-related media may view crimes more seriously, as they are probably anchored by the violent crime images constantly portrayed in the media. The effects should be stronger for the media most likely to present crime as graphic, random, and senseless: local television, crime info-tainment, and crime dramas.

Seventh, because of the simple morality plays presented on crime-related television programs, in which threats to the existing moral and social order are almost always resolved in favor of the forces of good, those who watch more crime-related television should have higher belief in a just world.

Finally, because of the inordinate emphasis on crime control as the primary solution to decrease crime, those who consume more crime-related media should be more punitive. They should be less likely to support rehabilitation, and more likely to support three strikes for a wider variety of offenses. Because newspapers are more likely to present detailed information about the criminal justice system, and of actual sentences received for particular criminal cases, they should have less of an impact on punitiveness compared to local television news, crime info-tainment, and crime dramas.

*Hypothesis 17:*     *Increases in television news and newspaper consumption will increase perceptions of neighborhood crime risk*

*Hypothesis 17.a:*  *The effects of crime-related media will be stronger for Blacks and Latinos*

*Hypothesis 18:*     *The greater the exposure to television news and crime info-tainment, the more likely the belief that state crime rates have increased. Newspapers decrease this perception.*

*Hypothesis 19:*    Crime-related media consumption is not related to feeling safe.

*Hypothesis 20:*    The greater the exposure to television news, crime info-tainment and newspapers, the higher the fear of crime. Crime dramas will have no effect.

*Hypothesis 20.a:*    The effects of crime-related media will be stronger for Blacks and Latinos.

*Hypothesis 21:*    The greater the exposure to crime-related media, the greater the belief in a just world.

*Hypothesis 21.a:*    Crime-related media will have stronger effects on the just world beliefs of Whites compared to Blacks or Latinos.

*Hypothesis 21.b:*    The effects of crime-related media on just world beliefs will vary across type of media. Specifically, the effects of crime info-tainment, local television news, and crime dramas will be stronger compared to the effects of newspapers.

*Hypothesis 22:*    The greater the exposure to crime-related media, the higher the rating of crime seriousness.

*Hypothesis 22.a:*    The effects of crime-related media on crime seriousness ratings will vary across type of media. Specifically, the effects of crime info-tainment, local television news, and crime dramas will be stronger than the effects of newspapers.

*Hypothesis 23:*    The greater the exposure to crime-related media, the lower support for rehabilitation.

*Hypothesis 23.a:*    Crime-related television will have stronger effects for Whites compared to Blacks or Latinos.

*Hypothesis 23.b:*    The effects of crime-related media on support for rehabilitation will vary across type of media. Specifically, the effects of crime info-tainment, local television news, and crime dramas will be stronger compared to the effects of newspapers.

*Hypothesis 24:*    *The greater the exposure to crime-related media, the higher the support for three strikes sentencing.*

*Hypothesis 24.a:*  *Crime-related media will have stronger effects on support for three strikes sentencing for Whites compared to Blacks or Latinos.*

*Hypothesis 24.b:*  *The effects of crime-related media on support for three strikes will vary across type of media. Specifically, the effects of crime info-tainment, local television news, and crime dramas will be stronger compared to the effects of newspapers.*

# NOTES

1. Most research is of media influence on political attitudes, beliefs and behaviors (eg., Iyengar et al., 1982; MacKuen and Coombs, 1981; McCombs and Shaw, 1972).

2. Entman and others contest the idea that media have minimal effects because they only impact what people think about (1989). Because media do set the public agenda of public discourse, they have significant impact on what people believe, especially on issues for which they have little direct experience. Similarly, Iyengar et al. (1982) argue what television *does not* broadcast is as important as what it does, because issues that do not receive media attention do not become part of the public discourse.

3. Research finds that the perceived reality of crime-related television is one of the largest influences on individuals' beliefs and understanding about crime (Slater and Elliott, 1982).

4. Victims' rights groups began mobilizing in the 1970's; most wanted better treatment from police and court personnel, and used the media to make their claims. Best (1997) suggests the victims' rights movement has transmogrified into a 'victim industry' supported by a media driven victim ideology, coupled with the interests of politicians and criminal justice personnel. For example, new legislation is often named for a slain victim. In the thirty years since the 'discovery of the victim' (Karmen, 2001), there have been numerous laws passed in the name of victims.

5. Uniform Crime Reports show Index crime rates were very low in the 1950's, rose steeply in the 1960's and continued to rise until 1980. They decreased slightly in the early 1980's but rose again until the early 1990's. Crime rates have declined precipitously over the last decade; they are at rates comparable to the early 1960's, although they appear to have stabilized.

6. *America's Most Wanted* is co-produced with the FBI's Public Affairs Office.

# CHAPTER 4

# Modeling Support for Three Strikes

Punitive attitudes are influenced by a number of factors. Media effects are hypothesized to directly influence support for three strikes and indirectly as they influence respondents' perceptions of the amount of crime, seriousness of crime, just world beliefs, support for rehabilitation, and fear of crime, which are treated as intervening factors of support for three strikes. In turn, crime-related media consumption, fear of crime, just world beliefs, perceptions of the amount of crime, the seriousness of crime, and direct crime experiences (as victim or offender) are directly influenced by a number of exogenous sociodemographic variables suggested by the literature: age, gender, political party, income, and education. An outline of the theoretical model is shown in figure 4.1.

## THE ANALYTICAL SCHEME

Since the theoretical model implies a causal link between crime-related media consumption, experiences with crime, crime perceptions, and other beliefs on support for three strikes, it is appropriate to analyze the data using structural equation modeling. This method uses the variance/covariance matrix of the model variables as input and provides maximum likelihood estimates of the coefficients in a set of linear structural equations of the variables. This allows for the simultaneous comparison of a set of independent (and intervening) variables to each other and of their unique contribution in explaining variation in a dependent construct.

**Figure 4.1   The Theoretical Model**

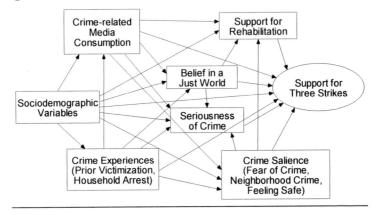

A simultaneous structural equations model was first estimated for the whole sample, treating Latino and African American groups as dummy variables, for which were found numerous statistically significant effects. This justified the use of a three-groups model comparing Whites, Latinos and African Americans. Equality constraints were placed to ascertain if both the measurement model and the structural model worked the same for all groups. The estimation of the parameters being constrained is based on the pooled variance of the race/ethnic groups, allowing for valid and easily interpretable comparisons of group processes.

The focus of this model is to determine which factors have the most influence on punitiveness, particularly the effects of media. Although a handful of prior studies have found modest correlations between media consumption and punitiveness, the question to be answered is whether these correlations hold when other factors are introduced. If not, this might suggest that earlier studies were capitalizing on spurious effects. Additionally, the control variables introduced in the model rest on theoretical grounds. As such, the analysis does not test competing theoretical models; but rather, tests the relative strength of the variables on support for three strikes, and compares their impact across race/ethnic groups. Consequently, nonsignificant parameters were retained in the model, to allow for a full explanation of the hypothesized effects.

Given the complexity of the research model, most of the variables used in the analysis could not be presented individually in figure 4.1, but are summarized in table 4.1. Detailed variable measurement is presented in the next chapter.

### Table 4.1 Variables Used in the Analysis

|  | *Variable Measurement* |
|---|---|
| ***Sociodemographic Variables*** | |
| Gender | Male = 1 |
| Age (30 and Under) | 'Age 31-59' omitted category |
| Age (60 and Over) | 'Age 31-59' omitted category |
| Education | Categorical – 5 categories |
| Income | Categorical – 9 categories |
| Republican | 'Independent/Other' omitted category |
| Democrat | 'Independent/Other' omitted category |
| ***Crime Experiences*** | |
| Prior Victimization | Scale (4 variables) |
| Household Arrest | Dummy coded |
| ***Crime-related Media Consumption*** | |
| Newspapers | Ratio (# of days per week) |
| Television News | Ratio (# of days per week) |
| Crime Info-tainment | Scale (4 variables) |
| Crime Dramas | Scale (4 variables) |
| Hours Watching Television | Ratio (# hours per week) |
| ***Crime Perceptions*** | |
| Local Crime Risk | Scale (7 variables) |
| State Crime Increased | Dummy coded |
| Feeling Safe | Scale (3 variables) |
| Fear of Crime | Scale (8 variables) |
| ***Seriousness of Crime*** | Scale (8 variables) |
| ***Belief in a Just World*** | Scale (5 variables) |
| ***Support for Rehabilitation*** | Dummy coded |
| ***Support for Three Strikes*** | Index (3 indices-12 variables total) |

## THE SAMPLE

The data come from a statewide survey of 4,245 California residents, stratified by race/ethnicity and county. In order to allow for statistical comparison by race/ethnicity, African Americans were oversampled. Certain geographic regions were also oversampled: the 'Inland Empire' of San Bernardino and Riverside counties, San Diego County, and the Central Valley region. Within each household, one adult respondent (18 years or older) was interviewed through a computer-assisted telephone interviewing system (which also ensured access to unlisted telephone numbers). The interview consisted of approximately 100 questions regarding fear of crime, media habits, support for three strikes sentencing and other criminal justice opinions, perceptions of crime, just world beliefs, and standard sociodemographic information (see appendix A for questions used in the analysis). The interviews averaged 35 to 40 minutes in length and were administered in Spanish, if necessary. 4245 completed interviews were collected from March to September 1999, for an average response rate of 69.9%; above average for telephone surveys (Weisberg, Krosnick, and Brown, 1989).

The collected sample included 2500 Whites, 777 Latinos, 435 African Americans, 312 Asians, 86 American Indians, 22 "others," and 113 who declined to state or did not know their race/ethnicity. Since over 95% of the Latinos sampled are of Mexican descent they are treated as a homogenous ethnic group in the analysis.

Because the Asian subsample consisted of several different ethnic groups that varied significantly in their support for three strikes, they could not be treated as one homogenous group and were dropped from the analysis. American Indians, "others" and those who declined to identify their race/ethnicity were not included because their numbers were too small to allow for valid statistical comparison. Therefore, the sample employed for this analysis retained 2500 White, 777 Latino and 435 African American respondents.

## SAMPLE DESCRIPTION

Table 4.2 presents the sociodemographic characteristics for the whole sample and by race/ethnicity. Women comprise almost 59% of the entire sample, but there are no significant differences in gender composition across race/ethnic categories. While the percent of women is higher than men, this is typical of survey data; and not of major concern since the effects of gender are controlled in the analysis. Approximately 19% of the entire sample are age thirty or younger, and

**Table 4.2   Sociodemographic Characteristics by Race/Ethnicity**

|  | *All* (n=3712) | *White* (n=2500) | *Latino* (n=777) | *Black* (n=435) |
|---|---|---|---|---|
| **Gender** | | | | |
| Male | 41.4% | 41.8% | 39.8% | 41.8% |
| Female | 58.6% | 58.2% | 60.2% | 58.2% |
| **Age** | | | | |
| 30 and Under | 18.8% | 13.6% | 35.4% | 18.9% |
| 60 and Over | 22.9% | 28.2% | 7.7% | 19.8% |
| **Political Party** | | | | |
| Republican | 26.4% | 35.2% | 11.3% | 3.2% |
| Democrat | 41.2% | 34.1% | 46.3% | 72.6% |
| **Education** | | | | |
| Not High School Grad | 8.1% | 3.2% | 23.3% | 9.0% |
| High School Graduate | 20.4% | 18.2% | 28.2% | 19.3% |
| Some College | 36.7% | 36.5% | 32.4% | 45.3% |
| College Graduate | 21.5% | 25.4% | 12.0% | 16.3% |
| Advanced Degree | 12.9% | 16.4% | 3.7% | 9.7% |
| **Household Income** | | | | |
| Less than $5,000 | 2.4% | 1.4% | 4.2% | 4.8% |
| $5,000 - $9,999 | 3.5% | 2.4% | 5.8% | 5.7% |
| $10,000 - $14,999 | 6.5% | 5.3% | 9.4% | 8.0% |
| $15,000 -$24,999 | 9.6% | 7.8% | 14.7% | 11.5% |
| $25,000 - $34,999 | 12.7% | 11.6% | 16.6% | 12.4% |
| $35,000 - $49,999 | 17.7% | 18.3% | 16.1% | 17.0% |
| $50,000 - $74,999 | 16.7% | 18.7% | 10.8% | 15.9% |
| $75,000 - $99,999 | 10.0% | 11.4% | 6.2% | 9.0% |
| $100,000 or more | 9.2% | 11.5% | 3.6% | 6.0% |

23% are age sixty and above. However, there are differences in age distributions across race/ethnicity. While both Black and Latino respondents were significantly younger than Whites, this is particularly so for Latinos; 35.4% are age thirty or under, compared to 18.9% of Blacks and 13.6% of Whites. Moreover, 28.2% of Whites sampled are age sixty or older, compared to 19.8% of Blacks, and only 7.7% of Latinos.

41.2% of the sample identified themselves as Democrats, and 26.4% as Republicans. Political party is also unevenly distributed across race/ethnicity. Fully 35.2% of Whites identified themselves as Republicans, compared to only 11.3% of Latinos, and a mere 3.2% of Blacks. Similarly, Whites had the lowest percentage of Democrats (34.1%) compared to 46.3% of Latinos and 72.6% of Blacks.

There are also differences of education and income levels across race/ethnicity; this imbalance is most evident in the highest and lowest values of the categories. For example, only 3.2% of Whites and 9.0% of African Americans had not finished high school compared to 23.3% of Latinos. Conversely, 16.4% of Whites had an advanced degree compared to less than 10% of Blacks and 4% of Latinos. Summing across the three lowest income categories, both Blacks and Latinos are twice as likely to report family incomes of less than $15,000 per year compared to Whites (18.5%, 19.4% and 9.1%, respectively). In contrast, 11.5% of Whites had annual family incomes of $100,000 or more, compared to only 3.6% of Latinos and 6.0% of Blacks.

## THE QUESTIONNAIRE

The questionnaire used for the study was designed to overcome a number of problems found in most surveys of public opinion of crime and crime policy. One of the chief concerns in the empirical research is the general public's lack of knowledge about crime issues. This problem is probably not as acute for this study, given the media spotlight on the Polly Klaas case and the groundswell of support for three strikes that resulted. Additionally, three strikes has engendered a lot of controversy and continued media coverage since it was passed in 1993. Some of the coverage has focused on the egregious uses of the law, (such as the worldwide media attention for the man who received a third strike for stealing a slice of pizza), and the topic appears with some regularity in the news. In short, the majority of Californians are likely to know of the three strikes law, although they may be unaware of its specific components. Nevertheless, respondents were read a brief statement that explained three strikes sentencing before they were asked about specific applications of the penalty.

Public opinion research on crime and crime policy also suffers from many methodological problems including superficial measurement techniques such as the use of global questions and dichotomous response categories, and over use of forced responses. Additionally, because question wording and question ordering can produce response set bias, questions should be presented in random order to average out these effects across a sample. Research also suggests that respondents tend to think of the worst type of criminal when they endorse habitual offender sentences, such as three strikes (Finkel et al., 1996). Thus, asking global questions about the application of three strikes will overestimate the extent of real support for the law. In order to ascertain the true extent of support for the three strikes law, the level of seriousness (and the type of crime) for the third offense (and priors) should be manipulated in a set of scenarios. The questionnaire was constructed to overcome these methodological concerns. To begin with, after respondents were read a brief statement that explained three strikes sentencing they were asked several questions about three strikes, which were manipulated along two dimensions: the type of crime (violent, property, and drug) and the seriousness of the offense (serious and less serious). Second, to reduce systematic bias introduced with question ordering, the type of crime category was randomized with the use of computer-assisted telephone interviewing.

Consequently, one respondent might start the section about three strikes with a question about drug crimes, another about violent crimes, and another about property crimes. Last, the use of the factorial design allowed for a great deal of variation across seriousness and crime type dimensions, which is reflected in the constructed index that ranges from zero to twelve (the questions used were dichotomous). Moreover, most other variables of interest used in the analysis are scales constructed from multiple Likert scale questions (detailed in the following chapter). However, with the exception of prior crime victimization, all of the questions are close ended, which may have forced responses, although 'no opinion' was offered as an option.

The following chapter describes the measures used in the analysis, and distribution of these variables for the entire sample, and by race/ethnic group. As will be seen, significant race/ethnic differences are found in the distributions of both the explanatory variables as well as support for three strikes. This underscores not only the importance of examining public opinion attitudes across race/ethnicity, but also the factors that lead to more punitive attitudes. Thus, after examining these differences, we will address whether they can be explained by differences in experiences or media consumption, or if these effects exist independent of the various explanatory and control variables used in the analysis.

The effects of media, which are presumed to be cumulative, are difficult to capture in cross-sectional research. When respondents were asked about media habits, the model assumes a constant diet over the course of time. Certainly, media habits change with factors such as age, education, and so forth, as one moves through the life cycle. Although the model attempts to control for such factors, it cannot fully capture this type of variability. In reality, the model likely underestimates the importance of media, since we are capturing media consumption at one point in time. This is an inherent problem for most types of cross-sectional social science research; and as such, suggests the coefficients must be interpreted with some caution. Moreover, because of the relatively large sample size, it is easy to capitalize on statistical significance. The size of the coefficients, rather than their significance levels, should remain the focus of the study, especially for those coefficients with moderate statistical significance. Therefore, after the model is examined, the relative impact of each of the statistically significant parameters is examined across race/ethnicity.

# CHAPTER 5

# Measuring Punitiveness and Related Factors

This chapter describes the measures used for the analysis. It begins by explaining how support for three strikes was captured, is followed by a detailed examination of the intervening variables, and ends with a brief description of the exogenous variables used in the analysis. Distributions of the variables are also shown to illustrate differences across race/ethnic groups.

## THREE STRIKES SENTENCING

Rather than asking global questions about support for three strikes (e.g., "should a person who has committed three felony offenses receive a sentence of 25 years to life?"), the survey questions were designed to uncover the threshold of support for three strikes depending on both severity of offense and type of crime. This was ascertained through a series of twelve questions that manipulated both the seriousness of offense (worded as either serious or less serious) and type of crime category (either violent, drug, or property offense). There were four possible questions that manipulated severity of offense within the three crime categories. For example, a respondent might first be asked if they supported a sentence of 25 years to life for someone who had committed three serious drug offenses. If they answered affirmatively, they were then asked if they supported a sentence of 25 years to life if the person had committed two serious and one less serious drug offenses. If they answered affirmatively, the manipulation of seriousness level would continue, until they finally said no, or until all three crimes were described as less serious. Each affirmative answer was coded a score of one, and combined into one of three different crime indexes: violent, drug, or property. This index measures the level of support of three strikes using the items that look at level of severity within each type of crime. For example, a person who supports three strikes for violent crimes even if all three are less serious would receive a higher index score on the violent crime index than someone who only supports three strikes for three serious violent crimes. Each index ranges from zero (doesn't support three strikes for any offense level) to four (supports three strikes even if all three crimes are less seriousness). As noted earlier, the computer-assisted telephone interviewing system allowed the types of crimes (violent, drug and property) to be randomly presented to reduce systematic bias.

The dependent variable used in the analysis is an endogenous factor constructed with the three indices of property, drug and violent offenses. The error terms for the drug and violent crime indices were allowed to correlate, since many people equate drug crime with violent crime (Doble, 1987; Sasson, 1995).

## *Californians' Support for Three Strikes*

One of the most noteworthy findings in this analysis is the overwhelming support of three strikes sentencing for third time serious violent offenders. 'Three strikes and you're out,' was a common refrain used in television campaign ads supporting the proposition, and repeatedly used by many politicians and government officials over the ensuing years. As illustrated in figure 5.1, it appears to have resonated with the California public. Approximately 93% of respondents support three strikes for a three time serious violent offender. But, respondents are much less supportive of three strikes for other types of crimes - even if they are described as three serious offenses. For example, 64% of the respondents are supportive of three strikes for three serious drug crimes, and only 46% support the sentence for three serious property crimes. Although respondents are less likely to endorse the application of three strikes sentencing for serious repeat drug and property offenders than they are for repeat violent offenders, the level of approval of three strikes is still relatively high. But does this punitive stance still hold when crimes are described as less serious?

**Figure 5.1 Percent Supporting Three Strikes for 3 Serious Offenses, by Type of Crime**

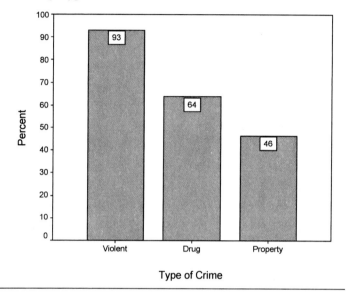

Table 5.1 disaggregates support for three strikes, by each type of crime category and level of seriousness for both the entire sample and across race/ethnic groups. As seen in the first column, on a scale of zero to four, the mean support for three strikes among the whole sample is highest for the violent crime index (2.130), second highest for the drug crime index (1.486), and lowest for the property crime index (1.031). Within each crime type, support for three strikes falls dramatically from when the description of the three crimes change from all three being serious, to two serious and one less serious. This erosion of support continues as more of the three crimes are described as less serious.

**Table 5.1 Means of Indicators for Support of Three Strikes by Race/Ethnicity**

|  | *All* (n=3712) | *White* (n=2500) | *Latino* (n=777) | *Black* (n=435) |
|---|---|---|---|---|
| ***Violent Crime Index*** | 2.130 | 2.294 | 1.889** | 1.618**,†† |
| All Three Serious | .932 | .948 | .900** | .894** |
| Two Serious, One Less | .555 | .604 | .498** | .375**,†† |
| One Serious, Two Less | .377 | .428 | .304** | .209**,†† |
| All Three Less Serious | .267 | .314 | .188** | .140**,†† |
| ***Drug Crime Index*** | 1.486 | 1.480 | 1.520 | 1.032**,†† |
| All Three Serious | .638 | .636 | .709** | .524**,†† |
| Two Serious, One Less | .363 | .379 | .386 | .234**,†† |
| One Serious, Two Less | .250 | .267 | .250 | .154**,†† |
| All Three Less Serious | .184 | .199 | .175 | .120** |
| ***Property Crime Index*** | 1.031 | 1.070 | 1.073 | .733**,†† |
| All Three Serious | .465 | .462 | .524* | .375**,†† |
| Two Serious, One Less | .255 | .267 | .260 | .177**,†† |
| One Serious, Two Less | .179 | .194 | .171 | .101**,†† |
| All Three Less Serious | .133 | .146 | .118 | .008** |

* p .01, ** p .001 for differences between Whites and Latinos, and Whites and Blacks.
† p .01, †† p .001 for differences between Latinos and Blacks

This is more clearly seen in figure 5.2, which documents the drop in support of three strikes as the number of serious violent crimes decreases - from 93% for an offender with three serious violent crimes, to 55% if one of the three violent offenses is less serious, to 38% if two of the three violent offenses are less serious, to 27% if all three violent offenses are less serious.

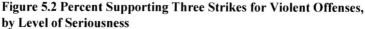

**Figure 5.2 Percent Supporting Three Strikes for Violent Offenses, by Level of Seriousness**

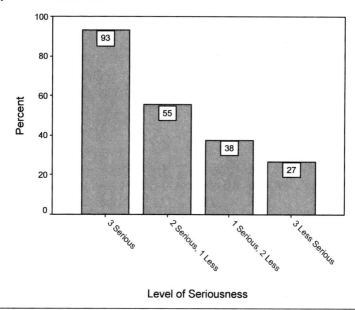

**Level of Seriousness**

Across all crime types, the largest drop in punitiveness occurs when the three offenses are all serious, to two serious and one less serious. Moreover, the percent decrease is very similar across each crime type - roughly a 40% to 45% reduction. For example, 46.5% of the sample supports three strikes for three serious property offenses, but only 25.5% do if only two of the property offenses are serious; a 45% drop in support.

## *Race/Ethnic Differences in Support for Three Strikes*

There are interesting differences in support for three strikes across race/ethnic groups. To begin with, Whites are much more likely to support three strikes for violent crimes across all seriousness levels than are Latinos or Blacks. As shown in table 5.1, the mean of the violent crime index for Latinos (1.889) and African Americans (1.618) is significantly lower than the 2.294 mean score for Whites (p < .001). However, as seen in figure 5.3, Latinos are more likely than Whites to support three strikes for three serious drug crimes and for three serious property crimes. There is no statistically significant difference between Latinos and Whites when property and drug crimes are less serious. In contrast, African Americans are much less likely than either Whites or Latinos to approve of three strikes for any of the crime types.

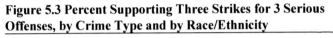

**Figure 5.3 Percent Supporting Three Strikes for 3 Serious Offenses, by Crime Type and by Race/Ethnicity**

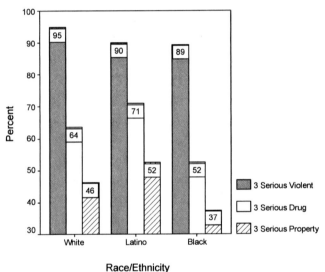

There are also race/ethnic differences in the drop of support for three strikes as one moves from three serious, to two serious and one less serious offense. Within all crime types, the drop is sharpest among African Americans, ranging from 58% (for violent crimes) to 53% (for property crimes). In contrast, among Whites, there is only a 37% drop in support for three strikes from three serious violent offenses to two serious and one less serious violent offense. Similarly, White support for three strikes drops roughly 40% for both drug and property crimes when one of the three offenses is less serious. Latinos' support for three strikes is reduced approximately 45% and 50% across all crime types when one of the offenses is described as less serious. Figure 5.4 illustrates the pattern of erosion in support for three strikes for violent crimes as the number of offenses become less serious.

**Figure 5.4 Percent Supporting Three Strikes for Violent Offenses, by Level of Seriousness and Race/Ethnicity**

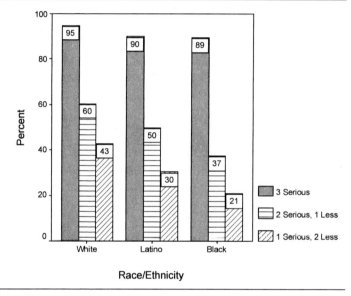

In short, there are interesting patterns in the distribution of support for three strikes across crime types, level of seriousness, and race/ethnicity. Support for three strikes is significantly higher for violent crimes, and almost universal for three serious violent crimes. However, support for three strikes erodes substantially when only one of the three offenses is described as less serious. Support continues to wane as the level of seriousness declines. A majority of the sample supports three strikes for three serious drug crimes, but barely one-third do if one of the offenses is described as less serious. Three strikes for three serious property offenses is supported by fewer than one-half of the respondents, and fewer than 10% support three strikes for three less serious property crimes.

Whites are more punitive than Latinos and African Americans for violent offenses (across all levels of seriousness), but Latinos are more punitive for drug and property offenses when all three are serious. African Americans are far less likely to support three strikes for any crime type or offense level compared to Latinos and Whites; moreover, their drop in support is largest when one of the offenses is described as less serious, for any given crime category. These patterns confirm prior research that finds Blacks are significantly less punitive than Whites (e.g., Blumstein and Cohen, 1980; Browning and Cao, 1992). Latinos are less likely to support three strikes compared to Whites, but are more likely to support three strikes than Blacks. The difference between White and Latino support for three strikes is explained wholly by their differences in the violent crime category. The large differences in support for three strikes sentencing between race/ethnic groups confirm that the study should compare the determinants of support to find where the differences originate.

# BELIEFS ABOUT CRIME AND THE CRIMINAL JUSTICE SYSTEM

## *Crime Seriousness*

Similar to the method used by Carlson and Williams (1993), respondents were asked to rate eight different felony crimes (aggravated assault, rape, robbery, theft, burglary, auto theft, drug possession and drug sales) in terms of their seriousness on a scale of zero to ten, with zero equal to not at all serious and ten extremely serious.[1] Research suggests that item order is important; namely, the perceived seriousness of a given item is influenced by the perceived seriousness of the preceding offense respondents are being asked to evaluate. Evans and Scott (1984) found ordering effects accounted for as much variation in seriousness as did the sociodemographic characteristics of respondents. Thus, to eliminate the influence of ordering, the list of eight crimes was randomly presented to respondents.

Several authors have noted that the use of a scale summing means of various types of offenses obfuscates the real differences between ratings of different types of crime (O'Connell and Whelan, 1996). For example, scores for the seriousness of graffiti are usually much lower than scores for serious violent offenses, such as homicide. This is important because prior research indicates that group differences are found for different dimensions of crime; using a summative scale masks these differences (Gottfredson, Warner, and Taylor, 1988).

Factor analysis was performed on the eight crime types to determine if there was more than one dimension. A principal factor analysis using varimax rotation produced two factors. The first, which accounted for approximately 34% of the variance, was comprised of all the non-drug related offenses. Only two offenses loaded on the second factor (the drug related offenses), which accounted for 22% of the variance. However, since a two-item construct cannot be treated as a scale, all eight items were combined into one seriousness scale. Individual item scores were totaled and divided through by the number of crime seriousness items The seriousness of crime scale, therefore, ranges from zero (not at all serious) to ten (most serious). The Cronbach's alpha reliability coefficient for the entire sample was .8550; for Whites, .8561; Latinos, .8523; and for African Americans, .8260.

Table 5.2 presents crime seriousness ratings for specific types of crimes for the entire sample and across race/ethnic categories. The crime seriousness index used in the analysis is shown in the bottom row of the table. All groups consider most of the crimes to be very serious (an 8.03 mean index score for the entire sample), given that the possible scores ranged from zero to ten. Moreover, Latinos rate crimes higher (8.51) than do Blacks (8.30), and Whites, who have the lowest crime seriousness ratings (7.84); a finding that confirms prior research on differences between Black and White assessments (e.g., Miethe, 1984; Rauma, 1991; Rossi and Berk, 1974).

There are important similarities and differences masked by the index. All three groups rate rape as the most serious crime, and there is no statistically significant difference between them, confirming prior studies that find a high degree of consensus on perceptions of serious violent crimes (e.g. Miethe, 1984; Rauma, 1991). Whites rate all crimes as less serious than do Latinos or African Americans. Latinos rate drug-related crimes as more serious than do Blacks, and there appears to be more consistency among Latinos in their perception of drug seriousness, as evidenced by the smaller standard deviation for these crime ratings. In contrast, there is a great deal of variation among White ratings of the seriousness of drug possession.

**Table 5.2 Means of Crime Seriousness Ratings by Race/Ethnicity**

|                    | *All* (n=3712) | *White* (n=2500) | *Latino* (n=777) | *Black* (n=435) |
|--------------------|---------------|-----------------|-----------------|-----------------|
| Rape               | 9.65          | 9.67            | 9.61            | 9.61            |
|                    | ( .97)        | (.85)           | (1.13)          | (1.28)          |
| Aggravated Assault | 8.77          | 8.73            | 8.93**          | 8.74            |
|                    | (1.56)        | (1.53)          | (1.55)          | (1.73)          |
| Drug Sales         | 8.34          | 8.07            | 9.01**          | 8.68**,††       |
|                    | (2.29)        | (2.42)          | (1.79)          | (2.05)          |
| Robbery            | 8.29          | 8.11            | 8.60**          | 8.73**          |
|                    | (1.75)        | (1.73)          | (1.78)          | (1.65)          |
| Burglary           | 7.89          | 7.70            | 8.32**          | 8.25**          |
|                    | (1.92)        | (1.88)          | (1.92)          | (2.02)          |
| Auto Theft         | 7.36          | 7.15            | 7.86**          | 7.68**          |
|                    | (2.18)        | (2.10)          | (2.22)          | (2.33)          |
| Theft              | 7.10          | 6.86            | 7.61**          | 7.51**          |
|                    | (2.20)        | (2.13)          | (2.22)          | (2.36)          |
| Drug Possession    | 6.90          | 6.44            | 8.13**          | 7.28**,††       |
|                    | (2.90)        | (2.95)          | (2.43)          | (2.71)          |
| Seriousness Index  | 8.03          | 7.84            | 8.51**          | 8.30**,††       |
|                    | (1.44)        | (1.44)          | (1.35)          | (1.38)          |

*Note:* Numbers in parentheses are standard deviations
\* $p \leq .01$, \*\* $p \leq .001$ for differences between Whites and Latinos, and Whites and Blacks
† $p \leq .01$, †† $p \leq .001$ for differences between Latinos and Blacks

Table 5.3 presents the relative ranking of the crime serious scores for specific crimes. Blacks and Whites have identical rankings: rape is most serious, followed by aggravated assault, robbery, drug sales, burglary, auto theft, theft, and drug possession. Recent studies of crime seriousness ranking find that drug crimes are being rated more seriously than they were in past decades (Roberts, 1992) but this was only found for Latino respondents. Drug sales are ranked as the second most serious offense by Latinos, and drug possession, the least serious offense for Blacks and Whites, is ranked sixth by Latinos.

The identical rankings for Blacks and Whites is consistent with some crime seriousness studies in the United States and Canada which find that race does not significantly affect the relative ranking of crime seriousness. However, it contradicts other research that finds Blacks rate crimes more seriously than do Whites (Miethe, 1984; Rauma).

**Table 5.3 Rank Order of Crime Seriousness Ratings by Race/Ethnicity**

| *All* | *White* | *Latino* | *Black* |
|---|---|---|---|
| Rape | Rape | Rape | Rape |
| Aggravated Assault | Aggravated Assault | Drug Sales | Aggravated Assault |
| Drug Sales | Robbery | Aggravated Assault | Robbery |
| Robbery | Drug Sales | Robbery | Drug Sales |
| Burglary | Burglary | Burglary | Burglary |
| Auto Theft | Auto Theft | Drug Possession | Auto Theft |
| Theft | Theft | Auto Theft | Theft |
| Drug Possession | Drug Possession | Theft | Drug Possession |

## *Support for Rehabilitation*

Respondents were asked to select the most important purpose to sentence adults for criminal penalties from among four possible reasons: deterrence, incapacitation, rehabilitation, and punishment.[2] Response categories were randomly presented to eliminate ordering bias. Prior research suggests that support for rehabilitation usually operates in different directions than does support for deterrence, punishment and incapacitation (Hamilton and Rytina, 1980). Exploratory data analyses bore this out. For example, there is a negative relationship between support for three strikes and rehabilitation as the primary purpose of criminal sentencing. In contrast, there is a positive relationship between support for three strikes and deterrence, incapacitation and punishment. Consequently, support for rehabilitation is included in the model as a dummy variable; incapacitation, deterrence, and punishment are treated as the excluded categories.

As outlined by Roberts (1992), two purposes of sentencing appear to be most salient to the general public - retribution and deterrence. Moreover, when asked to choose between the two, he found that retribution was by far the most popular reason to incarcerate. A recent national survey that used the same four choices used in this study found that 50% of respondents selected retribution as the most important reason to punish, followed by rehabilitation (21%), and deterrence and incapacitation (both 13%) (Gerber and Engelhardt-Greer, 1996).

**Table 5.4 Most Important Reason to Imprison by Race/Ethnicity**

|                | *All* (n=3712) | *White* (n=2500) | *Latino* (n=777) | *Black* (n=435) |
|----------------|------|--------|--------|-------|
| Deterrence     | 14.2% | 13.0% | 16.6% | 16.8% |
| Punishment     | 36.2% | 36.0% | 37.1% | 35.9% |
| Incapacitation | 22.9% | 27.6% | 13.5% | 12.9% |
| Rehabilitation | 24.4% | 20.9% | 30.8% | 32.6% |

Our analysis found similar results. As seen in table 5.4, respondents chose punishment as the most important reason to imprison (36%), followed by rehabilitation (24.4%), incapacitation (22.9%) and deterrence (14.2%). However, there are significant differences across race/ethnic groups. While all groups cite punishment or retribution as the most important reason to imprison and deterrence as the least important, Whites have much lower support for rehabilitation and far greater support for incapacitation than do Latinos or Blacks. Only 21% of Whites support rehabilitation as the most important reason to imprison compared to 31% of Latinos and almost 33% of Blacks. Moreover, 27.6% of Whites chose incapacitation as the most important reason, compared to 13.5% of Latinos and 12.9% of Blacks.

# BELIEFS ABOUT CRIME CAUSATION

## *Just World Beliefs*

The Just World Scale (Rubin and Peplau, 1975; a subset of the I-E Rotter Scale, 1966) is used to explore whether those that are more likely to believe the world is just are more supportive of three strikes than those that do not perceive the world as just. Eight questions from the twenty-item Just World Scale were asked of all respondents, but after reliability tests within race/ethnic groups, only five were retained for the analysis. Using a four point Likert scale, respondents were asked if they strongly disagreed, disagreed, agreed or strongly agreed with the following statements:

1) Basically, the world is a just place.
2) By and large, people deserve what they get.
3) Although evil people may hold political power for a while, in the general course of history, good wins out.
4) In almost any business or profession, people who do their job well rise to the top.
5) People who meet with misfortune have often brought it upon themselves.

The scale range was obtained by dividing the total score by the number of questions answered. Since there were five questions, the probability of losing too many cases precluded listwise deletion of respondents that did not answer all items. Instead, the mean score for the items that were answered by a given respondent replaced the other missing items. For example, if a respondent answered three of the five questions, the scores for the three items were summed and divided by three. This number was then used to replace the missing scores on the two unanswered questions. Respondents who only answered two or fewer questions were treated as missing cases as there was too little information to validly impute replacement means. The scale ranges from one (does not believe in a just world) to four (has very strong belief in a just world).

The Cronbach's alpha reliability coefficients were low: 5149 for the entire sample, .5095 for Whites, .5066 for Latinos, and .5088 for African Americans. But, the low reliability of the scale is similar to other studies that have used subsets of Rubin and Peplau's scale (e.g.,

Mohr and Luscri, 1995). Recent tests of Rubin and Peplau's Just World Scale argue the scale has low internal consistency because it taps into two dimensions: justness and *un*justness (Whatley, 1993). One of the five questions used measures unjustness, the other four measure justness. Studies that have used all twenty items of the Just World Scale typically find reliability coefficients in the high 60's and low 70's, but these tests are usually administered to relatively homogenous groups, such as college students. Thus, the relatively low coefficients obtained may also be explained by the diversity of the sample.

Prior research has found that those who have directly experienced social inequalities are far less likely to view the world as a just place. Thus, women, Blacks, and those with low income have less belief in a just world (Smith and Green, 1984; Calhoun and Cann, 1994). Only one study has compared the just world beliefs of Latinos, African Americans and Whites. Using a sample of southern Californians, Hunt (2000) found that Latinos had the strongest belief in a just world and Blacks the weakest. As seen in table 5.5, there are large differences in belief in a just world by race/ethnicity. African Americans have a group mean of 2.45, which is significantly lower than that of Whites (2.55). Latinos have the highest belief in a just world (2.64), which mirror Hunt's findings. It appears that country of origin makes a difference, as immigrants comprise about one-third of the Latino subsample. This is important for they have significantly higher belief in a just world compared to Latinos born in the United States (means of 2.71 vs. 2.59, respectively).

**Table 5.5 Means of Crime Experiences and Just World Beliefs by Race/Ethnicity**

|  | *All* (n=3712) | *White* (n=2500) | *Latino* (n=777) | *Black* (n=435) |
|---|---|---|---|---|
| Arrest in the Household | 0.17 | 0.16 | 0.17 | 0.23**,†† |
| Prior Victimization | 0.43 | 0.44 | 0.35* | 0.48 |
| Just World Beliefs Scale | 2.56 | 2.55 | 2.64** | 2.45**,†† |

\* $p \leq .01$, \*\* $p \leq .001$ for differences between Whites and Latinos, and Whites and Blacks
† $p \leq .01$, †† $\leq .001$ for differences between Latinos and Blacks

## DIRECT EXPERIENCES WITH CRIME: VICTIMS AND OFFENDERS

### *Prior Criminal Victimization*

Respondents were asked if they had been criminally victimized in the last three years. If they answered affirmatively, they were asked to describe the victimization. The responses yielded over thirty distinct criminal victimizations that were collapsed into four separate categories: serious and less serious property offenses and serious and less serious violent offenses. If a respondent reported multiple victimizations, only the most serious prior victimization was recorded. The categories are ranked on the basis of severity to create one variable that ranges from zero to four: zero equals no criminal victimizations within the previous three years and four equals a serious violent criminal victimization. Although this variable does not reflect the dimension of repeat victimization, which the literature suggests may make a difference, there were very few respondents with multiple victimizations (fewer than fifty).

The distribution of crime victimization is shown in table 5.5. The relatively low mean for prior criminal victimization (.4275 on a scale of zero to four) indicates that a large majority of the sample never experienced a prior criminal victimization or only a relatively minor one such as non-serious property crime. Latinos reported significantly lower victimization (.3488) compared to Whites (.4436) or Blacks, who experienced the highest victimization (.4759).

### *Household Arrest*

Respondents were asked if they or a member of their household had ever been arrested for a crime. Responses are dummy coded, yes = 1, no = 0. Never been arrested is the omitted category in the model. As seen in table 5.5, there are statistically significant differences in the distribution of household arrest across race/ethnicity. Fully 23% of Blacks reported that someone in their household had been arrested, compared to only 17% of Latinos and 16% of Whites. The higher percent of arrest and criminal victimization among Blacks may account for their lower belief in a just world.

## CRIME SALIENCE: FEAR OF CRIME, PERCEPTION OF NEIGHBORHOOD CRIME, AND FEELING SAFE

As supported by most recent literature on fear of crime, emotive fear of crime is treated as a separate construct from the perception of likelihood of neighborhood victimization, and feeling safe. To ascertain whether the distinctions are warranted, confirmatory factor analysis was performed using a principal components analysis with varimax rotation. As hypothesized, the solution produced three factors. Each of the items loaded as predicted: fear questions on one factor, the risk of neighborhood crime questions on second factor, and the safety questions on the third factor. Although correlations between each of the three constructed scales were high, (ranging from -.305 to .618) they were not high enough to suggest multicollinearity; tolerance tests did not find evidence of multicollinearity. Measurement for each of the crime salience variables is described below.

### *Fear of Crime*

Fear of crime is measured by eight questions which asked how fearful the respondent was of a number of potential victimizations: burglary of their home (while away and at home), attack with a weapon, sexual assault, auto theft, mugging, and their property being vandalized. One item asked how fearful they were of their loved ones being criminally victimized because studies find 'altruistic fear' is as, if not more, important than fear for one's personal safety (Warr, 1992). Respondents were asked to rate their fear of each crime on a scale of zero to ten in which zero equals not at all fearful and ten equals very fearful. Although some suggest that fear of property crimes be distinguished from fear of violent offenses (e.g., Warr, 1982), because of the high Cronbach's alpha reliability coefficient (.92 for all groups), these items are combined into a single scale for use in the model. Moreover, given the model's complexity, separating fear of crime into property and violent would add another level of unnecessary detail. Individual item scores were totaled and divided through by the number of fear of crime items. The fear of crime scale, therefore, ranges from 0 (not afraid of any crime) to 10 (extremely fearful of all crime). Respondents reported very low levels of fear overall; only a mean of 3.33 for the entire sample.

## Likelihood of Crime in the Neighborhood

Similar to the fear of crime questions, respondents were asked to rate the likelihood of seven specific crimes occurring in their neighborhood on a scale of zero to ten, where zero equals not at all likely and ten equals very likely. The seven crimes were: the likelihood of a house in the neighborhood being broken into while the owners were away, a house broken into while the owners were at home, someone in the neighborhood being attacked with a weapon, someone in the neighborhood being raped or sexually assaulted, someone in the neighborhood having their car stolen, someone in the neighborhood being mugged or robbed, and property in the neighborhood being vandalized. Again, because of the high Cronbach's alpha reliability coefficient (.93, with no differences across race/ethnic subsamples), and the model's complexity, all of the above items are used as a single scale in the model. As with the fear of crime scale, individual item scores were totaled and divided through by the number of questions. The scale ranges from 0 (does not perceive any crime risk in their neighborhood) to 10 (perceives the likelihood of crime in the neighborhood as extremely high).

## Feeling Safe

Feeling safe is treated as a single scale comprised of responses to three questions about safety rated on a scale from 0 to 10 where zero equals not at all safe and ten equals very safe. The questions were, "how safe from crime do you feel inside your home during the day?", "...at night?" and "...out alone in your neighborhood at night, say between sunset and 10 p.m.?" The Cronbach's alpha reliability coefficient is .7893 for the whole sample, but there are minor differences by race/ethnicity; for Whites the alpha coefficient is .7879, for Latinos it is .8120 and for African Americans, .7206. Again, the scale range of zero to ten was obtained by dividing the total scores by the number of safety questions asked.

## Perception of Crime in the State

Respondents were asked if they thought the amount of crime in the state over the last three years had gone down, stayed the same or gone up. Answers were dummy coded: gone up = 1; gone down or remained the same = 0. As seen in table 5.6, 42% of the respondents thought crime had gone up, even though crime rates had greatly declined in the seven years prior to the survey administration. Latinos were much more likely to believe crime had increased compared to African Americans or Whites.

There are large differences in the salience of crime by race/ethnicity. To begin with, as seen in table 5.6, only 38.5% of Whites believe crime in the state is increasing, compared to 43.0% of Blacks and 51.7% of Latinos. Blacks and Latinos also perceive a greater likelihood of crime in their neighborhoods compared to Whites, particularly for the likelihood of violent crime. Not surprisingly, Whites feel much safer than Blacks or Latinos. Although Blacks report a greater likelihood of neighborhood crime than Latinos, Latinos report higher fear of crime than Blacks. Compared to Whites, both African Americans and Latinos have statistically significant higher fear of property and violent crimes; confirming prior research (Braungart et al., 1980; Clemente and Kleiman, 1977; Liska et al., 1982; Moeller, 1989; Skogan and Maxfield, 1981; Stafford and Galle, 1984).

**Table 5.6 Means of Crime Salience Scales by Race/Ethnicity**

|  | *All* | *White* | *Latino* | *Black* |
|---|---|---|---|---|
|  | (n=3712) | (n=2500) | (n=777) | (n=435) |
| Crime in State is Increasing | 0.42 | 0.38 | 0.52** | 0.43[††] |
| Likelihood of Property Crime | 4.43 | 4.21 | 4.75** | 5.12** |
| Likelihood of Violent Crime | 3.15 | 2.83 | 3.71** | 4.01** |
| Likelihood of All Crime | 3.70 | 3.42 | 4.15** | 4.49** |
| Feeling Safe | 8.04 | 8.21 | 7.60** | 7.89* |
| Fear of Property Crime | 3.43 | 3.11 | 4.46** | 3.47*,[††] |
| Fear of Violent Crime | 2.80 | 2.87 | 4.47** | 3.48**,[††] |
| Fear of All Crime | 3.33 | 2.96 | 4.45** | 3.46**,[††] |

\* p≤.01, \*\* p≤.001 for differences between Whites and Latinos, and Whites and Blacks
[†] p≤.01, [††]≤.001 for differences between Latinos and Blacks

Table 5.7 details the differences across race/ethnic groups of the indicators that comprise the crime perception scales for likelihood of neighborhood victimization, feelings of safety, and fear of crime. There are statistically significant differences between Whites and Latinos across all the indicators. Compared to Whites, Latinos report significantly higher neighborhood crime risk, fear of crime, and feel much less safe. Blacks also report significantly higher neighborhood crime risk. Blacks are much more fearful than Whites of being attacked with a weapon, being robbed, and they are more fearful about the safety of their loved ones. However, Blacks do not feel less safe than Whites.

**Table 5.7 Means for Indicators of Crime Salience Scales by Race/Ethnicity**

|  | *All* | *White* | *Latino* | *Black* |
|---|---|---|---|---|
|  | (n=3712) | (n=2500) | (n=777) | (n=435) |
| ***Local Crime Risk*** |  |  |  |  |
| Home Broken Into When Away | 4.57 | 4.38 | 4.82** | 5.19** |
| Home Broken Into When Home | 2.84 | 2.65 | 3.18** | 3.30** |
| Attack with Weapon | 3.37 | 2.92 | 4.14** | 4.56** |
| Rape | 2.97 | 2.73 | 3.36** | 3.64** |
| Auto Theft | 4.27 | 3.99 | 4.69** | 5.08** |
| Robbery or Mugging | 3.45 | 3.06 | 4.11** | 4.56** |
| Property Vandalized | 4.46 | 4.26 | 4.76** | 5.10** |
| ***Feeling Safe*** |  |  |  |  |
| Inside Home - Day | 8.80 | 8.94 | 8.36** | 8.80† |
| Inside Home - Night | 8.14 | 8.31 | 7.63** | 8.09† |
| In Neighborhood at Night | 7.20 | 7.39 | 6.83** | 6.79 |
| ***Fear of Crime*** |  |  |  |  |
| Home Broken Into When Away | 3.67 | 3.35 | 4.70** | 3.63†† |
| Home Broken Into When Home | 2.45 | 2.15 | 3.50** | 2.32†† |
| Attack with Weapon | 3.23 | 2.78 | 4.46** | 3.61**,†† |
| Rape | 2.38 | 2.08 | 3.41** | 2.31†† |
| Auto Theft | 3.43 | 3.05 | 4.61** | 3.51*,†† |
| Robbery or Mugging | 3.16 | 2.73 | 4.34** | 3.51**,†† |
| Property Vandalized | 3.22 | 2.94 | 4.13** | 3.24†† |
| Safety of Loved Ones | 5.19 | 4.64 | 6.71** | 5.66**,†† |

\* $p \leq .01$, \*\* $p \leq .001$ for differences between Whites and Latinos, and Whites and Blacks
† $p \leq .01$, †† $p \leq .001$ for differences between Latinos and Blacks

There are only a few statistically significant differences between Latinos and Blacks. Compared to Blacks, Latinos feel much less safe inside their homes during both day and night, and they express greater fear of being attacked with a weapon.

To sum, Blacks and Latinos experience crime very differently than Whites. They are much more likely to live in high crime areas, which elevate their perception of crime, their fear of crime, and among Latinos, feeling safe. Blacks and Latinos also experience more criminal victimization than do Whites.

## CRIME-RELATED MEDIA CONSUMPTION

There are a number of variables employed in the model to measure exposure to crime related media. The survey contains eight questions that ascertain how often respondents watch specific crime dramas and crime info-tainment programs on a five-point Likert scale: never, occasionally, once a month, a few times each month, and every week. The selected programs aired on network television stations and were chosen because they had higher Nielsen ratings than other programs that dealt with crime in the year prior to the survey distribution. The four crime dramas chosen were *Law and Order*, *Homicide*, *NYPD Blue* and *Nash Bridges*. These are combined into a single scale; as are the four questions that ask about exposure to crime info-tainment programs. The four crime info-tainment programs are *Cops*, *American Justice*, *America's Most Wanted*, and *Justice Files*.

The Cronbach's alpha reliability coefficient of the crime info-tainment scale for the entire sample was .7285; for Whites, .7246, Latinos, .7085, and African Americans, .7112. The reliability coefficients for the crime drama scale are not as high as those for the crime info-tainment scale, but large enough to justify their use: .6678 for the entire sample; .6747 for Whites, .6582 for Latinos, and .6535 for African Americans.

Respondents were also asked about their exposure to crime-related news. Individuals were asked to estimate the number of days per week they watched local television news and read the newspaper. Respondents were also asked to estimate the number of hours they watched television per week. The news questions - the number of days per week that respondents watch local television news and read the newspaper - are retained as separate variables in the model, as is the number of hours spent watching television per week. This allows us to determine the relative impact of each form of news and to control for any spurious effects from simply watching a lot of television.

Table 5.8 presents the means of media consumption for the entire sample, and across race/ethnicity. All groups read newspapers fewer days per week than they watched television news (for the entire sample, 3.62 and 5.04 days, respectively). But there are significant differences in type and amount of television consumption across race/ethnic groups. On average, Whites read newspapers almost four days per week, compared to only 2.72 days for Latinos and 3.4 days for Blacks. Moreover, Whites watched local television news fewer days (4.78) than either Latinos (5.4) or Blacks (5.9). Blacks watched significantly more television overall, averaging 22.4 hours per week compared to roughly 17 hours per week for both Whites and Latinos. Blacks also watched more television crime dramas than Latinos and Whites, but both Latinos and Blacks watched crime info-tainment shows more frequently than Whites.

**Table 5.8 Means of Crime-related Media Consumption by Race/Ethnicity**

|  | *All* (n=3712) | *White* (n=2500) | *Latino* (n=777) | *Black* (n=435) |
|---|---|---|---|---|
| ***Days Per Week*** |  |  |  |  |
| Read Newspaper News | 3.62 | 3.94 | 2.72** | 3.40**,†† |
| Watch Local T.V. News | 5.04 | 4.78 | 5.40** | 5.90**,†† |
| Weekly T.V. Hours | 17.60 | 17.00 | 16.50 | 22.40**,†† |
| ***Monthly T.V. Crime Viewing*** *(0 = Never; 5 = Weekly)* |  |  |  |  |
| Crime Drama | 1.78 | 1.78 | 1.70 | 1.96**,†† |
| Crime Info-tainment | 1.88 | 1.73 | 2.16** | 2.20** |

* $p \leq .01$, ** $p \leq .001$ for differences between Whites and Latinos, and Whites and Blacks
† $p \leq .01$, †† $p \leq .001$ for differences between Latinos and Blacks

# MEASUREMENT OF SOCIODEMOGRAPHIC CORRELATES

*Age.* Prior research suggests a curvilinear relationship age and fear of crime (e.g. Ortega and Myles, 1987). With this in mind, treating age as a single continuous variable would mask its effects. Therefore, age is collapsed into three dummy variables: 18-30; 31-59 and 60 and over. The 18-30 age group and the 60 and over age group are dummy variables in the model and compared to the middle age range of 30-59 which is treated as the omitted age category.

*Gender.* Male = 1; female = 0. Female is the excluded category in the model.

*Completed Education.* The highest level of education completed is treated as an interval level variable, although it was an ordinal measure. The five categories of education are: less than high school (which includes no formal education up through completion of the 11th grade), high school graduate (or equivalent), some college or trade school, college graduate (bachelor's degree) and advanced degree (which includes master's, doctorate or professional degree). The higher the number, the higher the level of education completed.

*Income.* Income is treated as an interval level variable with nine categories of annual household income (before taxes): less than $5,000, $5,000 to $9,999, $10,000 to $14,999, $15,000 to 24,999, $25,000 to $34,999, $35,000 to $49,999, $50,000 to $74,999, $75,000 to $99,999, and $100,000 or more. The higher the number, the higher the level of household income.

*Political Party.* Political party was coded as Democrat, Republican, Independent/no party, or other, to the question, "Generally speaking, do you consider yourself to be a Democrat, Republican, Independent, or something else?" The four categories are treated as dummy variables; Democrats and Republicans are included in the model, Independents/no party and others comprise the omitted category.

# NOTES

1. Homicide was not included because the literature documents little variation in public opinion of its seriousness. The public views homicide as the most serious crime.
2. See Appendix A for exact wording.

# CHAPTER 6

# Explaining Punitiveness

This chapter presents the coefficients for the full structural equations model.[1] The model's complexity and size precludes presenting all of the coefficients in one table. Instead, the coefficients are displayed in tables 6.1 through 6.12. The tables are organized to reflect the order of variables in the model. They begin with an examination of the estimated coefficients of the exogenous sociodemographic variables on the intervening variables of media consumption and crime experiences. The next set of tables look at the unstandardized regression coefficients for the many intervening variables in the model: the perception of crime risk in one's neighborhood, the perception of state crime rates, feeling safe, fear of crime, belief in a just world, crime seriousness ratings, and support for rehabilitation, in that order. The last table shows all of the sociodemographic correlates and the influence of the intervening variables on the dependent variable - support for three strikes.

In order to determine if media variables and beliefs about crime and crime causation work similarly across race/ethnic groups, the model simultaneously analyzes all three, thus allowing for valid comparisons of estimated parameters. Moreover, the analysis can test for the statistical significance of any dissimilarity between groups. If the differences are not large, the parameters can be constrained equal across groups. This is also a more efficient method than running separate multivariate analyses for each race/ethnic group. Since the model was run as a three-groups model, the unstandardized coefficients are displayed to show equality constraints between race/ethnic groups. Every regression weight was tested for equality constraints, even those that were not statistically significant.[2] It is important to note that there were no relationships that could not be constrained equal in some way -

in other words, for any given relationship, estimated parameters could be constrained equal for at least two of the three race/ethnic groups. In cases where the coefficient for one of the groups could not be constrained equal to the other two race/ethnic groups, it is both *italicized* and <u>underlined</u> in the tables. Asterisks after the coefficients show the level of statistical significance; the absence of an asterisk indicates the coefficient is not statistically significant.

# THE SOCIODEMOGRAPHIC CORRELATES OF MEDIA CONSUMPTION AND CRIME EXPERIENCES

## *Media Consumption*

The specific forms of media intake vary greatly by gender, age, race/ethnicity, education, and income. As seen in table 6.1, newspaper readers are more educated and have higher incomes. Older respondents

**Table 6.1 Unstandardized Regression Coefficients of Newspaper and Television News Consumption by Race/Ethnicity**

|  | *White* (n=2500) | *Latino* (n=777) | *Black* (n=435) |
|---|---|---|---|
|  | *Newspapers* | | |
| Gender | .138 | *.827*** | .138 |
| 30 and Under | -.449*** | -.449*** | -.449*** |
| 60 and Over | *1.743*** | .754** | .754** |
| Education | .474*** | .474*** | .474*** |
| Income | .213*** | .213*** | .213*** |
|  | *Television News* | | |
| Gender | -.288*** | -.288*** | -.288*** |
| 30 and Under | -.188 | -.188 | -.188 |
| 60 and Over | .972*** | .972*** | .972*** |
| Education | *-.257*** | -.078 | -.078 |
| Income | -.027 | -.027 | -.027 |

*p≤.05; **p≤.01; ***p≤.001

read newspapers much more frequently compared to middle age respondents; and middle-aged respondents read newspapers more often than do those under thirty. Only among Latinos do men read newspapers more frequently than women.

Gender and age are strongly related to watching television news. Women watch local television news more frequently than men, and older respondents are much more likely to watch the news compared to middle age or younger respondents. Education is negatively related to television news watching, but the relationship is only statistically significant among Whites.

As seen in table 6.2, the largest predictors of viewing crime dramas are age and education. Middle-aged respondents watch crime dramas more frequently than older and younger respondents. Women watch a little more frequently than do men, and among Latinos only; education is positively correlated with viewing. Income is negatively correlated with viewing, but the relationship is rather weak.

Crime info-tainment viewing is strongly related to gender, age, income, and education. Men watch crime 'info-tainment' shows such as *COPS* and *America's Most Wanted* much more frequently than women.

**Table 6.2 Unstandardized Regression Coefficients of Crime Drama and Crime Info-tainment Consumption by Race/Ethnicity**

| | *White* (n=2500) | *Latino* (n=777) | *Black* (n=435) |
|---|---|---|---|
| | ***Crime Dramas*** | | |
| Gender | -.076* | -.076* | -.076* |
| 30 and Under | -.134*** | -.134*** | -.134*** |
| 60 and Over | .114** | .114** | .114** |
| Education | -.017 | *.116*** | -.017 |
| Income | -.024** | -.024** | -.024** |
| | ***Crime Info-tainment*** | | |
| Gender | .078** | .078** | .078** |
| 30 and Under | -.094* | *.071* | -.094* |
| 60 and Over | -.208*** | -.208*** | -.208*** |
| Education | -.195*** | *-.052* | -.195*** |
| Income | -.050*** | -.050*** | -.050*** |

*p≤.05; **p≤.01; ***p≤.001

In general, middle-aged respondents watch more crime info-tainment than either older or younger respondents. Income is negatively correlated with consumption. Education is also negatively correlated with crime info-tainment viewing, but only among Whites and Blacks; there are no effects of education among Latinos.

As seen in table 6.3, age, income and education are strongly related to the sheer number of hours spent watching television. Those thirty and younger watch significantly less television compared to middle-aged respondents, but the parameter could not be constrained equal across race/ethnicity. Younger Whites and African Americans are less likely to watch television compared to middle-aged respondents in their respective race/ethnic groups than are Latino respondents. Among older respondents, only Whites watch more television compared to their middle-aged counterparts. Education has a strong negative effect on hours of television watched among Whites and Blacks, but not among Latinos. Income is also negatively related to frequency of television watching, but the effect is strongest among African Americans.

As noted earlier, one of the criticisms of research that finds a relationship between media consumption and fear of crime is that these studies may be merely exploiting spurious effects. According to this viewpoint, it is not television that drives fear; but rather, fear television viewing.

**Table 6.3 Unstandardized Regression Coefficients of Hours Spent Watching Television per Week by Race/Ethnicity**

|  | *White* (n=2500) | *Latino* (n=777) | *Black* (n=435) |
|---|---|---|---|
|  | ***Hours Spent Watching TV*** | | |
| Gender | -.011 | -.011 | -.011 |
| 30 and Under | -2.963*** | *-.509* | -2.963*** |
| 60 and Over | *5.330****** | 1.139 | 1.139 |
| Education | -1.904*** | *-.357* | -1.904*** |
| Income | -.654*** | -.654*** | *-1.684****** |
| Prior Victim | .248 | .248 | .248 |
| Arrest | *3.316****** | .233 | .233 |

*$p \le .05$; **$p \le .01$; ***$p \le .001$

Because the empirical model is already very complicated, the reciprocal effects between television viewing and fear of crime are not examined. However, controls for prior crime experience (household arrest and prior victimization) on hours spent watching television are included. People who have been victimized may be more fearful of crime, and consequently, stay indoors more and watch television. Similarly, those who have been arrested for a crime may be on parole and have restrictions placed on them, or they may be unemployed, and therefore, watch more television.

No relationship was found between prior victimization and hours spent watching television, but Whites who have a member in the household that has been arrested spend more hours watching television compared to Whites that do not have someone in their household that has been arrested. This relationship was not found among Latino and African American respondents.

To sum, media consumption varies significantly across demographic groups; the strongest effects are found for gender, age and race. Women watch more television news and crime dramas than men, and much less crime info-tainment. In general, respondents age sixty and older read newspapers more often than respondents in the other age groups, and they watch more television, except for crime info-tainment. The effects of education and income are strong only for newspaper reading; newspaper readers are more educated and have higher incomes. Education is also negatively related to frequency of crime info-tainment viewing, but the relationship is weak among Latinos. Income is negatively correlated with frequency of both crime drama and crime info-tainment viewing.

## Prior Experiences with Crime

As seen in table 6.4 there are several important sociodemographic correlates of prior criminal victimization.[3] Of note, is the lack of gender difference among White and Latino respondents. However, Black men report more serious victimization than Black women; a finding that confirms what we know about the distribution of crime, especially of violent victimization. In all three race/ethnic groups, those thirty and younger report much more victimization compared to middle-aged respondents. Older respondents report much less serious victimization compared to their middle-aged counterparts; but only among Black and

White respondents; there is no difference in victimization between older and middle age Latinos. Education is not correlated with prior victimization of White and Black respondents, but it is positively related to victimization among Latinos. Conversely, while income has a negative effect on victimization among Whites and Blacks, it is not related to victimization of Latinos.

**Table 6.4 Unstandardized Regression Coefficients of Prior Victimization and Household Arrest**

|  | *White* (n=2500) | *Latino* (n=777) | *Black* (n=435) |
|---|---|---|---|
| | *Prior Victimization* | | |
| Gender | .008 | .008 | *.243** |
| 30 and Under | .189*** | .189*** | .189*** |
| 60 and Over | -.299*** | *.040* | -.299*** |
| Education | .023 | *.095*** | .023 |
| Income | -.054*** | *.021* | -.054*** |
| | *Household Arrest* | | |
| Gender | .090*** | *.024* | .090*** |
| 30 and Under | *-.065*** | .076** | .076** |
| 60 and Over | *-.177**** | -.077* | -.077* |
| Education | -.028*** | -.028*** | -.028*** |
| Income | *-.027**** | -.009 | -.009 |

*p≤.05; **p≤.01; ***p≤.001

In White and Latino households, men are more likely than women to live with someone that has been arrested, but gender makes no difference among African Americans.[4] Age is also related to household arrest, but operates differently across race/ethnicity. Younger Whites are less likely to live with household members that have been arrested than are middle-aged Whites; in contrast, younger Latinos and Blacks are more likely to live with household members that have been arrested than their middle age counterparts. Older respondents are also less likely to live with someone that has been arrested than middle-aged respondents. As one would expect, education is negatively correlated with household arrest; but the negative effects of income are only statistically significant for Whites.

# EXPLAINING CRIME SALIENCE

## *Perception of Neighborhood Crime Risk*

Table 6.5 presents the unstandardized regression coefficients of respondents' perceptions of neighborhood crime risk. The strongest determinants of perceptions of crime risk are gender, age, income and prior victimization. Compared to men, women perceive more neighborhood crime risk. Older respondents perceive much less crime risk than their middle age counterparts. Not surprisingly, income is negatively correlated; moreover, the effects of income are so much greater among Blacks that this coefficient could not be constrained equal to that of Whites and Latinos. Victims have significantly higher perceptions of crime risk in their neighborhoods compared to respondents that have not been victimized. Contrary to prior research, education does not appear to effect the perception of neighborhood crime risk.

**Table 6.5 Unstandardized Regression Coefficients of the Perception of Neighborhood Crime by Race/Ethnicity**

|  | *White* (n=2500) | *Latino* (n=777) | *Black* (n=435) |
|---|---|---|---|
| Gender | -.259*** | -.259*** | -.259*** |
| 30 and Under | -.233* | -.233* | -.233* |
| 60 and Over | -.474*** | -.474*** | -.474*** |
| Education | -.072 | -.072 | -.072 |
| Income | -.129*** | -.129*** | *-.377**** |
| Prior Victim | .490*** | .490*** | .490*** |
| Newspapers | -.012 | -.012 | -.012 |
| Television News | .050** | .050** | *.202*** |
| Info-tainment | .073 | .073 | .073 |
| Crime Drama | .100* | .100* | .100* |
| Hours of TV | .005 | .005 | *-.017** |

*p≤.05; **p≤.01; ***p≤.001

Some forms of media also elevate the perception of neighborhood crime risk. Specifically, local television news and crime drama viewing increases the perception of neighborhood crime risk; among Black respondents, watching local news heightens this perception even more so than it does for Latinos and Whites. The effects of viewing local television on perceptions of neighborhood crime risk is expected; the greater effect upon Black respondents' perceptions indicate support for the resonance hypothesis – that media effects are strongest when they reflect lived reality.

## Perception of Increased Crime in the State

There are many factors that influence the perception that crime in California had risen over the three years prior to the survey administration. As seen in table 6.6, women are far more likely to believe that crime in California had increased; this is particularly true for Black women. Education and income is negatively associated. Democrats are less likely to believe that crime had increased. Experiences with crime appear to color perceptions of state crime rates. Victims of crime and those that perceive greater neighborhood crime risk are much more likely to believe state crime rates had increased.

**Table 6.6 Unstandardized Regression Coefficients of the Perception that State Crime had Increased by Race/Ethnicity**

|  | *White* (n=2500) | *Latino* (n=777) | *Black* (n=435) |
|---|---|---|---|
| Gender | -.120*** | -.120*** | -.229*** |
| 30 and Under | -.007 | -.007 | -.007 |
| 60 and Over | .015 | .015 | .015 |
| Education | -.051*** | -.051*** | -.051** |
| Income | -.012** | -.012** | -.012** |
| Republican | .015 | .015 | .015 |
| Democrat | -.069*** | -.069*** | -.069*** |
| Prior Victim | .015** | .015** | .015** |
| Newspapers | -.007** | -.007** | -.007** |
| Television News | .006 | .006 | .006 |
| Info-tainment | .035*** | .035*** | .035*** |
| Crime Drama | -.002 | -.002 | -.002 |
| Hours of TV | .000 | .000 | .000 |
| Local Risk | .014*** | .014*** | .014*** |

*p≤.05; **p≤.01; ***p≤.001

As hypothesized, those who read newspapers more frequently are slightly less inclined to believe that crime has increased. In contrast, crime info-tainment viewers are much more likely to believe crime has risen, confirming prior research (Oliver and Armstong, 1998). Surprisingly, television news consumption has no effect.

## Feeling Safe from Crime

Consistent with the extant literature, as seen in table 6.7, one of the largest determinants found for feeling safe is gender: men feel much safer than women. Interestingly, and unlike other studies, age does not appear related to feeling safe from crime.

The positive effects of education are found only among Latinos; the higher the education achieved, the safer respondents feel. Income has small positive effects on feeling safe for Whites and Latinos, but much larger positive effects for Blacks. Victims feel less safe, as do respondents that perceive greater neighborhood crime risk, and those that believe state crime had increased. Media do not affect feeling safe whatsoever.

**Table 6.7 Unstandardized Regression Coefficients of Feeling Safe by Race/Ethnicity**

|  | *White* (n=2500) | *Latino* (n=777) | *Black* (n=435) |
|---|---|---|---|
| Gender | .395*** | .395*** | .395*** |
| 30 and Under | .020 | .020 | .020 |
| 60 and Over | -.059 | -.059 | -.059 |
| Education | -.046 | *.258*** | -.046 |
| Income | .042* | .042* | *.116** |
| Prior Victim | -.083** | -.083** | -.083** |
| Newspapers | -.010 | -.010 | -.010 |
| Television News | -.010 | -.010 | -.010 |
| Info-tainment | -.028 | -.028 | -.028 |
| Crime Drama | .056 | .056 | .056 |
| Hours of TV | -.001 | -.001 | -.001 |
| Local Risk | -.281*** | -.281*** | -.281*** |
| Crime Increased | -.124* | -.124* | -.124* |

*p≤.05; **p≤.01; ***p≤.001

## Fear of Crime

There are several determinants of fear of crime, as displayed in table 6.8. As expected, men have much lower fear of crime than women; moreover, this difference is very large. Younger respondents have slightly higher fear of crime than their middle-aged counterparts, but those sixty and over report much lower fear of crime. This finding supports prior research (Chadee and Ditton, 2003), but contradicts studies that find the relationship between age and fear is curvilinear (Ortega and Myles, 1987; Rountree and Land, 1996). In all race/ethnic groups, increased education is associated with slight reductions in fear, but the negative effect of income is only statistically significant for Whites. Victims are much more fearful than nonvictims. Those that live with someone who has been arrested have much lower fear. As expected, given the multi-dimensional quality of 'fear of crime,' perceptions of neighborhood crime risk, the belief that state crime is increasing, and feeling safe are all strongly related to fear of crime.

**Table 6.8 Unstandardized Regression Coefficients of Fear of Crime by Race/Ethnicity**

|  | *White* (n=2500) | *Latino* (n=777) | *Black* (n=435) |
|---|---|---|---|
| Gender | -.605*** | -.605*** | -.605*** |
| 30 and Under | .195* | .195* | .195* |
| 60 and Over | -.290*** | -.290*** | -.290*** |
| Education | -.066* | -.066* | -.066* |
| Income | *.068*** | -.017 | -.017 |
| Prior Victim | .157*** | .157*** | .157*** |
| Household Arrest | -.268*** | -.268*** | -.268*** |
| Newspapers | .020* | .020* | .020* |
| Television News | .029** | .029** | .029** |
| Info-tainment | .096** | .096** | .096** |
| Crime Drama | .041 | *-.275** | .041 |
| Hours of TV | *-.002* | .011** | .011** |
| Local Risk | .433*** | .433*** | .433*** |
| Crime Increased | .175** | .175** | .175** |
| Feeling Safe | *-.355*** | -.253*** | -.253*** |

*p≤.05; **p≤.01; ***p≤.001

All forms of media influence fear of crime, but the effects are variable by type. As hypothesized, more frequent viewing of television news and crime info-tainment greatly increases fear; increased newspaper reading also elevates fear of crime, but the effect is not as strong. The more hours spent watching television, the greater the fear, supporting the cultivation hypothesis, but this relationship is not found for Whites. Viewing crime dramas has no effect on Whites and Blacks, but it is associated with decreased fear of crime among Latinos.

## EXPLAINING BELIEFS ABOUT CRIME AND CRIME CAUSATION

### *Just World Beliefs*

As presented in table 6.9, belief in a just world is affected by a number of sociodemographic factors but these vary considerably across race/ethnicity. Men are more likely than women to view the world as just, confirming prior research (Smith and Green, 1984); although the effects are only statistically significant for Whites and Blacks. Age does not appear to be related to just world beliefs; but prior evidence on this relationship is mixed (Benson, 1992; Rubin and Peplau, 1973). In all race/ethnic groups, education is negatively correlated with just world beliefs, but the effects of income are more complex. Among Latinos and Blacks, there is a negative relationship between income and just world beliefs; but income has no effect on the just world beliefs of Whites. Black and White Republicans are more likely to view the world as just compared to their Independent counterparts, although this is not true for Latino Republicans. Prior criminal victimization slightly decreases belief in a just world, as do increases in perception of neighborhood crime risk. White and Black respondents who believe state crime has increased are less likely to perceive the world as just.

As hypothesized, increases in consumption of television news, crime info-tainment, and crime drama elevate belief in a just world. Although the effects are only moderately statistically significant, the findings are in the hypothesized direction, and found only amongst the forms of media in which 'good guy' and 'bad guy' imagery is most often simplistically presented.

**Table 6.9 Unstandardized Regression Coefficients of Belief in a Just World by Race/Ethnicity**

|                  | *White* (n=2500) | *Latino* (n=777) | *Black* (n=435) |
|------------------|------------------|------------------|-----------------|
| Gender           | .088***          | *.026*           | .088***         |
| 30 and Under     | .030             | .030             | .030            |
| 60 an d Over     | -.000            | -.000            | -.000           |
| Education        | -.025***         | -.025***         | -.025***        |
| Income           | *.000*           | -.026***         | -.026***        |
| Republican       | .099***          | *-.018*          | .099***         |
| Democrat         | .013             | .013             | .013            |
| Prior Victim     | -.015*           | -.015*           | -.015*          |
| Arrest           | -.034            | -.034            | -.034           |
| Newspapers       | .001             | .001             | .001            |
| Television News  | .008*            | .008*            | .008*           |
| Info-tainment    | .016*            | .016*            | .016*           |
| Crime Drama      | .014*            | .014*            | .014*           |
| Hours of TV      | .000             | .000             | .000            |
| Local Risk       | -.010**          | -.010**          | -.010**         |
| Crime Increased  | -.039**          | *.036*           | -.039**         |
| Feeling Safe     | .001             | .001             | .001            |
| Fear of Crime    | .004             | .004             | .004            |

*p≤.05; **p≤.01; ***p≤.001

## *Crime Seriousness*

Table 6.10 presents the coefficients for crime seriousness. Women rate crimes much more seriously than men. Consistent with prior research, there is a positive linear relationship between age and views of crime seriousness; and a negative relationship with education and income (Cullen et al., 1974; Rossi et al., 1974) though the negative effect of education is only found among Whites and Latinos. Education has no effect on Blacks' views of crime seriousness. Confirming prior research (Rauma, 1991), Republicans rate crimes as more serious compared to Independents; but the effect of Democrat status is not so strong. The only relationship found is a modest decrease in crime seriousness ratings among White Democrats compared to White Independents.

**Table 6.10 Unstandardized Regression Coefficients of Crime Seriousness by Race/Ethnicity**

|  | White (n=2500) | Latino (n=777) | Black (n=435) |
|---|---|---|---|
| Gender | -.278*** | -.278*** | -.278*** |
| 30 and Under | -.463*** | -.463*** | -.463*** |
| 60 and Over | .254*** | .254*** | .254*** |
| Education | -.196*** | -.196*** | *-.019* |
| Income | -.052*** | -.052*** | -.052*** |
| Republican | .340*** | .340*** | .340*** |
| Democrat | *-.155** | .095 | .095 |
| Prior Victim | -.034 | -.034 | -.034 |
| Arrest | -.391*** | -.391*** | -.391*** |
| Newspapers | -.009 | -.009 | -.009 |
| Television News | .061*** | .061*** | .061*** |
| Info-tainment | .052* | .052* | .052* |
| Crime Drama | -.049* | -.049* | -.049* |
| Hours of TV | -.003 | -.003 | -.003 |
| Local Risk | .022* | .022* | .022* |
| Crime Increased | .264*** | .264*** | .264*** |
| Feeling Safe | .007 | .007 | .007 |
| Fear of Crime | .054*** | .054*** | .054*** |
| Just World Beliefs | .232*** | .232*** | .232*** |

*p≤.05; **p≤.01; ***p≤.001

People with higher just world beliefs have much higher crime seriousness ratings. As predicted, respondents who live with household members that have been arrested view crimes as less serious. Of the four crime salience variables, the belief that state crime is increasing and higher fear of crime are strongly associated with higher crime seriousness ratings; greater perception of neighborhood crime risk is weakly associated with higher crime seriousness ratings.

The effects of media consumption on crime seriousness are variable across media types. As expected, increases in television news and crime info-tainment viewing are associated with increases in crime seriousness ratings. The effects of other media are slight or nonexistent.

## *Support for Rehabilitation*

As seen in table 6.11, there are relatively few sociodemographic factors that influence support for rehabilitation; those there are indicate significant interactions by race/ethnicity. Republicans are less likely to support rehabilitation compared to Independents. As one would expect, those that live with someone that has been arrested are more likely to support rehabilitation. Belief in a just world and crime seriousness ratings are negatively associated. Interestingly, none of the crime salience variables have any influence. Viewing crime drama decreases support for rehabilitation; similarly, the more hours spent watching television, the less likely respondents are to support rehabilitation.

**Table 6.11 Unstandardized Regression Coefficients of Support for Rehabilitation by Race/Ethnicity**

|  | *White* (n=2500) | *Latino* (n=777) | *Black* (n=435) |
|---|---|---|---|
| Gender | -.016 | -.016 | -.016 |
| 30 an d Under | .097*** | .001 | .001 |
| 60 and Over | .006 | .006 | .006 |
| Education | .006 | .006 | .006 |
| Income | -.009 | -.033*** | -.009 |
| Republican | -.056** | -.056** | -.056** |
| Democrat | .068*** | -.042 | -.042 |
| Prior Victim | .004 | .004 | .004 |
| Arrest | .054** | .054** | .054** |
| Newspapers | .001 | .001 | .001 |
| Television News | -.002 | -.002 | -.002 |
| Info-tainment | -.012 | -.012 | -.012 |
| Crime Drama | -.016* | -.016* | -.016* |
| Hours of TV | -.002*** | -.002*** | -.002*** |
| Local Risk | .003 | .003 | .003 |
| Crime Increased | -.018 | -.018 | -.018 |
| Feeling Safe | .004 | .004 | .004 |
| Fear of Crime | .003 | .003 | .003 |
| Just World Beliefs | -.069*** | -.069*** | -.069*** |
| Crime Seriousness | -.021*** | -.021*** | -.021*** |

*p≤.05; **p≤.01; ***p≤.001

# WHAT ELEVATES SUPPORT FOR THREE STRIKES?

Only a handful of variables have a direct effect on support for three strikes. The strongest predictors are political party, household arrest, just world beliefs, crime seriousness and support for rehabilitation. Age, income, the belief that state crime is increasing, and fear of crime are weakly related to support for three strikes.

**Table 6.12 Unstandardized Regression Coefficients of Support for Three Strikes by Race/Ethnicity**

|                            | *White* (n=2500) | *Latino* (n=777) | *Black* (n=435) |
|----------------------------|------------------|------------------|-----------------|
| Gender                     | -.024            | -.024            | -.024           |
| 30 and Under               | .028             | .028             | .028            |
| 60 and Over                | -.100*           | -.100*           | -.100*          |
| Education                  | -.019            | -.019            | -.019           |
| Income                     | .016             | *.095***         | .016            |
| Republican                 | .180***          | .180***          | .180***         |
| Democrat                   | *-.156**         | -.036            | -.036           |
| Prior Victim               | -.011            | -.011            | -.011           |
| Arrest                     | -.259***         | -.259***         | -.259***        |
| Newspapers                 | -.007            | -.007            | -.007           |
| Television News            | -.010            | -.010            | -.010           |
| Info-tainment              | .014             | .014             | .014            |
| Crime Drama                | -.007            | -.007            | -.007           |
| Hours of TV                | -.002            | -.002            | -.002           |
| Local Risk                 | -.007            | -.007            | -.007           |
| Crime Increased            | .065*            | .065*            | .065*           |
| Feeling Safe               | .011             | .011             | .011            |
| Fear of Crime              | .021*            | .021*            | .021*           |
| Just World Beliefs         | .178***          | .178***          | .178***         |
| Crime Seriousness          | *.220***         | .112***          | .112***         |
| Support for Rehabilitation | -.313***         | -.313***         | -.313***        |

*p≤.05; **p≤.01; ***p≤.001

As seen in table 6.12, support for three strikes is much higher among Republicans, those with higher belief in a just world, those that believe crime rates have increased, and those with higher fear of crime.

Those that rate crimes as more serious are also more likely to support three strikes for a greater number of offenses; among Whites, this relationship is extremely strong. Among Latinos only, those with higher incomes are more likely to support three strikes.

Respondents age sixty and older are less likely to support three strikes compared to middle-aged respondents. There is no difference between young and middle-aged respondents in support for three strikes. Those that live with someone that has been arrested are much less likely to support three strikes, as do respondents that believe the primary purpose of imprisonment should be rehabilitation. Interestingly, none of the media variables influence support for three strikes, neither does prior criminal victimization, nor education. As predicted, feeling safe and perceptions of neighborhood crime risk are not associated with support for three strikes.

## SUMMARY OF VARIABLE EFFECTS

The coefficients have been described in terms of their relative impact on the endogenous variables in the model, and on the dependent variable, support for three strikes. In this section we review the unstandardized regression coefficients under a different schema. This section reviews the effects of each exogenous or intervening variable on the various endogenous constructs. This gives us a snapshot look at the effects of a given variable, such as gender, throughout the entire model. Rather than examining what influences a particular construct, this enables us to see which variables have the most effects, and whether those effects are clearly patterned.

### *Sociodemographic Correlates*

#### Gender
There are numerous differences between men and women, and these differences are quite large. Women are much more likely than men to perceive higher crime risk in their neighborhoods and to believe that crime rates in the state had increased. Consistent with numerous studies of fear of crime, women feel much less safe than men, and they report significantly higher levels of fear of crime. They also have lower beliefs in a just world, rate crimes less seriously, and are more likely to support rehabilitation; all findings consistent with prior research (e.g.,

Smith and Green, 1984; Haghighi and Lopez, 2000). Of all the variables of interest, only in support for three strikes, is no gender effect found. This confirms prior research that finds gender differences usually disappear in multivariate analyses (e.g., Applegate and Cullen, 1996; Rossi and Berk, 1997).

*Age*

There are many statistically significant effects of age, although the results are quite complex. Middle-aged respondents perceive more neighborhood crime risk than do younger or older respondents; but older respondents are the least fearful. There are no age differences found for the belief that state crime had increased, in feeling safe, or in belief in a just world. Age is positively correlated with views of crime seriousness. Older respondents are less likely to support three strikes compared to middle-aged and younger respondents. These findings confirm prior studies that find middle-aged respondents are somewhat more punitive than older or younger respondents (e.g., Rossi and Berk, 1997)

*Education*

Unlike many other studies of public opinion of crime sentencing, there are few educational effects. The higher the level of education, the less likely respondents are to believe that crime rates had increased, and the lower their fear of crime. Education is also negatively correlated with belief in a just world and views of crime seriousness. Education has no effect on neighborhood crime risk perceptions, support for rehabilitation, or support for three strikes. Diagnostic tests were run to determine if the lack of educational effects were due to multicollinearity between income and education in this complex model, but this was not confirmed. In any event, the lack of educational effects on punitiveness contradicts some prior research (e.g., Rossi and Berk, 1997; Roberts and Stalans, 1997), but it mirrors the findings of a small public opinion survey of three strikes (Applegate and Cullen, 1996).

*Income.*

Income affects all of the endogenous variables, but quite differently across race/ethnic groups. Respondents with higher incomes perceive lower neighborhood crime risks; this relationship is particularly strong for Blacks. Similarly, higher levels of income work to increase feeling safe, but only among Blacks. In contrast, Whites with higher incomes report higher levels of fear of crime compared to Whites with lower incomes. Among all race/ethnic groups, income is negatively associated with the belief that state crime had increased. Among Blacks and Latinos, higher income reduces belief in a just world. Individuals with higher incomes also have higher crime seriousness ratings. Among Latinos only, higher income reduces support for rehabilitation, but elevates support for three strikes.

## Experiences with Crime

### Prior Victimization
Prior victimization seems to influence a variety of crime perceptions and beliefs. Victims are more likely to believe that crime in California had increased, and perceive much more neighborhood crime risk. Victimization also reduces feeling safe and greatly increases fear of crime. On the other hand, prior criminal victimization is not related to support for three strikes, consistent with prior research (e.g., Hough and Roberts, 1999; Rossi et al., 1985; Rossi and Berk, 1997). The effects of victimization on the above perceptions and beliefs do not vary across race/ethnic groups. Interestingly, the severity of prior criminal victimization does not impact crime seriousness ratings.

Prior victimization also decreases belief in a just world. The modest decrease in just world beliefs is more difficult to explain. Intuitively, we would expect that individuals who have suffered a criminal victimization would view the world as less just. That they do not do so to any significant degree suggests that respondents may have been satisfied with the outcome of their victimization (i.e., their stolen property was found or returned; the offender was caught and punished; they received restitution, and so forth); an idea put forth by Agnew (1985), but never tested heretofore.

### Household Member Arrested
Although the model tested relatively few effects of household arrest the relationships found are very strong. Interestingly, respondents that live with someone that has been arrested are less fearful of crime than those that do not live with someone that has been arrested. As predicted, respondents with a household arrest view crime less seriously, are more likely to support rehabilitation, and are much less likely to support three strikes. As with prior victimization, the effects of household arrest do not vary across race/ethnicity.

## Crime Salience

### Perception of Neighborhood Crime

Those who perceive more crime risk in their neighborhoods are more likely to believe that state crime had increased. They also feel considerably less safe, and have higher fear of crime. They are less likely to perceive the world as just, and rate crime seriousness higher than do those that perceive less crime in their neighborhoods. Yet, as hypothesized, and consistent with other studies (e.g., Rossi and Berk, 1997), the perception of neighborhood crime does not influence support for three strikes.

### Belief that Crime in the State had Increased

The perception that crime in the state had increased influences a number of other beliefs and attitudes about crime and crime policy. Respondents that believe crime had increased feel less safe, and have higher fear of crime than those that do not think crime had increased. Respondents who think crime had increased also view crimes as much more serious as others, and as hypothesized, are more likely to support three strikes.

### Feeling Safe

The effects of feeling safe do not appear to impact other beliefs and opinions about crime, with the exception of fear. Respondents that feel safe from crime have much lower fear of crime; this is particularly so for Whites. Feeling safe does not influence just world beliefs, crime seriousness, and support for rehabilitation or, as hypothesized, support for three strikes.

### Fear of Crime

Respondents with higher fear of crime view crimes as more serious than respondents with lower levels of fear. Consistent with prior studies (e.g., McCorkle, 1993), higher fear is not associated with support for rehabilitation, but is associated with a slight elevation in support for three strikes.

## Beliefs about Crime and Crime Causation

### Political Ideology

Consistent with prior research, the effects of political ideology are quite strong, especially for Republicans. They are more likely to believe that crime rates have increased in the state, and view crimes as much more serious compared to Independents and Democrats. Republicans view the world as just, and consistent with prior research (e.g., Miethe, 1984), are much less likely to support rehabilitation and much more likely to support three strikes sentencing (e.g., Applegate and Cullen, 1996). Conversely, Democrats are much less likely to believe crime had increased, and they have lower belief in a just world. Democrats have lower crime seriousness ratings, are more likely to support rehabilitation, and are much less likely to support three strikes. However, statistically significant differences between Democrats and Independents are only found among Whites, suggesting little difference between Latino and Black Independents and Democrats in their views of crime policy.

*Just World Beliefs*

Higher just world beliefs are negatively related to support for rehabilitation. Those with higher just world beliefs have higher crime seriousness ratings, and greater support for three strikes sentencing, as some research in this area suggests (e.g., Finamore and Carlson, 1987).

*Crime Seriousness*

Those who rate crimes more seriously are much less likely to support rehabilitation. Consistent with prior research, crime seriousness is the largest positive coefficient of support for three strikes (e.g., Blumstein and Cohen, 1980; Hamilton and Rytina, 1980), moreover, its effects are even stronger among Whites compared to blacks and Latinos.

*Support for Rehabilitation*

Support for rehabilitation as the most important reason to imprison offenders is related to much lower level of support for three strikes across all race/ethnic groups, confirming prior research (e.g., Hamilton and Rytina, 1980).

## Media Effects on Attitudes and Beliefs about Crime, and Support for Three Strikes

Although media have no direct effects on support for three strikes, they do indirectly influence three strikes through their impact on perceptions and beliefs about crime, although these effects are variable across specific forms of crime-related media. To begin with, there are very few effects of newspaper reading, but many more effects of television viewing. The more frequent newspaper reading, the *less* likely respondents are to believe that crime in the state is increasing, but the greater their fear of crime (although this effect is relatively small).

Watching crime-related drama produces small increases in the perception of neighborhood crime, belief in a just world, and decreases support for rehabilitation. Those that watch crime-related dramas also have higher ratings of crime seriousness. Among Latinos only, watching crime drama is associated with a fairly large decrease in fear of crime.

As hypothesized, the largest media effects are found for crime info-tainment and television news. Watching reality-based crime programs increases the perception that crime in the state has increased, raises fear of crime, increases crime seriousness ratings, and elevates belief in a just world. Similarly, television news consumption is positively correlated with fear of crime, crime seriousness ratings, and just world beliefs. Viewing television news increases perceptions of neighborhood crime risk in all race/ethnic groups, but the relationship is especially strong amongst Blacks, indicative of support for the resonance hypothesis. Television news coverage of violent crime is more likely to cover areas of Black residential concentration, thus elevating Blacks' perceptions of local crime risk even higher than White or Latino respondents.

## WHITE, LATINO AND AFRICAN AMERICAN DETERMINANTS OF PUNITIVENESS

This section compares race/ethnic group differences of the statistically significant standardized regression coefficients that determine support for three strikes. Examining the standardized effects allows for valid comparisons of the relative ranking of these determinants between race/ethnic groups. More simply, we can ascertain whether the most influential factors of punitiveness are the same for Latinos as they are for Blacks, or for Whites. Tables 6.13 to 6.18 examine the most important effects of exogenous and intervening variables on the following attitudes and beliefs about crime and punishment: support for three strikes, support for rehabilitation, crime seriousness, just world beliefs, fear of crime, feeling safe, and beliefs about statewide crime trends, in that order. Each variable is ranked in order of importance within each race/ethnic group column as ascertained from the size of its associated standardized regression coefficient; the value of the beta weight is also presented. We begin by examining the factors that determine support for three strikes.

## Race/Ethnic Differences in Support for Three Strikes

Table 6.13 compares the determinants of three strikes support between Whites, Latinos, and African Americans. As with other studies, crime seriousness is the most important determinant of support for three strikes but this effect is found only among Whites and Blacks. Crime seriousness has a much larger effect for Whites ($\beta = .311$) than either Latinos or Blacks ($\beta = .168$ and $\beta = .182$, respectively). The second and third largest determinants of support for three strikes among Whites and Blacks are support for rehabilitation and household arrest (both negatively related).

**Table 6.13 Rank Order of Statistically Significant Standardized Effects of Support for Three Strikes Sentencing by Race/Ethnicity**

| White (n=2500) | | Latino (n=777) | | Black (n=435) | |
|---|---|---|---|---|---|
| Seriousness | .311 | Income | .205 | Seriousness | .182 |
| Support Rehab | -.126 | Seriousness | .168 | Support Rehab | -.173 |
| Arrest | -.095 | Support Rehab | -.158 | Arrest | -.128 |
| Republican | .085 | Arrest | -.106 | Just World | .085 |
| Democrat | -.073 | Just World | .074 | Fear of Crime | .064 |
| Just World | .067 | Fear of Crime | .062 | 60 and Over | -.048 |
| Fear of Crime | .045 | Republican | .062 | Republican | .038 |
| 60 and Over | -.045 | Crime Increased | .036 | Crime Increased | .038 |
| Crime Increased | .031 | 60 and Over | -.030 | | |

*Note:* Numbers on right side of column are standardized regression coefficients. All are statistically significant (p-values of .05 or smaller).

In contrast, among Latinos, the most important determinant of support for three strikes is income, followed by crime seriousness, support for rehabilitation and household arrest. Although there are similarities in the rank order of determinants, support for rehabilitation and household arrest have larger negative effects for Blacks and Latinos than for Whites. Political party affiliation appears more important for Whites; political party is the fourth and fifth largest determinant of punitiveness among Whites. In contrast, Democrat party identification did not influence punitiveness among Latinos and Blacks, and Republican status was only marginally influential.

The effects of just world beliefs and fear of crime operate similarly for each race/ethnic group. Just world beliefs are somewhat stronger determinants of support for three strikes among African Americans compared to Whites and Latinos, but the difference is not large. The effects of fear of crime are of about equal importance for all race/ethnic groups: higher fear leads to higher support for three strikes.

In general, although there are some differences in determinants of punitiveness between race/ethnic groups, there are more similarities than dissimilarities. The two largest differences are the importance of income in determining Latino punitiveness and of political party influences on White's support for three strikes.

As demonstrated earlier, although media do not directly influence support for three strikes, they appear work to indirectly through their influence on the attitudes and beliefs determinant of support for three strikes. The importance of crime seriousness ratings, support for rehabilitation, just world beliefs and fear of crime on support for three strikes warrants further examination of the determinants of these intervening variables.

## Race/Ethnic Differences in Support for Rehabilitation

As seen in table 6.14, the determinants of support for rehabilitation vary across race/ethnicity. The largest coefficient among Whites is age. White respondents age thirty and younger are more likely to support rehabilitation compared to middle-aged Whites ($\beta = .082$). In contrast, age is not relevant for Latinos and Blacks. Instead, the largest determinant of support for rehabilitation among Latinos is income, followed by crime seriousness, both of which are negatively related to support for rehabilitation ($\beta = -.141$ and $\beta = -.062$, respectively). Democrat party affiliation has the second largest effect on support for rehabilitation among Whites ($\beta = .080$).

Among Blacks, the largest influence on support for rehabilitation is hours spent watching television ($\beta = -.069$). In contrast, television viewing is only the fourth largest determinant among Latinos and the sixth largest among Whites; nonetheless, the coefficient sizes are almost equivalent in all groups. The relative influence of crime seriousness and just world beliefs are equal among Latinos and Blacks, and not dissimilar from Whites. Crime seriousness is the second largest determinant of support for rehabilitation among Latinos and Blacks; just world beliefs are ranked third. Among Whites, crime seriousness is ranked third and just world beliefs, fifth. Republican status is a much more important determinant of support for rehabilitation among Whites ($\beta$ = -.066) than either Latinos or Blacks ($\beta$ = -.038 and $\beta$ = -.021, respectively). Household arrest has more of an impact on African Americans and Latinos compared to Whites. Finally, crime drama viewing has similarly small, negative effects for all groups.

**Table 6.14 Rank Order of Statistically Significant Standardized Effects of Support for Rehabilitation by Race/Ethnicity**

| *White* (n=2500) | | *Latino* (n=777) | | *Black* (n=435) | |
|---|---|---|---|---|---|
| 30 and Under | .080 | Income | -.141 | TV Hours | -.069 |
| Democrat | .082 | Crime Serious | -.062 | Crime Serious | -.062 |
| Crime Serious | -.073 | Just World | -.057 | Just World | -.059 |
| Republican | -.066 | TV Hours | -.047 | Arrest | .049 |
| Just World | -.065 | Arrest | .044 | Crime Drama | -.032 |
| TV Hours | -.061 | Republican | -.038 | Republican | -.021 |
| Arrest | .049 | Crime Drama | -.030 | | |
| Crime Drama | -.036 | | | | |

*Note:* Numbers on right side of column are standardized regression coefficients. All are statistically significant (p-values of .05 or smaller).

## *Race/Ethnic Differences in Crime Seriousness Ratings*

As with support for three strikes there are significant differences in the relative importance of determinants of crime seriousness across race/ethnicity. To begin with, as seen in table 6.15, education has the largest effect among Whites and the second largest among Latinos; the coefficients are also nearly equal in size ($\beta$ = -.145 and $\beta$ = -.154, respectively), but education has no effect on Blacks' views of crime seriousness. The second largest determinant of crime seriousness ratings among Whites is political party - Republicans rate crimes as more serious ($\beta$ = .114). Although Latino and Black Republicans view crimes as more serious compared to their Independent counterparts ($\beta$ = .078 and $\beta$ = .043, respectively), the importance of political party is much lower in its relative importance in determining crime seriousness ratings among Latinos and Blacks.

The effects of younger age and household arrest are large for all groups, although strongest for Latinos and Blacks. Younger age and household arrest are the largest determinants of crime seriousness ratings among Blacks, ranked first and third in their relative importance among Latinos, but only third and fifth among Whites. Additionally, the effects of fear of crime are much stronger for Latinos and Blacks compared to Whites; it is the third largest determinant of crime seriousness ratings among Blacks, the fourth largest among Latinos, but only the eighth largest among Whites.

**Table 6.15 Rank Order of Statistically Significant Standardized Effects of Seriousness of Crime by Race/Ethnicity**

| *White* (n=2500) | | *Latino* (n=777) | | *Black* (n=435) | |
|---|---|---|---|---|---|
| Education | -.145 | 30 and Under | -.161 | 30 and Under | -.133 |
| Republican | .114 | Education | -.154 | Arrest | -.118 |
| 30 and Under | -.112 | Arrest | -.106 | Fear of Crime | .100 |
| TV News | .108 | Fear of Crime | .105 | Gender | -.099 |
| Arrest | -.102 | TV News | .100 | Crime Increased | .095 |
| Gender | -.096 | Gender | -.098 | TV News | .086 |
| Crime Increased | .090 | Crime Increased | .097 | Income | -.081 |
| Fear of Crime | .082 | Republican | .078 | 60 and Over | .074 |
| 60 and Over | .081 | Income | -.075 | Just World | .067 |
| Income | -.071 | Just World | .064 | Republican | .043 |
| Just World | .062 | 60 and Over | .050 | Crime Risk | .041 |
| Democrat | -.052 | Crime Risk | .042 | Info-tainment | .038 |
| Crime Risk | .036 | Info-tainment | .038 | Crime Drama | -.033 |
| Info-tainment | .032 | Crime Drama | -.031 | | |
| Crime Drama | -.031 | | | | |

*Note:* Numbers on right side of column are standardized regression coefficients. All are statistically significant (p-values of .05 or smaller).

The importance of media works relatively similar across all race/ethnic groups. Television news viewing is positively related to crime seriousness ratings, although the effects are stronger for Whites ($\beta$ = .108) and Latinos ($\beta$ = .100) than Blacks ($\beta$ = .086). Television news viewing is the third largest determinant of crime seriousness among Whites, fifth among Latinos, and sixth among African Americans. Crime drama and crime info-tainment viewing have modest effects on crime seriousness ratings, and are ranked last in terms of their relative importance among all three race/ethnic groups.

## *Race/Ethnic Differences in Just World Beliefs*

The determinants of just world beliefs vary substantially across groups. As displayed in table 6.16, income is not relevant to Whites' beliefs in a just world, but it is the most influential factor of Latinos and Blacks. Among them, the higher the income, the lower the belief in a just world. Again, political party is most salient for Whites - Republican status is the largest determinant of just world beliefs among Whites, the sixth largest for Blacks, but it is not at all relevant to Latinos. Gender is

**Table 6.16 Rank Order of Statistically Significant Standardized Effects of Just World Beliefs by Race/Ethnicity**

| *White* (n=2500) | | *Latino* (n=777) | | *Black* (n=435) | |
|---|---|---|---|---|---|
| Republican | .123 | Income | -.136 | Income | -.139 |
| Gender | .114 | Education | -.071 | Gender | .108 |
| Education | -.069 | Crime Risk | -.070 | Education | -.065 |
| Crime Risk | -.061 | TV News | .047 | Crime Risk | -.065 |
| Crime Increased | -.049 | Info-tainment | .044 | Crime Increased | -.048 |
| TV News | .045 | Arrest | -.034 | Republican | .043 |
| Info-tainment | .038 | Prior Victim | -.033 | Info-tainment | .042 |
| Prior Victim | -.037 | Crime Dramas | .033 | TV News | .039 |
| Crime Dramas | .034 | | | Prior Victim | -.037 |
| Arrest | -.033 | | | Arrest | -.036 |
| | | | | Crime Dramas | .034 |

*Note:* Numbers on right side of column are standardized regression coefficients. All are statistically significant (p-values of .05 or smaller).

the second largest determinant of just world beliefs among Whites and Blacks - in both groups, men are more likely to see the world as just. In contrast, there are no gender differences in just world beliefs among Latinos.

Perceived neighborhood crime risk lowers belief in a just world and is of similar importance across race/ethnic groups. However, the perception that crime has increased is only salient for Whites and Blacks. Television news, crime drama and crime info-tainment increase belief in a just world similarly across all three race/ethnic groups, although these effects are smaller than most of the other determinants.

## Race/Ethnic Differences in Fear of Crime

As seen in table 6.17, the most significant determinants of fear of crime do not differ across race/ethnic groups. The largest coefficients are neighborhood crime risk, feeling safe, and gender, in that order. Prior victimization is of about equal influence in engendering fear. Of note,

**Table 6.17 Rank Order of Statistically Significant Standardized Effects of Fear of Crime by Race/Ethnicity**

| *White* (n=2500) | | *Latino* (n=777) | | *Black* (n=477) | |
|---|---|---|---|---|---|
| Crime Risk | .471 | Crime Risk | .429 | Crime Risk | .442 |
| Safety | -.288 | Safety | -.223 | Safety | -.214 |
| Gender | -.139 | Gender | -.110 | Gender | -.116 |
| Prior Victim | .069 | Crime Dramas | -.090 | TV Hours | .077 |
| Income | .061 | TV Hours | .050 | Prior Victim | .062 |
| 60 and Over | -.061 | Prior Victim | .050 | 60 and Over | -.046 |
| Arrest | -.046 | Info-tainment | .036 | Arrest | -.044 |
| Info-tainment | .039 | 30 and Under | .035 | Info-tainment | .038 |
| Crime Increased | .039 | Crime Increased | .033 | Crime Increased | .034 |
| TV News | .035 | 60 an d Over | -.029 | 30 and Under | .030 |
| Education | -.032 | Education | -.027 | Education | -.027 |
| 30 and Under | .031 | Arrest | -.037 | Newspapers | .023 |
| Newspapers | .028 | TV News | .025 | TV News | .022 |
| | | Newspapers | .021 | | |

*Note:* Numbers on right side of column are standardized regression coefficients. All are statistically significant (p-values of .05 or smaller).

income is only important for Whites, among whom higher income produces higher fear. Older respondents, especially Whites, are less fearful. Household arrest and education have similar negative effects on fear of crime across all groups.

## Race/Ethnic Differences in the Perception of State Crime

As seen in table 6.18, the rank of determinants of the perception that crime had increased are remarkably similar across race/ethnic groups. To begin with, the first and second most important determinants are the same. Gender and education are both negatively related to the perception that crime had increased. Among all race/ethnic groups, Democrats are less likely to believe that crime had increased, as are those with higher incomes.

In all race/ethnic groups, respondents that watch crime info-tainment are more likely to think that crime had increased statewide; moreover, this is one of the more important determinants. Among Blacks, it is the third largest effect and the fourth largest for Latinos and Whites. Among all race/ethnic groups, increases in newspaper reading equally reduce the belief that state crime had increased

**Table 6.18 Rank Order of Statistically Significant Standardized Effects of the Perception that Crime in the State had Increased by Race/Ethnicity**

| *White* (n=2500) | | *Latino* (n=777) | | *Black* (n=435) | |
|---|---|---|---|---|---|
| Gender | -.123 | Gender | -.117 | Gender | -.227 |
| Education | -.110 | Education | -.109 | Education | -.107 |
| Democrat | -.067 | Crime Risk | .073 | Info-tainment | .073 |
| Crime Risk | .067 | Info-tainment | .071 | Crime Risk | .072 |
| Info-tainment | .063 | Democrat | -.068 | Democrat | -.061 |
| Income | -.048 | Income | -.047 | Income | -.052 |
| Newspapers | -.046 | Newspapers | -.041 | Newspapers | -.044 |

*Note:* Numbers on right side of column are standardized regression coefficients. All are statistically significant (p-values of .05 or smaller).

## *Summary of Media Effects*

Although mass media do not directly influence support for three strikes sentencing, they appear to have a sizeable influence on other attitudes and beliefs which are important determinants of support for three strikes sentencing; namely, crime seriousness, support for rehabilitation, just world beliefs, fear of crime, and the belief that crime in the state has increased. As hypothesized, the effects of media vary dependent upon their specific forms. Crime-related television programs, no matter what the type, appear to have much stronger effects than reading about crime in the newspaper. Increased viewing of television news elevates in crime seriousness ratings, belief in a just world, and fear of crime, all of which are positively related to support for three strikes. Increased viewing of crime-based reality programs not only leads to increased crime seriousness ratings, belief in a just world, and fear of crime, but also the belief that state crime has increased. Crime drama viewing is positively related to crime seriousness, just world beliefs; and among Latinos, fear of crime. It also reduces support for rehabilitation among all groups, as do increases in the amount of television watched. In turn, support for rehabilitation is negatively related to support for three strikes, therefore, increases in crime drama and hours of overall television viewing indirectly increase support for three strikes sentencing. Increases in television viewing also increase fear of crime among Latinos and Blacks.

While the effects of television indirectly increase support for three strikes, the effects of newspapers are more complex. Newspaper reading increases fear of crime, yet, decreases belief that crime in the state is increasing. Moreover, unlike television, the sizes of the effects of newspaper reading on attitudes and beliefs about crime are relatively small.

Overall, the effects of media on support for three strikes sentencing are complex as they work through and are conditioned by other attitudes and beliefs determinant of punitiveness. Although the effects of appear to be of less importance than other attitudinal, experiential, and sociodemographic factors, they are too numerous to ignore. Moreover, the importance of media is complicated by their variable effects across media formats, and audience composition, particularly that of race/ethnicity.

# NOTES

1. Model chi-square = 846.823; 517 df; p< .001. Although the chi-square fit is less than .001, given the model complexity (153 regression weights estimated for each race/ethnic group), the resultant 1.63 chi-square per degree of freedom indicates a very good fit given the sample size (n = 3712). Other indicators of fit also suggest the model fits the data quite well; Root mean square residual is .013.

2. The full model was also run with nonsignificant parameters free. Although the model fit was not as good as the fully constrained model, releasing the constrained nonsignificant parameters did not change the values of the coefficients that were statistically significant and constrained equal.

3. Recall that the victimization variable reflects the seriousness of prior victimization (if any victimization occurred), not the frequency.

4. Respondents may have been the person in the household that was arrested. The question asked if they or any member of their household had ever been arrested.

CHAPTER 7
# Summing Up

The intent of this study was to explore the effects of crime-related media on punitive attitudes in multivariate models using individual level data. Many important relationships were uncovered in the analyses that remained even after controlling for a large number of sociodemographic, experiential and attitudinal factors. This chapter summarizes these relationships and implications of the results. The hypotheses are clustered, indicative of their thematic content, and presented in the order they were discussed in the theoretical discussion.

## *The Importance of Race/Ethnicity*

Hypothesis 1:   *Whites are more supportive of three strikes than African Americans and Latinos.* **Strongly Supported**

Hypothesis 2:   *Latinos are less supportive of three strikes compared to Whites, but more supportive than Blacks.* **Strongly Supported**

The difference in support for three strikes by race/ethnicity is substantial. As hypothesized, Whites are much more likely to support three strikes than Latinos and African Americans. This is not surprising given prior research that documents the higher punitiveness of Whites (e.g., Surette, 1985). In this study, the large difference between Black and White respondents can be partially attributed to their higher arrest rates, greater support for rehabilitation, and the fact that very few are Republican (approximately 3%).

Latino endorsement of three strikes is considerably lower than Whites, but much higher than Blacks. The lower support of three strikes among Latinos relative to Whites is also due in part, to their smaller percentage of Republicans (11%), and greater support for rehabilitation. However, Latinos are much more fearful of crime, have higher belief in a just world, view crimes as more serious, and are more likely to think that crime had increased in the state compared to Whites; all of which are positively related to support for three strikes. This suggests that the lower punitiveness of Latinos relative to Whites may be attributed to other factors.

Very few of the structural and experiential variables included in the analysis contribute significant direct effects to punitive attitudes, but rather, primarily have indirect influence through other attitudes and beliefs. However, although there are differences in the distribution of structural, experiential, and attitudinal factors across race/ethnic groups, the process by which these factors work do not substantially differ. Recall there very few parameters that could not be constrained equal; and those that could not be were most often the exogenous variables related to media consumption and experiences with crime. Thus, the race/ethnic differences in support for three strikes are not explained by differential impact of the intervening variables.

An examination of the data suggests there are other factors that contribute to the lower punitiveness of Latinos and Blacks that are not captured in the analytical model. The squared-multiple correlations (analogous to $R^2$) for the structural equations indicate the model fits the data best for Whites. The model explains 19.4% of the variance in White support for three strikes, but only 13.3% of the variance in Latino support and 11.9% of the variance in Black support. Clearly, our theoretical models are much better at predicting White attitudes and opinions of criminal punishment than they are in predicting those of other race/ethnic groups.

The model does not include other race-related variables, such as perceptions of the fairness of the criminal justice system, or of structural inequality. As research suggests, Blacks and other nonwhites perceive significantly more race discrimination within the criminal justice system than do Whites (Macmillan et al., 1997; Wortley, 1996), and not without reason. The ongoing 'War on Drugs' has had a deleterious impact on impoverished Black communities and has catapulted the number of Blacks imprisoned for drug-related offenses. Additionally, anti-gang policing also ramped up in the 1980's and 1990's, primarily in Latino and Black communities.

For example, Latino and Black neighborhoods in Los Angeles were regularly impacted by the crime control efforts of the Los Angeles Police Department, particularly the anti-gang unit known as CRASH (disbanded in 2000 after significant police corruption was uncovered). During the 1980's and 1990's police routinely used battering rams to raid 'crack houses,' and the CRASH unit often conducted early morning neighborhood sweeps in which they would round up dozens of residents suspected of gang crime. Most of these neighborhood sweeps netted only a handful of arrests, and were finally discontinued after sustained negative publicity.

Approximately 40% of the Black subsample was pulled from census tracts with 30% or higher concentration of Blacks; most of these tracts were the impoverished areas of South Central Los Angeles, Inglewood, Compton, and Oakland. These communities have suffered significant economic decline since the 1960's, and all of them have had bouts of serious civil disturbance. For example, the flashpoint of the Los Angeles riots after the Rodney King verdict in 1994 occurred in one of the neighborhoods used in the sample. These were also the neighborhoods targeted by the anti-gang and drug policing activities. However, Blacks who lived in these neighborhoods were no less likely to endorse three strikes than Blacks who came from other areas of the state. Thus, although Blacks have much higher fear of crime and neighborhood crime risk that typically elevate punitive attitudes; they appear reticent to endorse criminal laws that will further harm Black communities and individuals.

These types of crime control activities may explain why Blacks are much less likely to support three strikes, particularly for drug-related offenses, compared to Latinos or Whites. However, policing activities and other crime control policies that also affect Latino neighborhoods do not appear to lower their punitiveness because of all race/ethnic groups, Latinos are most supportive of three strikes for drug offenders.

## *The Importance of Crime Seriousness*

> *Hypothesis 3:*   The higher the rating of crime seriousness,
>                   the greater the support for three strikes
>                   **Strongly Supported**

As predicted, crime seriousness ratings are the largest determinants of support for three strikes among Whites and Blacks, and the second largest for Latinos. Crime seriousness is an especially strong predictor of White punitiveness. The findings confirm the numerous studies that find crime seriousness is the most important determinant of punitiveness (Blumstein and Cohen, 1980; Gebotys and Roberts, 1987; Hamilton and Rytina, 1980).

## *The Importance of Support for Rehabilitation*

> *Hypothesis 4:*   Support for rehabilitation is negatively
>                   related to support for three strikes.
>                   **Strongly Supported**

Support for rehabilitation is a very strong negative correlate of support for three strikes, as one would expect. Clearly, those that are more likely to support three strikes for relatively minor offenses are probably less likely to perceive rehabilitation efforts as the primary reason to incarcerate offenders. However, what the data cannot reveal is if this attitude stems from a retributive stance, or a belief that criminals are not amenable to change.

Latinos and African Americans are much more supportive of rehabilitation compared to Whites, but the analytical model could not determine the source of difference, as the coefficients between race/ethnic groups could be constrained equal. However, as discussed earlier, those with household arrests are much more supportive of rehabilitation. Since Blacks have significantly higher household arrests, this may explain their higher support of rehabilitation. On the other hand, because Latino arrest rates are almost identical to Whites, this explanation cannot account for Latinos' larger support of rehabilitation.

A question in the survey (not included in the analytical model) asked if a household member had ever served time in jail or prison. The answers reveal that among Latinos the percentage of households with a member who had been incarcerated is almost identical to the percentage with household arrests. This suggests that when Latinos are arrested, they are more likely to serve time in jail or prison. Although it is logical to reason that this may account for some of their higher support of rehabilitation, crosstabulations show that Latinos who have had a household member in jail or prison are no more likely to support rehabilitation (34%) than Whites (32%), (compared to over 50% of African Americans). In short, negative experiences with the criminal justice system do not appear to be the factor that makes Latinos more supportive of rehabilitation, although it does appear to have a significant effect among Blacks.

Political party affiliation may account for some of the race/ethnic differences in support for rehabilitation. Only among Whites are Democrats more supportive of rehabilitation compared to political Independents. In contrast, Latino and African American Democrats are actually less supportive of rehabilitation than their Independent counterparts (although the difference is not statistically significant). Because many Latinos are political Independents (43%), this may be one of the primary reasons why Latino support for rehabilitation is so much higher than Whites.

## *The Importance of Prior Criminal Victimization*

| | |
|---|---|
| *Hypothesis 5:* | *The more serious the prior criminal victimization, the higher the fear of crime.* **Strongly Supported** |
| *Hypothesis 6:* | *The more serious the prior criminal victimization, the greater the support for three strikes.* **Not Supported** |

The largest impact of prior criminal victimization is on fear of crime, which significantly increases as the severity of victimization increases. Victimization also leads to significant increases in the perception of neighborhood crime risk, modest increases in the belief that state crime has increased, and it makes individuals feel less safe.

As discussed earlier, analyses of prior criminal victimization on fear of crime have produced mixed results; some of which may be caused by inadequate measures of victimization. Because there were too few cases of serious criminal victimization in the sample (less than fifty), what the data cannot reveal is if there is a particular point on the severity of offense continuum that triggers these responses to victimization, or if *any* victimization tends to increase feelings and perceptions of vulnerability to crime.

The severity of prior criminal victimization does not predict support for three strikes sentencing. This finding lends credence to the argument posited by Taylor et al. (1979) more than twenty years ago. As they suggested, those who are criminally victimized are more likely to employ pragmatic solutions such as purchasing an alarm system to reduce the chances of further victimization, rather than seek indirect solutions such as demanding longer prison sentences for convicted criminals. As they suggest, "there is a weaker...logical connection between...victimization on one hand and support for harsher penalties on the other" (1979: 414).

## The Importance of Prior Arrest

> *Hypothesis 7:*      *Respondents with a household member that has been arrested will be less supportive of three strikes compared to respondents that have not had a household member arrested.*
> **Strongly Supported**

Prior household arrest is one of the largest determinants of support for three strikes. As hypothesized, individuals that live in households in which a member had been arrested are far less supportive of three strikes compared to households without an arrested member. Furthermore, the effects of household arrest do not differ across race/ethnicity. Clearly, households that have had members in trouble with the law are more likely to view mandatory sentences such as California's three strikes law with a more jaundiced eye, for such laws are more likely to directly effect them. Similarly, Clear and Rose (1999) find that those that either know someone who has been incarcerated or have been incarcerated themselves, are less supportive of formal social control than those who have not; moreover, they have less confidence in the fairness of the criminal justice system.

Prior household arrest also significantly decreases crime seriousness ratings, and modestly elevates support for rehabilitation. As such, prior household arrest significantly decreases support for three strikes both directly and indirectly as it works through crime seriousness ratings and support for rehabilitation.

## *The Importance of Just World Beliefs*

*Hypothesis 8:*    *The higher the belief in a just world, the higher the ratings of crime seriousness.*
**Strongly Supported**

*Hypothesis 9:*    *The higher the belief in a just world, the less likely the support for rehabilitation.*
**Strongly Supported**

*Hypothesis 10:*    *The higher the belief in a just world, the higher the support for three strikes.*
**Strongly Supported**

As hypothesized, the higher the belief in a just world, the greater the support for three strikes; these beliefs appear to have slightly stronger effects for Latinos and Blacks. People with high just world beliefs are also much less likely to support rehabilitation and view crimes as more seriousness. Therefore, just world beliefs are an important determinant of public opinion of crime policies.

Belief in a just world appears to be measuring belief in free will and 'just deserts.' Given the linear relationship between just world beliefs and support for three strikes, it appears that respondents with high just world beliefs do not view offenders as 'victims' of a harsh law. This was confirmed when the correlations between just world beliefs and support for three strikes for less serious crimes was examined (not shown). Although the relationship between just world and support for three strikes weakened as the crimes were described as less serious, the relationship was never negative. There was still a positive relationship between just world beliefs and support for three strikes sentencing even when all three offenses were described as less serious property offenses; moreover, this positive correlation held in all race/ethnic groups. Thus, respondents with that are more likely to perceive the world as just do not seem to perceive three strikes as unduly harsh punishment even for non-violent offenders, but rather, that offenders get what they deserve. Clearly, just world beliefs are an important determinant of punitiveness, and warrant further research.

## *The Importance of Political Beliefs*

*Hypothesis 11:*    *Republicans will be less likely to support rehabilitation compared to Independents or Democrats.* **Strongly Supported**

*Hypothesis 12:*    *Republicans will be more supportive of three strikes than Independents or Democrats.* **Strongly Supported**

Political party is a very important determinant of punitiveness. As expected, Republicans are far more supportive of three strikes sentencing than Democrats or Independents. Moreover, because the parameter could be constrained equal across all three race/ethnic groups, the strength of Republican membership appears to work similarly for all groups. The effects of Democrat membership were not so strong. Only White Democrats are far less supportive of three strikes compared to their Republican or Independent counterparts; there is no statistical difference in support for three strikes between Latino Democrats and Independents, or between African American Democrats and Independents.

These findings suggest two explanations: White Independents may be more similar to White Republicans than to White Democrats; and/or Latino and Black Democrats may be more similar to Latino and Black Independents. A comparison of bivariate correlations (not shown) across race/ethnic groups between political party and support for three strikes reveal significant differences in the manner in which political party influences support for three strikes.

For example, among Blacks, political party does not usually differentiate support for three strikes, regardless of offense type. The exception is for property crimes; Black Republicans are much more supportive of three strikes compared to Black Independents or Democrats. In contrast, both White and Latino Republicans are much more likely than their Independent or Democrat counterparts to support three strikes for all crime types - violent, drug, and property offenses.

White Democrats are significantly less likely than White Independents to support three strikes for property and drug crimes, but there was no statistical difference between the two with respect to support for three strikes for violent offenses. In contrast, there was no clear cut pattern of Democrat status on Latino support of three strikes.

Latino Democrats are only slightly less likely to support three strikes for property crimes compared to Latino Independents, but slightly more likely to endorse the sentence for drug offenders.

These findings suggest that White Democrats are much less supportive of three strikes compared to White Independents, who in turn, are much less supportive of three strikes compared to White Republicans. In contrast, there is little difference between Latino Independents and Latino Democrats, but Latino Republicans are more likely than either group to support three strikes. The same can be said for African Americans: Democrats and Independents are very similar in their support of three strikes, but Republicans are more supportive, although the increase in support is not as large among Black Republicans as it is among Latino Republicans. Of all, White Republicans are considerably more punitive than any other group.

Political party is also predictive of other attitudes and opinions about crime that are related to support for three strikes. Republicans are far less likely to support rehabilitation, and in all race/ethnic groups, they rate crimes as more serious than do Independents and Democrats. However, only White and African American Republicans view the world as more just compared to their Independent counterparts.

To sum, Republican status appears to have a much stronger effect on an individual's attitudes and beliefs than do other political party affiliations. More importantly, these beliefs appear to operate similarly across race/ethnic groups. In contrast, the effects of Democrat status appear to work most strongly and most often on Whites. Compared to Independents, only White Democrats rate crimes as less serious, only White Democrats are more likely to support rehabilitation, and as noted earlier, only White Democrats are less supportive of three strikes.

## The Importance of Crime Salience

*Hypothesis 13:*  *The higher the emotional fear of crime, the greater the support for three-strikes.* **Moderately Supported**

*Hypothesis 14:*  *Belief that crime in the state has risen increases support for three strikes.* **Moderately Supported**

Hypothesis 15:  Feeling safe is not related to support for three strikes. **Supported**

Hypothesis 16:   Perception of neighborhood crime risk is not
                 related to support for three strikes.
                 **Supported**

The direct effects of crime salience on support for three strikes
sentencing differ according to the type of crime salience. The emotional
fear of crime and cognitive belief that crime in the state had increased
are both positively related to support for three strikes, although the
relationships are relatively modest, and less important determinants
than crime seriousness, support for rehabilitation, household arrest,
political party (among Whites only), and just world beliefs.

Nevertheless, while fear of crime and the belief that state crime is
increasing are only modestly related to direct support for three strikes,
they also contribute significant indirect support. For example, fear of
crime is one of the largest determinants of crime seriousness, which is
the largest determinant of direct support for three strikes. Increases in
fear increase crime seriousness ratings, particularly among Blacks and
Latinos. The belief that state crime is increasing is also associated with
increases in crime seriousness, just world beliefs, and fear of crime; all
of which are directly related to increased support for three strikes.

As hypothesized, feeling safe and the perception of neighborhood
crime risk are not directly related to support for three strikes. However,
increases in the perception of neighborhood crime risk and decreases in
feeling safe are the two largest determinants of fear of crime. This
suggests that cognitive perceptions of immediate risk and vulnerability
(not feeling safe) may work to increase support for three strikes as they
work indirectly through fear. Neighborhood crime risk also colors
perceptions of state crime rates.

Perceptions of neighborhood crime risk are also associated with
increases in crime seriousness ratings and decreases in just world
beliefs, both of which are directly related to increased support for three
strikes. However, feeling safe is not associated with crime seriousness
or belief in a just world; and neither neighborhood risk nor feeling safe
is associated with support for rehabilitation.

Taken together, the constellation of crime salience variables is
important to the development of attitudes and beliefs about crime and
crime policy. Of all the crime salience variables, the emotional fear of
crime has the largest impact on support for three strikes as it works
directly and indirectly through crime seriousness.

The only cognitive assessment of crime risk related to punitiveness is when individuals perceive that crime rates in the state are increasing. The perception that neighborhood crime is high is not directly tied to support for three strikes. This supports the idea, as discussed earlier, that individuals do not respond to risks in their immediate environment with demands for changes on a broader (and therefore, more remote) level. Instead, they are more likely to respond with changes to their local environment, or daily routine, to reduce their chances of victimization. Nonetheless, the perception of neighborhood crime risk indirectly influences crime policy because it dramatically elevates fear of crime.

Both local and societal level judgments of crime risk are related to increases in crime seriousness ratings, (although the perception that state crime had increased has a larger impact than the perception of neighborhood risk). This suggests that crime seriousness ratings are not strictly independent assessments of the perceived harm that is caused by criminal acts, but rather, such assessments are filtered through the perception of risk. When the amount of crime is perceived as relatively high and/or increasing, people are more likely to perceive crime as more serious than when the amount of crime is thought to be lower and/or decreasing. This finding underscores the importance of crime-related media, which impact perceptions of both neighborhood risk and state crime rates. If the media message is distorted and hyperbolic, people may tend to see criminal acts as more serious and increase demand for tougher crime policies (Gebotys et al., 1988).

Increases in both types of perceptions of crime risk increase fear of crime, although the perception that crime is increasing in the neighborhood is the largest determinant by far. This supports Forde's (1993) finding that judgments of crime risk have far greater effects on the emotional fear of crime when the risks are perceived as local and immediate. Last, vulnerability (feeling safe) is only related to increases in fear of crime; again, supporting the idea that while one's perceived vulnerability to crime may increase one's fear, it may be more likely to produce changes in one's daily routine or environment to reduce vulnerability, than to produce demands for policy changes as these do nothing to change one's vulnerability to local crime.

The finding that the perceptions of neighborhood crime risk and feeling safe are not directly related to punitiveness is supported by prior research that tested the relationship between fear of crime and punitiveness (e.g., Baron and Hartnagel, 1996; Cullen et al., 1985). However, the measures these studies employed to capture fear of crime were really measures of vulnerability or feeling safe - the typical questions about feeling safe inside one's home or walking alone in the neighborhood at night – the same questions that comprise the feeling safe scale in this research. As with our analysis using these indicators, these studies did not find a link between fear and punitiveness.

Clearly, it matters how crime salience is measured. Different measures yield important differences in attitudes about crime and crime policy. The emotive fear of crime is the most important crime salience variable in that it has the biggest impact on support for three strikes. The cognitive perception that state crime is increasing also directly increases support for three strikes, although the association is not as large. In contrast, the more localized measures of neighborhood risk and feeling safe do not directly influence support for three strikes.

This discussion does not negate the importance of local environment on public opinion of crime policy. As Taylor et al. (1979) argue, people living in high crime areas think more about crime issues because they are confronted with crimes on a regular basis. This is important because much public opinion research has discovered that increased salience of a phenomenon leads to an increase in ideological coherence, or what is termed 'cognitive consistency' (Converse, 1964). Simply stated, when people think more about an issue, their supportive beliefs and opinions are more apt to be logically cohesive.

As Stinchcombe et al. (1980) argue, the end result is a polarization of opinions and attitudes about the salient issue. Thus, with respect to criminal sentencing, those who are somewhat inclined to favor harsher sentences should become even more supportive of these views when faced with the issue of crime on a more frequent basis, as would those who live in high crime areas. Conversely, those who are less inclined to favor harsh punishment, become more 'liberal' when crime is more salient to their personal lives. Thus, people who live in high crime areas will have more consistent views on criminal sentencing than those that do not live in high crime areas.

Although Stinchcombe et al. (1980) did not use actual crime rates to measure the amount of crime in the neighborhood, the voluminous literature on the issue merits discussion. Most of this research centers on the relationship of actual crime rates (crimes reported to the police) in the neighborhood to respondents' fear of crime. As noted earlier, some studies find an apparent paradox of fear of crime - those who live in high crime areas report lower fear of crime than those who live in comparatively low crime areas.

However, it is not so much what is true or factual, but instead, that which is perceived by individuals to be factual, that should be relevant to beliefs and opinions about crime. What matters is what people believe to be true, not what is actually true. Consequently, a consistently punitive attitude should more likely be found when people *believe* that state or neighborhood crime is increasing, or when their own perceptions of neighborhood crime risk or fear of crime are high, irrespective of the amount of actual crime in their environment(s). If this is true, it is not so much whether one actually lives in a high crime area that increases cognitive consistency, but merely the *belief* that one resides in a high crime area, or the *belief* that crime is rising that should increase cognitive consistency.

To test this hypothesis, Taylor et al. (1979) examined bivariate correlations of various opinions about crime between respondents who perceived that they lived in high crime areas and those that did not. They also examined differences between respondents with high and low fear of crime. They found that although the degree of support for capital punishment was no greater among respondents who lived in high crime areas than those who lived in communities with less crime, beliefs and attitudes about crime and crime control were more highly correlated among residents of high crime areas, thus supporting the theory of cognitive consistency. Similarly, those with higher fear of crime also displayed greater cognitive consistency about crime issues than those with lower fear of crime.

To test the idea of ideological consistency, bivariate correlations (not shown) of support for three strikes, crime seriousness, just world beliefs, and support for rehabilitation were conducted for each race/ethnic group between respondents with high fear of crime and low fear of crime, and between those that perceived the level of neighborhood crime risk as high and those that perceived it as low. Although there are problems associated with assuming what constitutes a 'high' level of fear, or 'high' neighborhood crime risk, for this analysis, fear of crime and perception of neighborhood risk were dichotomized as 'high' if the score was one standard deviation or above the aggregate means for the sample, and 'low' for all others.

Unlike the findings of Taylor et al. (1979), perceptions of neighborhood risk and fear of crime do not appear to determine ideological consistency. The correlations of the crime items are no higher among respondents with 'high' fear or 'high' perception of neighborhood crime than for respondents with lower levels of each.

Reasoning that low-income respondents were more likely to live in high crime areas, an additional analysis was conducted between respondents with high and low incomes. Bivariate correlations also compared the cognitive consistency of crime issues between those who believe state crime had increased and those that believe it had remained the same or decreased. Still, no difference was found in ideological consistency between these groups.

Based on these analyses, it appears that environmental cues and fear of crime do not affect the cognitive consistency of crime related issues. However, fear of crime and the belief that state crime is increasing do increase punitiveness directly, as does perception of neighborhood risk as it works indirectly through fear of crime.

These are important findings for they hint at the potential impact of media. As detailed in the pages to follow, crime-related media consumption has much more impact on emotive fear of crime and the perception that state crime is increasing than it does on the perception of neighborhood risk or feelings of safety. In fact, feeling safe is not impacted whatsoever by crime-related media consumption. Moreover, of all the crime-related media examined, only increases in local television news consumption leads to significant increase in the perception of neighborhood crime risk. This suggests that the effects of mediated or vicarious crime experiences are more influential on attitudes about criminal punishment than they are on perceptions of risk and vulnerability to crime in one's immediate environment.

## *The Importance of Crime-Related Media*

*Hypothesis 17:*    *Increases in television news and newspaper consumption will increase perceptions of local crime risk.* **Partially Supported**

*Hypothesis 17.a:* *The effects of crime-related media will be stronger for African Americans and Latinos.* **Partially Supported**

The effects of heavy consumption of local news media on perceptions of local crime risk are mixed. Increases in television news viewing modestly increase the perception of neighborhood crime risk, but newspaper consumption is not related. These findings are analogous to other studies that found increased television consumption was not related to fear of crime, but it did increase concern about the amount of crime in the community (Tyler, 1980; Tyler and Cook, 1984). These studies also found that although media increased the belief that crime in the community was increasing, it did not alter perceptions of one's crime risk in the immediate neighborhood. Since we specifically asked about 'neighborhood' crime risk, our results do lend support for television news influence on one's immediate environment.

A very interesting finding is that the influence of local television news is so much larger for Blacks compared to Whites or Latinos, the coefficient could not be constrained equal. Given that African Americans are more likely to live in low-income and high-crime areas associated with television news coverage of crime, this suggests that media has more impact when what is portrayed resonates with real-world experiences (Gerbner et al., 1994).

> *Hypothesis 18:*    *The greater the exposure to television news and crime info-tainment, the more likely the belief that state crime rates have increased. Newspaper consumption decreases this perception.* **Partially Supported**

Crime-related media effects on perceptions of state crime trends vary by the type of media. In short, those who watch more crime info-tainment programming are more likely to perceive that crime in the state is increasing. In comparison, those who read newspapers more frequently are less likely to perceive that state crime is increasing; not surprising, since newspapers are the most likely media to discuss crime trends in detail. Consequently, more frequent readers of newspapers receive a more balanced and informative view of state crime trends. It is important to note that the effects of newspaper reading on the perception of state crime are independent of income and education. Consumption of other crime-related media and number of hours spent watching television are not related to the perception of state crime rates.

I offer two post hoc explanations for why crime info-tainment consumption is related to the belief that state crime had increased. First, the more sensationalistic portrayal of crime found in crime info-tainment, such as that shown on *Cops*, may lead viewers to believe that crime 'out there' is more rampant than it actually is. But if this were the reason, surely television news exposure would have impacted the perception of increasing state crime, but it did not.

Another explanation is that people who are more inclined to see the world as increasingly crime-ridden are anxious and worried. They seek out shows like *Cops* to alleviate this anxiety because these shows usually have an unambiguous response to deviance. As noted earlier, the police are portrayed as effective, and most always, criminals are successfully apprehended. As such, it is not that viewing crime info-tainment makes one more likely to believe that crime in the state is increasing, but rather, those that already believe this seek out crime info-tainment. As the data used in the analysis is cross-sectional, causality cannot be determined.

> *Hypothesis 19:*  *Crime-related media consumption decreases feeling safe.* **Supported**
>
> *Hypothesis 20:*  *The greater the exposure to television news, crime info-tainment and newspapers, the higher the fear of crime. Crime dramas will have no effect.* **Partially Supported**
>
> *Hypothesis 20.a: The effects of crime-related media will be stronger for African Americans and Latinos.* **Not Supported**

Media has no impact on feeling safe, thus it appears that our crime salience measures do disentangle vulnerability from fear, and from cognitive perceptions of crime. All crime-related media variables were however, related to fear of crime, but with variations across race/ethnicity and type of media.

To begin with, consumption of most crime-related media increases fear of crime. As hypothesized, the effects are strongest for crime info-tainment and local television news, but only marginally related to newspaper reading. This supports prior research that finds the impact of television news on fear is much stronger than the impact of newspapers (Chiricos et al., 1997; O'Keefe and Reid-Nash, 1987). However, the results of increased crime drama viewing are not in the specified direction - increases in viewing crime drama lead to *decreases* in fear of crime. This supports the idea that crime dramas do not exacerbate our fears, but instead, provide a sense of reassurance. Although they display the world as a mean and scary place, this is ameliorated by the dramatic actions of heroes who restore the forces of justice in a familiar and routinized manner (Sparks 1992; Zillman and Wakshlag, 1985). But this effect is only found among Latino respondents – crime drama consumption does not impact fear of crime among Blacks or Whites.

The effects of the other forms of crime-related media consumption do not differ across race/ethnicity. This is important, and against expectations. Recent studies suggest that television has different effects on fear of crime for different audiences. Specifically, those who are disproportionately portrayed as victims in the media are more fearful compared to those that are not. Because White women are disproportionately depicted as victims compared to Black and Latino women (Dixon and Linz, 2000), they tend to be more fearful, independent of prior victimization, income, or feelings of vulnerability (Chiricos et al., 1997).

In our study, women of all race/ethnic groups have very high and similar levels of fear of crime. Additionally, African American women suffer considerably more victimization than either White or Latino women. It may be that the sources of fear for White women are more often vicarious than they are for Black women; and among Black women sources of fear more often come from direct experiences - the net result is increased fear for both.

To examine this idea more closely, comparisons of bivariate correlations of the various crime-related media with fear of crime, controlling for gender, reveal results similar to those reported by Chiricos et al. (1997). Crime info-tainment consumption has strong positive effects on fear of crime among White women, but not Latino or African American women, who are less likely to be depicted as victims in this genre. Crime info-tainment also significantly increases fear of crime among White men (the coefficient is almost the same as for White women), and it also increases fear among African American men. Similarly, television news consumption also significantly increases fear among White women and White men, and also Black women. But neither form affects Latinos, regardless of gender. Together, these correlations suggest that media do appear to have variable effects, but why they do is not readily apparent. If it were a simple matter of audience composition and victim portrayal, the correlation of fear of crime and crime-related media consumption would be uniformly larger for White women.

Although the focus of this study is not to explain why media effects are different across race/ethnicity, the above findings do suggest some variability in audience effects not easily explained by the misrepresentation of victim groups in terms of race/ethnicity and gender. As discussed earlier, some suggest the effects of crime-related media are conditioned more by one's environment than by infrequent direct personal experiences such as victimization. This line of reasoning assumes that the effects of crime-related media might actually be stronger for those who are confronted with the realities of street crime on a more regular basis - those who live in high crime areas (Doob and Macdonald, 1979; Gunter, 1987). Yet, other researchers believe that the effects of media are stronger for those who have no direct experience with the phenomenon being portrayed (known as the substitution hypothesis).

To explore this issue more deeply, we ran bivariate correlations between crime-related media and fear of crime, controlling for area crime rates (using income as a proxy). Table 7.1 compares these correlations between those that have less than $15,000 annual household income and those that have more. Because the low-income group is small, size of the correlations, not statistical significance, is most relevant. Focusing on correlation sizes of .10 and larger, there are no clear patterns for race/ethnicity, media type, or income seen in the table. Poor Whites became more fearful when they read newspapers, but poor Blacks become less fearful. Poor Latinos became more fearful with increased television news viewing, but television news has no effect on poor African Americans or Whites. On the other hand, watching crime dramas decreases the fear of poor Latinos, but elevates it among poor Blacks. Thus, these data do not support the resonance hypothesis.

Instead, crime-related media consumption appears more influential on increasing fear among those with higher income. Television news and crime info-tainment consumption increases fear among Whites and African Americans. Among Latinos, the more television watched, the higher the fear; newspaper consumption decreased fear.

**Table 7.1 Bivariate Correlations of Fear of Crime and Crime-Related Media Consumption by Family Income and Race/Ethnicity**

|  | *Annual Family Income* | |
|---|---|---|
|  | *Below $15,000* | *Above $15,000* |
| *Fear × Local TV News* | | |
| Whites | .070 | .103*** |
| Latinos | .115 | .030 |
| African American | .058 | .142** |
| *Fear × Newspapers* | | |
| Whites | .131* | -.017 |
| Latinos | -.050 | -.106** |
| African American | -.128 | -.036 |
| *Fear × Crime Info-tainment* | | |
| Whites | .122* | .115*** |
| Latinos | -.043 | .055 |
| African American | -.007 | .125* |
| *Fear × Crime Drama* | | |
| Whites | .059 | .047* |
| Latinos | -.173* | -.036 |
| African American | .165 | .177*** |
| *Fear × TV Hours* | | |
| Whites | -.015 | .036 |
| Latinos | .034 | .128*** |
| African American | .230* | .014 |

*p≤.05; **p≤.01; ***p≤.001

In short, crime-related media consumption appears to have more effects upon those who have higher incomes. If income is a good proxy for the amount of crime in one's environment, these findings contradict Doob and Macdonald's (1979) work, and underscore the idea that media effects are strongest for those that do not have any (or many) direct experiences with crime, particularly on a daily basis. Moreover, none of the media examined were uniform in their effects across all three race/ethnic groups.

The results may be due to the threshold effects of low income. If fear of crime among the poor is already very high, media is not likely to have much of an impact. As seen in table 7.2, there *are* statistically significant differences in fear of crime between income groups. Within each race/ethnic category, low-income groups have much higher levels of fear. Nevertheless, the highest group mean reported is 4.93 on a ten-point scale. Thus, threshold effects can not account for the relatively low impact of crime-related media on fear of crime among the poor.

**Table 7.2 Comparisons of Means of Fear of Crime by Family Income and Race/Ethnicity**

|  | *Annual Family Income* | |
| --- | --- | --- |
|  | *Below $15,000* | *Above $15,000* |
| Whites | 3.327 | 2.920*** |
| Latinos | 4.931 | 4.338*** |
| African Americans | 4.729 | 3.188*** |

*p≤.05; **p≤.01; ***p≤.001

It appears that although high-income groups have lower fear of crime overall, the correlations in table 7.1 suggest they are more impacted by the media messages. The more plausible explanation is that crime-related media have stronger effects on engendering fear among the groups least likely to be victimized. This evidence supports the substitution hypothesis and also suggests that crime-related media may have greater effects on other attitudes and beliefs about crime held by those that are least likely to be exposed to street crime on a daily basis.

*Hypothesis 21:*   *The greater the exposure to crime-related media, the greater the belief in a just world.* **Moderately Supported**

*Hypothesis 21.a:* *Crime-related media will have stronger effects on the just world beliefs of Whites than Blacks or Latinos.* **Not Supported**

*Hypothesis 21.b*: The effects of crime-related media on just world beliefs will vary across type of media. Specifically, the effects of crime info-tainment, local television news, and crime dramas will be stronger compared to the effects of newspapers. **Strongly Supported**

As hypothesized, increases in crime-related media consumption increase belief in a just world, with the exception of newspapers, which essentially have no effect. These findings lend credence to the suggestion that television promotes a narrow ideological view of crime and crime control. To begin with, television privileges resolutions to crime that restore the moral and social order. All crime-related television programs focus on the capture, arrest, and convictions of deviant criminals; eventually, those who break the law are apprehended and justly punished. Moreover, criminal wrongdoing is attributed to individual responsibility. Without an understanding of the structural causes of crime (or of structured inequality), viewers may be inclined to believe that the world operates in a relatively fair manner for those who work hard enough.

When the 'game' is presented as fair, and criminals as those who play against the 'rules,' it should not be surprising to find that those who watch more crime related television believe that the world operates fairly - and individuals earn their just deserts. Thus, it may be that the primary effect of crime-related television is not so much its impact on opinions about specific crime policies, but its influence on shaping attributions of responsibility. Little research has investigated the relationship between television viewing and just world beliefs; clearly, more research is needed in this area.

*Hypothesis 22*: The greater the exposure to crime-related media, the higher the rating of crime seriousness. **Moderately Supported**

*Hypothesis 22.a*: The effects of crime-related media on crime seriousness ratings will vary across type of media. Specifically, the effects of crime info-tainment, local television news, and crime dramas will be stronger than the effects of newspapers. **Partially Supported**

Increases in crime-related television news and crime info-tainment consumption lead to higher ratings of crime seriousness; newspaper reading is not related. Television news is the most influential media form on crime seriousness ratings. Prior research on crime seriousness finds that individuals will rate all crimes more seriously when violent crime is more salient to them. Because news media information is perceived as factual, the inordinate amount of coverage devoted to sensational violent street crime is apt to influence perceptions of the seriousness of crime. Thus, it is not surprising to see that television news consumption significantly elevates crime seriousness ratings. Moreover, as found in prior research, the less information respondents have, the more likely they are to view the crime as serious (Gebotys et al., 1988). Relative to newspapers, crime news and crime info-tainment present little detail about crime events or criminal offenders, thus, increases in consumption should increase crime seriousness.

Increases in viewing crime dramas decrease crime seriousness ratings. This is more difficult to explain. It may be that viewers approach crime dramas with more skepticism than crime news or info-tainment because they know it is fictional. Viewers may not attend to the presentations as carefully as crime news or info-tainment, and therefore, disregard much of what is presented. But if this were the reason, there should be *no* relationship between viewing crime drama and perceptions of crime seriousness.

Another plausible explanation centers on the items used in the study to capture crime seriousness ratings: solely street crimes. Because crime dramas are more apt to present other crimes and criminals besides violent street crime and offenders, (such as corporate or white collar crime and criminals), respondents who watch more media in which white-collar crimes and criminals are regularly presented may not view some street crimes as harmful as the effects of corporate crime, and may use this reference as an anchor when rating the street crimes used in the study.

However, if this were true, one would expect to find a similar negative relationship between newspaper reading and crime seriousness ratings since they have more detailed stories about corporate and white-collar crime than television news and crime info-tainment. Thus, one would expect to see a negative relationship between newspaper consumption and crime seriousness, as we do, although the relationship is not statistically significant.

*Hypothesis 23:*    *The greater the exposure to crime-related media, the lower support for rehabilitation.* **Weakly Supported**

*Hypothesis 23.a:* Crime-related television will have stronger effects for Whites compared to Blacks or Latinos. **Not Supported**

*Hypothesis 23.b:* The effects of crime-related media on support for rehabilitation will vary across type of media. Specifically, the effects of crime info-tainment, local television news, and crime dramas will be stronger compared to the effects of newspapers. **Partially Supported**

There is only modest evidence to support the hypothesis that the greater the exposure to crime-related media, the less likely one is to support rehabilitation as the primary purpose of imprisonment. Specifically, increases in crime drama consumption, and the number of hours of television viewing reduce support for rehabilitation. There are no significant effects for newspaper, television news or crime info-tainment consumption.

The relationship is particularly strong for the number of hours spent watching television. This suggests that the most important effects of crime-related television may be cumulative and over time, manifest themselves in the shaping of values, beliefs and opinions of the American public. If the primary discourse around crime is reduced to rather simplistic presentations of good and evil, if criminal wrongdoing is only explained in terms of individual level causes, and if the criminal justice system and rehabilitation efforts are consistently presented as ineffective, then support for rehabilitation efforts is apt to be reduced. Besides crime-related programs, other television shows also deliver the same consistent message: deviance is caused by poor morals or inexplicable evil, and deviants get what they deserve in the long run. Not surprisingly, heavy television viewers are far less supportive of rehabilitation.

Crime drama consumption is the only crime-related media that decreases support for rehabilitation. This may be due to the different foci of crime, criminals, and the criminal justice system employed by this type of genre. Television news and crime info-tainment shows are the least likely television formats to cover all components of the criminal justice system. On the other hand, crime dramas more frequently portray other facets of the criminal justice system. For example, shows such as *Law and Order* and *Homicide* focus on solving crimes and prosecuting alleged offenders. In the process, criminal justice personnel are often shown dealing with prison inmates to solve crimes or obtain convictions. These inmates are usually portrayed as unscrupulous types, such as jailhouse snitches or repeat felons who haven't learned from prior incarceration(s). The script often includes cynical remarks made by police and prosecution characters that deride the efficacy of the prison system. Heavy viewing of these programs may ultimately decrease support for rehabilitation.

> *Hypothesis 24:*    *The greater the exposure to crime-related media, the higher the support for three strikes sentencing.* **Not Supported**
>
> *Hypothesis 24.a:* *Crime-related media will have stronger effects on support for three strikes sentencing for Whites compared to Blacks or Latinos.* **Not Supported**
>
> *Hypothesis 24.b:* *The effects of crime-related media will vary across type of media. Specifically, the effects of info-tainment crime programs, local television news, and crime television dramas will be stronger compared to the effects of newspapers.* **Not Supported**

Consumption of crime-related media is *not* directly related to support for three strikes sentencing. None of the media variables had any statistically significant effect on punitiveness. However, as detailed above, although crime related media consumption does not directly influence support for three strikes, it does strongly influence other attitudes and beliefs related to support for three strikes. Interestingly, the effects of media consumption did not differ across race/ethnicity. The parameters for media consumption on three strikes could be constrained equal across race/ethnicity, no matter what the type of media. It appears media were equally unimpressive across race/ethnic groups in their lack of direct influence on punitive attitudes.

## Conclusion

Simply put, the effects of media on punitiveness are not direct, but rather, operate indirectly through their effects on other attitudes and beliefs related to punitiveness. It may be that the effects of crime-related media work to increase ideological consistency about crime issues. Thus, media may not necessarily create beliefs and attitudes about crime and crime policy, but they may strengthen and align an individual's beliefs and attitudes that are created and shaped from former experiences with crime, political ideology, and so forth. Analogous to the earlier tests of cognitive consistency, a post hoc examination of bivariate correlations (not shown) of the various attitudes and beliefs about crime between heavy and non-heavy consumers of crime-related media, found little support for this explanation. This may be due to the spurious structural effects that pattern both media consumption and other attitudes and beliefs about crime; or it may have been due to inadequate measurement of 'heavy consumption.'

Nevertheless, the findings are clear. Net of a large number of other factors known to affect attitudes and beliefs about crime, media have strong indirect effects on punitiveness. Increases in crime-related media consumption increase fear of crime, the perception that state crime is increasing, the perception of crime risk in one's neighborhood, just world beliefs, crime seriousness, and decrease support for rehabilitation. Moreover, there are no differences across race/ethnic groups in the impact of media on these intervening variables, with the exception of their impact on perceptions of neighborhood crime risk and fear of crime. But for all other intervening variables, the effects of media could be constrained equal.

This is no small matter. In prior research, crime seriousness has been the most significant determinant of punitive attitudes, which is found in this analysis as well. More importantly, this analysis finds crime-related media greatly impacts crime seriousness perceptions. Television news consumption, in particular, is one of the largest determinants of crime seriousness among Whites; only slightly smaller in size than the coefficient for Republican status, and much larger than fear of crime. Among Latinos and Blacks, television news consumption is equivalent to fear of crime in its impact on crime seriousness. Thus, media, especially television news, is very important in structuring individuals' perceptions of the seriousness of crime, and thus, in elevating punitive attitudes.

The significance of media is even greater when one considers the pervasiveness of its use. Although type (and frequency) of media consumption is conditioned by age, gender, education, and income, most everyone appears to be getting some form of mediated information about crime. This is even more significant as the vast majority of Americans cite the media as their primary source of information about crime. Almost 100% of the respondents were exposed to some crime-related media; fewer than 1% never watched television news, crime info-tainment, crime dramas, or read the newspaper in the course of a given week or month. Moreover, a large percent of respondents were *heavy* consumers of crime-related media, especially of the news. Fully one-quarter of the sample watched a local television news program and read a newspaper on a daily basis.

As Garland and Spark (2000) note, although mass media may not directly influence individual attitudes and beliefs about crime policy, they have certainly institutionalized crime. Mass media have made the issue more salient, so that protection from crime is an organizing principle of modern daily life. In particular, television coverage of crime is so pervasive, and narrowly focused, that crime *is* violence. As Altheide (2002) demonstrates, the word "crime" is now coupled with "violence," particularly in television news portrayals. "As the audience becomes more familiar with the meaning of the term [violence] and the context of its use, it becomes redundant to state 'violent crime' since the mass-mediated experience suggests that 'crime is violent'" (39). In much the same way crime is not only linked to violence, but is also linked to specific types of offenders – the predatory criminal (Surette, 1994) – and more specifically, the Black predatory criminal (Altheide, 2002; Entman, 1989). Thus, as crime remains a salient feature of modern culture, and as crime continues to be associated with violent predators, the public's response is essentially visceral – lock 'em up.

Given the nature of crime-related media content, the most significant effect of crime-related media may be "broadly ideological rather than narrowly attitudinal or behavioral" (Sacco, 1995:153). The findings from this analysis lend much support for this statement. The data suggest that media contour the broad outlines of a set of beliefs and values about crime. Heavier media consumers are more likely to possess a conservative framework of attitudes and beliefs that indirectly support a crime control stance and increase punitiveness. Television, in particular, seems to present a very limited understanding and discourse of crime and crime policy.

As we have seen in this analysis, the most influential effects of crime-related media consumption were found for crime-related television, particularly television news and crime info-tainment. The more individuals watch these programs, the more fearful they become, the more they view crime as serious, the more likely they are to believe crime is increasing, and the more they likely they are to believe the world operates justly. In short, television news media and crime info-tainment appear to elevate punitive attitudes as they influence other attitudes that support a crime control stance.

One of television's most invidious effects may be in promoting a simplistic view of the world. As noted throughout this book, the heroes and villains are easily identifiable in crime-related television programs. Criminals are exceedingly heinous, and their actions are attributed to individual causes such as a lack of morals. On the other hand, heroes, even when they violate the law, usually operate from a morally centered base. Good usually triumphs over evil in due course. Such presentations promote a simple version of justice, and perpetuate the idea that only guilty parties are dealt with in the criminal justice system.

These findings parallel those of a recent study that compared the relationship between 'complex media' and more simplistic forms, such as crime info-tainment and talk shows. Sotirovic (2001) found that viewers of more complex media were much more likely to support crime prevention efforts than viewers of 'simple' media, who were more likely to support punitive policies. More specifically, 'simple' media presentations appear to inhibit complex thinking about crime and crime control, but stimulate affective responses, namely fear. Other research suggests that those who hold 'black and white' views of justice may be more punitive, as are those who believe the application of crime control is administered equitably (Benson, 1992).

But the most important long-term effect of heavy crime-related consumption may be the constriction of discourse about crime. The importance of crime-related media in shaping ideological responses to crime may lay not so much in what is presented, but in what is lacking. The presentation of crime, particularly in the news, tends to portray the views of law enforcement and other criminal justice agencies.

Alternative points of view are seldom broadcast. Even viewpoints from criminologists are secondary to that of law enforcement and politicians, who are treated as *the* primary definers of crime (Welch, Fenwick, and Roberts, 1997). Moreover, research indicates that even when alternative views are portrayed, they are presented long after public sentiment about a particular issue has solidified, as was the case with newspaper coverage of California's Three Strikes Law (Surette, 1996).

By framing crime as an individual problem, media have directed attention away from any structural explanations. This is extremely important as the rise in crime during the 1970's and 1980's could have been explained as a by-product of deindustrialization and globalization of capital. The economic cleavages created in the wake of these massive shifts in labor markets since the early 1970's have hit predominately Black communities very hard; over thirty years later there are still few opportunities for residents of inner-cities. As people turned to informal economies, such as the much maligned crack cocaine market, the state responded by increasing police surveillance of inner-city neighborhoods, ratcheting up drug penalties, and by embracing an all out 'war' on drugs. Twenty-five years later, the result is an enormous increase in imprisonment, and an unprecedented gap in the ratio of White to Black incarceration rates. All the while, media were there to report on the war, to demonstrate the pernicious effects of crack cocaine, and to remind us, through vivid imagery, just how drugs can ruin entire communities and make us all unsafe.

Yet, the story could have been framed differently than what was presented to the American public. Would we have two million people incarcerated today if the links to deindustrialization and globalization had been made in the media? If nothing else, the stories about inner-cities could have focused on the economic plight of individuals in these communities; there could have been a humanizing aspect to the frames. Instead, the most common frames were of ruthless drug dealers that used lethal violence to establish control of inner city drug markets and of addicts that would do anything to get their fix. Although the scripts have since shifted away from the evils of crack cocaine, we are still inundated with stories about inner-city crime, and with images of Black violence.

As Gamson notes, "one realm of media discourse is uncontested. It is the realm where the social constructions rarely appear as such to the reader...They appear as transparent descriptions of reality, not as interpretations, and are apparently devoid of political content. Journalists feel no need to get different points of view for balance when they deal with images in this realm." (1993:199).

By excluding information about the actual distribution of crime, by not reassuring viewers that the likelihood of violent crime is very rare, by not portraying alternative solutions to incarceration, by not informing viewers of what *is* effective in preventing crime, and by not framing crime as a function of other social problems, the media have wielded enormous influence on the public's understanding of crime. Instead, the information the public *does* receive is filtered through short, affective frames - especially those of fear and tragedy. Crime is senseless violence, criminals are predatory young Black males, victims are innocent and hapless, and crime is the result of inexplicable or unchangeable individual pathology. Any decreases in crime are applauded as the success of incarceration.

As discussed earlier, individuals tend to view crime as more serious, and believe sentences are too lenient when they receive limited information. Prior research finds that individuals, who are dissatisfied with the courts and criminal sentencing, usually believe the courts are much more lenient than they really are (Doob and Roberts, 1984; Stalans and Diamond, 1990). This suggests that criminologists can play an important role in educating the public about crime and crime policies.

The findings of this study suggest that media shape a set of beliefs and values about crime that are not policy specific, but more symbolic and ideological in nature. Thus, criminologists should be more active in media dissemination of crime information on a more regular and sustained basis. As Roberts et al. chide, "Scholars have too often developed an isolationist approach" by limiting critical assessments of current penal practices to "like-minded peers" (2003:174). As Barak (1994b) outlines, although difficult, criminologists can gain access to news media, because they already rely heavily on criminal justice organizational sources for information about crime. He argues that although the media are part of the central institutions of social control, the principles that guide news professionals - objectivity, fairness, and public service - provide ample space for 'newsmaking criminologists' to operate.

Almost all Americans get their information about crime from mediated rather than direct experiences. If the effects of media are cumulative, and over time, homogenize beliefs and attitudes, this will likely further narrow the current constricted public discourse of crime and crime policy. The task at hand for criminologists is to become a steady source of specialized knowledge about crime, and over time, influence media presentations to provide a more balanced view of crime, criminals, and crime control.

# APPENDIX A
# Survey Questions

## *Just World (order randomized)*
For each of the following items please tell me whether you strongly agree, agree, disagree, or strongly disagree.

1.  I've found that people rarely deserve the reputation they have.
2.  Basically the world is a just place.
3.  By and large, people deserve what they get.
4.  Good deeds often go unnoticed and unrewarded.
5.  Although evil people may hold political power for a while, in the general course of history good wins out.
6.  In almost any business or profession, people who do their job well rise to the top.
7.  People who meet with misfortune have often brought it on themselves.
8.  Many people suffer through absolutely no fault of their own.

## *Crime in the Media*

Now I am going to ask you about a number of programs that are currently on television. For each program, please tell me if you watch it every week, a few weeks each month, once a month, occasionally or never.

1.  How often do you watch Law and Order?
2.  How often do you watch Cops?
3.  How often do you watch Homicide?
4.  How often do you watch American Justice?
5.  How often do you watch NYPD Blue?
6.  How often do you watch America's Most Wanted?
7.  How often do you watch Nash Bridges?
8.  How often do you watch Justice Files?

## *Crime in the Media, con't.*

9.  How many days a week would you say you read the national or local news section of a newspaper?

    No days
    1 day
    2 days
    3 days
    4 days
    5 days
    6 days
    Every day

10. How many days a week would you say you listen to the national or local news on the radio?

11. How many days a week would you say you watch the local news on television?

12. How many days a week would you say you watch the national news on television?

13. On the average, how many hours per week do you watch television?

    Number of Hours _____

## *Support for Rehabilitation*

There are four purposes for criminal penalties that we would like to ask you about. These are 1) to discourage others from committing crimes, 2) to separate offenders from society, 3) to train, educate and counsel offenders, and 4) to give offenders the punishment they deserve.

1.  Please tell me which of these four purposes you think should be the most important in sentencing adults? (Responses Randomized)

    To discourage others from committing crimes
    To separate offenders from society
    To train, educate and counsel offenders
    To give offenders the punishment they deserve

## Crime Seriousness *(order randomized)*

We'd like to know your opinion about the seriousness of certain felony crimes. On a scale of zero to ten, where zero equals not at all serious and ten equals extremely serious, rate the seriousness of...

1. Aggravated assault
2. Rape
3. Robbery
4. Theft
5. Burglary
6. Auto theft
7. Drug possession
8. Drug sales

## Three Strikes Offense Matrix *(Section Order Randomized)*

The state of California has a three strikes law that states that a person convicted of a third felony receives a sentence of 25 years to life. Currently, there is a lot of debate over the types of crimes that should be included in a three strikes law.

Violent:    Should a person receive a sentence of 25 years to life if all three crimes are serious violent offenses?

            Yes

            No    [Skip to Property or Drugs]

            Should a person still receive a sentence of 25 years to life if one of the three violent crimes is less serious?

            Yes

            No    [Skip to Property or Drugs]

            Should a person still receive a sentence of 25 years to life if two of the three violent crimes are less serious?

            Yes

            No    [Skip to Property or Drugs]

| | |
|---|---|
| Violent: cont.: | Should a person still receive a sentence of 25 years to life if all three crimes are for less serious violent offenses? |

Yes [Skip to Property or Drugs]
No [Skip to Property or Drugs]

| | |
|---|---|
| Property: | Should a person receive a sentence of 25 years to life if all three crimes are serious property offenses? |

Yes
No [Skip to Drugs]

Should a person still receive a sentence of 25 years to life if one of the three property crimes is less serious?

Yes
No [Skip to Drugs]

Should a person still receive a sentence of 25 years to life if two of the three property crimes are less serious?

Yes
No [Skip to Drugs]

Should a person still receive a sentence of 25 years to life if all three crimes are for less serious property offenses?

Yes [Skip to Drugs]
No [Skip to Drugs]

| | |
|---|---|
| Drugs: | Should a person receive a sentence of 25 years to life if all three crimes are serious drug offenses? |

Yes
No

Should a person still receive a sentence of 25 years to life if one of the three drug crimes is less serious?

Yes
No

Should a person still receive a sentence of 25 years to life if two of the three drug crimes are less serious?

Yes
No

Should a person still receive a sentence of 25 years to life if all three crimes are for less serious drug offenses?

Yes
No

# CRIME PERCEPTIONS

## *Neighborhood Crime* (order randomized)

Next I would like to know how you feel about crime in your neighborhood. Using a scale of zero to ten, where zero equals not at all likely and ten equals very likely, please tell me the likelihood that the crime will happen in your neighborhood.

1. How likely is it that a home in your neighborhood will be broken into while the occupants are away?

2. How likely is it that a home in your neighborhood will be broken into while the occupants are at home?

3. How likely is it that someone in your neighborhood will be attacked by someone with a weapon?

4. How likely is it that someone in your neighborhood will be raped or sexually assaulted?

5. How likely is it that someone in your neighborhood will have their car stolen?

6. How likely is it that someone in your neighborhood will be robbed or mugged?

7. How likely is it that property in your neighborhood will be vandalized?

## *Fear of Crime* (order randomized)

For the next set of questions, please tell me how fearful you are that certain crimes will happen to you. Using a scale of zero to ten, where zero equals not at all fearful and ten equals very fearful …

1. How fearful are you that your home will be broken into while you are away?

2. How fearful are you that your home will be broken into while you are at home?

3. How fearful are you that you will be attacked by someone with a weapon?

4. How fearful are you that you will be raped or sexually assaulted?

5.  How fearful are you that your car will be stolen?

6.  How fearful are you that you will be robbed or mugged?

7.  How fearful are you that your property will be vandalized?

8.  How fearful are you for the safety of your loved ones (i.e. spouse, partner, children, or other family members)?

## Feeling Safe

For the next three questions in this section, using a scale of zero to ten where zero equals not at all safe and ten equals very safe...

1.  How safe from crime do you feel inside your home during the day?

2.  How safe from crime do you feel inside your home during the night?

3.  How safe from crime do you feel out alone in your neighborhood at night, say between sunset and 10pm?

## Amount of Crime in the State

Do you think the amount of crime in the state over the last three years has...

Gone down
Stayed the same
Gone up

## Crime Experiences

1.  Do you or does anyone in your family work in any criminal justice related field?
    Yes [specify]
    No

2.  Have you been a victim of a crime in the last three years?
    Yes [specify]
    No

3.  Have you or has anyone in your household ever been arrested or convicted of a crime?
    Yes
    No

## *Demographic Questions*

1.  In what year were you born?

2.  What is the highest level of education you have completed?

    Less than high school
    High school graduate
    Some college or trade school
    College graduate
    Advanced degree

3.  Generally speaking, do you consider yourself to be a Democrat, Republican, independent, or something else?

    Democrat
    Republican
    No party or independent
    Other party [specify]

4.  How would you describe your racial background?

    White
    Latino/Hispanic/Mexican
    American/Other Latin Country
    African American or Black
    Asian [specify]
    American Indian
    Other [specify]

5.  Please stop me when I reach the category that best describes your total family annual income, before taxes. Would you say that it was...

    Less than $5,000
    $5,000 to under $10,000
    $10,000 to under $15,000
    $15,000 to under $25,000
    $25,000 to under $35,000
    $35,000 to under $50,000
    $50,000 to under $75,000
    $75,000 to under $100,000
    $100,000 or more

6.  Respondent gender – do not ask:

# The Full Model

The following tables (1.A to 1.O) show the structural equations for the full model. All parameters were tested for equality constraints. In cases where the coefficient could be constrained equal, it is both italicized and underlined. *Note*: Model $\chi^2$ = 846.823; df. = 517 (p<.001).

**Table 1.A Unstandardized Regression Coefficients of the Effects of Gender by Race/Ethnicity**

|  | *White* (n=2500) | *Latino* (n=777) | *Black* (n=435) |
|---|---|---|---|
| ***Gender on Media Consumption*** | | | |
| Gender → Newspapers | .138 | *.827*** | .138 |
| Gender → Television News | -.288*** | -.288*** | -.288*** |
| Gender → Crime Info-tainment | .078** | .078** | .078** |
| Gender → Crime Drama | -.076* | -.076* | -.076* |
| Gender → Hours Watching TV | -.011 | -.011 | -.011 |
| ***Gender on Crime Experiences*** | | | |
| Gender → Prior Victimization | .008 | .008 | *.243** |
| Gender → Household Arrest | .090*** | *.024* | .090*** |
| ***Gender on Crime Perceptions and Beliefs*** | | | |
| Gender → Local Crime Risk | -.259*** | -.259*** | -.259*** |
| Gender → Crime Up in State | -.120*** | -.120*** | *-.229*** |
| Gender → Feeling Safe | .395*** | .395*** | .395*** |
| Gender → Fear of Crime | -.605*** | -.605*** | -.605*** |
| Gender → Crime Seriousness | -.278*** | -.278*** | -.278*** |
| Gender → Just World Beliefs | .088*** | *.026* | .088*** |
| Gender → Rehabilitation | -.016 | -.016 | -.016 |
| **Gender → Support for 3 Strikes** | **-.024** | **-.024** | **-.024** |

*p≤.05; **p≤.01; ***p≤.001

**Table 1.B Unstandardized Regression Coefficients of the Effects of Age under 30 by Race/Ethnicity**

| | *White* (n=2500) | *Latino* (n=777) | *Black* (n=435) |
|---|---|---|---|
| ***Age: Under 30 on Media Consumption*** | | | |
| Under 30 → Newspapers | -.449*** | -.449*** | -.449*** |
| Under 30 → Television News | -.188 | -.188 | -.188 |
| Under 30 → Crime Info-tainment | -.094* | *.071* | -.094* |
| Under 30 → Crime Drama | -.134*** | -.134*** | -.134*** |
| Under 30 → Hours Watching TV | -2.963*** | *-.509* | -2.963*** |
| ***Under 30 on Crime Experience*** | | | |
| Under 30 → Prior Victimization | .189*** | .189*** | .189*** |
| Under 30 → Household Arrest | *-.065*** | .076** | .076** |
| ***Under 30 on Crime Perceptions and Beliefs*** | | | |
| Under 30 → Local Crime Risk | -.233* | -.233* | -.233* |
| Under 30 → Crime Up in State | -.007 | -.007 | -.007 |
| Under 30 → Feeling of Safe | .020 | .020 | .020 |
| Under 30 → Fear of Crime | .195* | .195* | .195* |
| Under 30 → Crime Seriousness | -.463*** | -.463*** | -.463*** |
| Under 30 → Just World Beliefs | .030 | .030 | .030 |
| Under 30 → Rehabilitation | *.097*** | .001 | .001 |
| **Under 30 → Support for 3 Strikes** | **.028** | **.028** | **.028** |

*p≤.05; ** p≤.01; ***p ≤.001

**Table 1.C Unstandardized Regression Coefficients of the Effects of Age 60 and Over by Race/Ethnicity**

|  | *White* (n=2500) | *Latino* (n=777) | *Black* (n=435) |
|---|---|---|---|
| ***Age 60 and Over on Media Consumption*** | | | |
| Over 60 → Newspapers | *1.743*\*\*\* | .754\*\* | .754\*\* |
| Over 60 → Television News | .972\*\*\* | .972\*\*\* | .972\*\*\* |
| Over 60 → Crime Info-tainment | -.208\*\*\* | -.208\*\*\* | -.208\*\*\* |
| Over 60 → Crime Drama | .114\*\* | .114\*\* | .114\*\* |
| Over 60 → Hours Watching TV | *5.330*\*\*\* | 1.139 | 1.139 |
| ***Age 60 and Over on Crime Experiences*** | | | |
| Over 60 → Prior Victimization | -.299\*\*\* | *.040* | -.299\*\*\* |
| Over 60 → Household Arrest | *-.177*\*\*\* | -.077\* | -.077\* |
| ***Age 60 and Over on Crime Perceptions and Beliefs*** | | | |
| Over 60 → Local Crime Risk | -.474\*\*\* | -.474\*\*\* | -.474\*\*\* |
| Over 60 → Crime Up in State | .015 | .015 | .015 |
| Over 60 → Feeling Safe | -.059 | -.059 | -.059 |
| Over 60 → Fear of Crime | -.290\*\*\* | -.290\*\*\* | -.290\*\*\* |
| Over 60 → Crime Seriousness | .254\*\*\* | .254\*\*\* | .254\*\*\* |
| Over 60 → Just World Beliefs | -.000 | -.000 | -.000 |
| Over 60 → Rehabilitation | .006 | .006 | .006 |
| **Over 60 →Support for 3 Strikes** | **-.100**\* | **-.100**\* | **-.100**\* |

\*p≤.05; \*\* p≤.01; \*\*\*p≤.001

**Table 1.D Unstandardized Regression Coefficients of the Effects of Education by Race/Ethnicity**

| | *White* (n=2500) | *Latino* (n=777) | *Black* (n=435) |
|---|---|---|---|
| ***Education on Media Consumption*** | | | |
| Education → Newspapers | .474*** | .474*** | .474*** |
| Education → Television News | <u>-.257***</u> | -.078 | -.078 |
| Education → Crime Info-tainment | -.195*** | <u>-.052</u> | -.195*** |
| Education → Crime Drama | -.017 | <u>.116***</u> | -.017 |
| Education → Hours Watching TV | -1.904*** | <u>-.357</u> | -1.904*** |
| ***Education on Crime Experiences*** | | | |
| Education → Prior Victimization | .023 | <u>.095**</u> | .023 |
| Education → Household Arrest | -.028*** | -.028*** | -.028*** |
| ***Education on Crime Perceptions and Beliefs*** | | | |
| Education → Local Crime Risk | -.072 | -.072 | -.072 |
| Education → Crime Up in State | -.051*** | -.051*** | -.051** |
| Education → Feeling Safe | -.046 | <u>.258***</u> | -.046 |
| Education → Fear of Crime | -.066* | -.066* | -.066* |
| Education → Crime Seriousness | -.196*** | -.196*** | <u>-.019</u> |
| Education → Just World Beliefs | -.025*** | -.025*** | -.025*** |
| Education → Rehabilitation | .006 | .006 | .006 |
| **Education → Support of 3 Strikes** | **-.019** | **-.019** | **-.019** |

*p≤.05; ** p≤.01; ***p≤.001

**Table 1.E Unstandardized Regression Coefficients of the Effects of Income by Race/Ethnicity**

| | White (n=2500) | Latino (n=777) | Black (n=435) |
|---|---|---|---|
| ***Income on Media Consumption*** | | | |
| Income → Newspapers | .213*** | .213*** | .213*** |
| Income → Television News | -.027 | -.027 | -.027 |
| Income → Crime Info-tainment | -.050*** | -.050*** | -.050*** |
| Income → Crime Drama | -.024** | -.024** | -.024** |
| Income → Hours Watching TV | -.654*** | -.654*** | *-1.684*** |
| ***Income on Crime Experiences*** | | | |
| Income → Prior Victimization | -.054*** | *.021* | -.054*** |
| Income → Household Arrest | *-.027*** | -.009 | -.009 |
| ***Income on Crime Perceptions and Beliefs*** | | | |
| Income → Local Crime Risk | -.129*** | -.129*** | *-.377*** |
| Income → Crime Up in State | -.012** | -.012** | -.012** |
| Income → Feeling Safe | .042* | .042* | *.116** |
| Income → Fear of Crime | *.068*** | -.017 | -.017 |
| Income → Crime Seriousness | -.052*** | -.052*** | -.052*** |
| Income → Just World Beliefs | *.000* | -.026*** | -.026*** |
| Income → Rehabilitation | -.009 | *-.033*** | -.009 |
| **Income → Support for 3 Strikes** | **.016** | ***.095**** | **.016** |

*p≤.05; ** p≤.01; *** p≤.001

**Table 1.F Unstandardized Regression Coefficients of the Effects of Political Party by Race/Ethnicity**

| | *White* (n=2500) | *Latino* (n=777) | *Black* (n=435) |
|---|---|---|---|
| ***Republican on Crime Perceptions and Beliefs*** | | | |
| Republican → Crime Up in State | .015 | .015 | .015 |
| Republican → Crime Seriousness | .340*** | .340*** | .340*** |
| Republican → Just World Beliefs | .099*** | *-.018* | .099*** |
| Republican → Rehabilitation | -.056** | -.056** | -.056** |
| **Republican → Support of 3 Strikes** | **.180***** | **.180***** | **.180***** |
| ***Democrat on Crime Perceptions and Beliefs*** | | | |
| Democrat → Crime Up in State | -.069*** | -.069*** | -.069*** |
| Democrat → Crime Seriousness | *-.155** | .095 | .095 |
| Democrat → Just World Beliefs | .013 | .013 | .013 |
| Democrat → Rehabilitation | *.068*** | -.042 | -.042 |
| **Democrat → Support of 3 Strikes** | ***-.156**** | **-.036** | **-.036** |

*p≤.05; **p ≤.01; ***p≤.001

**Table 1.G Unstandardized Regression Coefficients of the Effects of Victimization by Race/Ethnicity**

|  | *White* (n=2500) | *Latino* (n=777) | *Black* (n=435) |
|---|---|---|---|
| ***Victimization on Media Consumption*** | | | |
| Victimization → Hrs Watching TV | .248 | .248 | .248 |
| ***Victimization on Crime Perceptions and Beliefs*** | | | |
| Victimization → Local Crime Risk | .490*** | .490*** | .490*** |
| Victimization → Crime Up in State | .015** | .015** | .015** |
| Victimization → Feeling Safe | -.083** | -.083** | -.083** |
| Victimization → Fear of Crime | .157*** | .157*** | .157*** |
| Victimization → Crime Seriousness | -.034 | -.034 | -.034 |
| Victimization → Just World Beliefs | -.015* | -.015* | -.015* |
| Victimization → Rehabilitation | .004 | .004 | .004 |
| **Victimization → Support for 3 Strikes** | **-.011** | **-.011** | **-.011** |

*p≤.05; **p ≤.01; ***p≤.001

**Table 1.H. Unstandardized Regression Coefficients of the Effects of Household Arrest by Race/Ethnicity**

|  | *White* (n=2500) | *Latino* (n=777) | *Black* (n=435) |
|---|---|---|---|
| ***Arrest on Media Consumption*** | | | |
| Arrest → Hours Watching TV | *3.316*** | .2323 | .233 |
| ***Arrest on Crime Perceptions and Beliefs*** | | | |
| Arrest → Crime Seriousness | -.391*** | -.391*** | -.391*** |
| Arrest → Just World Beliefs | -.034 | -.034 | -.034 |
| Arrest → Rehabilitation | .054** | .054** | .054** |
| **Arrest → Support for 3 Strikes** | **-.259***** | **-.259***** | **-.259***** |

*p≤.05; **p ≤.01; ***p≤.001

**Table 1.I Unstandardized Regression Coefficients of the Effects of News Media by Race/Ethnicity**

| | *White* (n=2500) | *Latino* (n=777) | *Black* (n=435) |
|---|---|---|---|
| ***Newspapers on Crime Perceptions and Beliefs*** | | | |
| Newspapers → Local Crime Risk | -.012 | -.012 | -.012 |
| Newspapers → Crime Up in State | -.007** | .007** | -.007** |
| Newspapers → Feeling Safe | -.010 | -.010 | -.010 |
| Newspapers → Fear of Crime | .020* | .020* | .020* |
| Newspapers → Crime Seriousness | -.009 | -.009 | -.009 |
| Newspapers → Just World Beliefs | .001 | .001 | .001 |
| Newspapers → Rehabilitation | .001 | .001 | .001 |
| **Newspapers → Support for 3 Strikes** | **-.007** | **-.007** | **-.007** |
| ***Television News on Crime Perceptions and Beliefs*** | | | |
| TV News → Local Crime Risk | .050** | .050** | _.202_** |
| TV News → Crime Up in State | .006 | .006 | .006 |
| TV News → Feeling Safe | -.010 | -.010 | -.010 |
| TV News → Fear of Crime | .029** | .029** | .029** |
| TV News → Crime Seriousness | .061*** | .061*** | .061*** |
| TV News → Just World Beliefs | .008* | .008* | .008* |
| TV News → Rehabilitation | -.002 | -.002 | -.002 |
| **TV News → Support for 3 Strikes** | **-.010** | **-.010** | **-.010** |

\*p≤.05; \*\*p≤.01; \*\*\*p≤.001

**Table 1.J Unstandardized Regression Coefficients of the Effects of Crime-related Entertainment Media by Race/Ethnicity**

| | *White* (n=2500) | *Latino* (n=777) | *Black* (n=435) |
|---|---|---|---|
| ***Info-tainment on Crime Perceptions and Beliefs*** | | | |
| Info-tainment → Local Crime Risk | .073 | .073 | .073 |
| Info-tainment → Crime Up in State | .035*** | .035*** | .035*** |
| Info-tainment → Feeling Safe | -.028 | -.028 | -.028 |
| Info-tainment → Fear of Crime | .096** | .096** | .096** |
| Info-tainment → Crime Seriousness | .052* | .052* | .052* |
| Info-tainment → Just World Beliefs | .016* | .016* | .016* |
| Info-tainment → Rehabilitation | -.012 | -.012 | -.012 |
| **Info-tainment → Support for 3 Strikes** | **.014** | **.014** | **.014** |
| ***Crime Drama on Crime Perceptions and Beliefs*** | | | |
| Crime Drama → Local Crime Risk | .100* | .100* | .100* |
| Crime Drama → Crime Up in State | -.002 | -.002 | -.002 |
| Crime Drama → Feeling Safe | .056 | .056 | .056 |
| Crime Drama → Fear of Crime | .041 | *-.275*** | .041 |
| Crime Drama → Crime Seriousness | -.049* | -.049* | -.049* |
| Crime Drama → Just World Beliefs | .014* | .014* | .014* |
| Crime Drama → Rehabilitation | -.016* | -.016* | -.016* |
| **Crime Drama → Support for 3 Strikes** | **-.007** | **-.007** | **-.007** |

*p≤.05; ** p≤.01; ***p≤.001

**Table 1.K Unstandardized Regression Coefficients of the Effects of Hours Spent Watching Television by Race/Ethnicity**

|  | *White* (n=2500) | *Latino* (n=777) | *Black* (n=435) |
|---|---|---|---|
| ***Hours of T.V. on Crime Perceptions and Beliefs*** | | | |
| Hours of T.V. → Local Crime Risk | .005 | .005 | -.017* |
| Hours of T.V. → Crime Up in State | .000 | .000 | .000 |
| Hours of T.V. → Feeling Safe | -.001 | -.001 | -.001 |
| Hours of T.V. → Fear of Crime | -.002 | .011** | .011** |
| Hours of T.V. → Crime Seriousness | -.003 | -.003 | -.003 |
| Hours of T.V. → Just World Beliefs | .000 | .000 | .000 |
| Hours of T.V. → Rehabilitation | -.002*** | -.002*** | -.002*** |
| **Hours of T.V. → Support for 3 Strikes** | **-.002** | **-.002** | **-.002** |

*p≤.05; ** p≤.01; ***p≤.001

**Table 1.L Unstandardized Regression Coefficients of the Effects of Perceptions of Local Crime Risk by Race/Ethnicity**

|  | *White* (n=2500) | *Latino* (n=777) | *Black* (n=435) |
|---|---|---|---|
| ***Local Crime Risk on Crime Perceptions and Beliefs*** | | | |
| Crime Risk → Crime Increased | .014*** | .014*** | .014*** |
| Crime Risk → Feeling Safe | -.281*** | -.281*** | -.281*** |
| Crime Risk → Fear of Crime | .433*** | .433*** | .433*** |
| Crime Risk → Crime Seriousness | .022* | .022* | .022* |
| Crime Risk → Just World Beliefs | -.010** | -.010** | -.010** |
| Crime Risk → Support for Rehab. | .003 | .003 | .003 |
| **Crime Risk → Support 3 Strikes** | **-.007** | **-.007** | **-.007** |

*p≤.05; ** p≤.01; ***p≤.001

**Table 1.M Unstandardized Regression Coefficients of the Effects of Crime Salience Perceptions by Race/Ethnicity**

| | *White* (n=2500) | *Latino* (n=777) | *Black* (n=435) |
|---|---|---|---|
| **Crime Increased on Crime Perceptions and Beliefs** | | | |
| Crime Increased → Feeling Safe | -.124* | -.124* | -.124* |
| Crime Increased → Fear of Crime | .175** | .175** | .175** |
| Crime Increased → Crime Seriousness | .264*** | .264*** | .264*** |
| Crime Increased → Just World Beliefs | -.039** | _.036_ | .039** |
| Crime Increased → Support for Rehabilitation | -.018 | -.018 | -.018 |
| **Crime Increased → Support for 3 Strikes** | **.065*** | **.065*** | **.065*** |
| **Feeling Safe on Crime Perceptions and Beliefs** | | | |
| Feeling Safe → Fear of Crime | _-.355_*** | -.253*** | -.253*** |
| Feeling Safe → Just World Beliefs | .001 | .001 | .001 |
| Feeling Safe → Crime Seriousness | .007 | .007 | .007 |
| Feeling Safe → Support for Rehab. | .004 | .004 | .004 |
| **Feeling Safe → Support for 3 Strikes** | **.011** | **.011** | **.011** |
| **Fear of Crime on Crime Perceptions and Beliefs** | | | |
| Fear of Crime → Crime Seriousness | .054*** | .054*** | .054*** |
| Fear of Crime → Support for Rehabilitation | .003 | .003 | .003 |
| **Fear of Crime → Support for 3 Strikes** | **.021*** | **.021*** | **.021*** |

*p≤.05; ** p≤.01; ***p≤.001

**Table 1.N Unstandardized Regression Coefficients of the Effects of Belief in a Just World by Race/Ethnicity**

|  | *White* (n=2500) | *Latino* (n=777) | *Black* (n=435) |
|---|---|---|---|
| Just World Beliefs → Support for Rehabilitation | -.069[***] | -.069[***] | -.069[***] |
| Just World Beliefs → Crime Seriousness | .232[***] | .232[***] | .232[***] |
| **Just World Beliefs → Support for 3 Strikes** | .178[***] | .178[***] | .178[***] |

*p≤.05; ** p≤.01; ***p≤.001

**Table 1.O Unstandardized Regression Coefficients of the Effects of Crime Seriousness and Support for Rehabilitation by Race/Ethnicity**

|  | *White* (n=2500) | *Latino* (n=777) | *Black* (n=435) |
|---|---|---|---|
| *Crime Seriousness on Crime Perceptions/Beliefs* | | | |
| Crime Seriousness → Support for Rehabilitation | -.021[***] | -.021[***] | -.021[***] |
| **Crime Seriousness → Support for 3 Strikes** | *.220*[***] | .112[***] | .112[***] |
| *Support for Rehabilitation* | | | |
| **Support for Rehabilitation → Support for 3 Strikes** | -.313[***] | -.313[***] | -.313[***] |

*p≤.05; ** p≤.01; ***p≤.001

# References

Adatto, Kiku. 1993. *Picture Perfect: The Art and Artifice of Public Image Making.* New York: Basic Books.

Agnew, Robert S. 1985. "Neutralizing the Impact of Crime." *Criminal Justice and Behavior*, 12(2):221-239.

Altheide, David L. 2002. *Creating Fear: News and the Construction of Crisis.* New York: Aldine de Gruyter.

Antunes, George E. and Patricia A. Hurley. 1977. "The Representation of Criminal Events in Houston's Two Daily Newspapers." *Journalism Quarterly*, 54:756-760.

Applegate, Brandon K. and Francis T. Cullen. 1996. "Assessing Public Support for Three-Strikes and You're Out Laws: Global Versus Specific Attitudes." *Crime and Delinquency*, 42(4):517-535.

Applegate, Brandon K., Francis T. Cullen, and Bonnie S. Fisher. 1997. "Public Support for Correctional Treatment: The Continuing Appeal of the Rehabilitative Ideal." *Prison Journal*, 77:237-258.

Austin, James. 1996. "The Effects of 'Three Strikes and You're Out' on Corrections." Pp. 155-174 in *Three Strikes and You're Out: Vengeance as Public Policy*, edited by D. Shichor and D. Sechrest. Thousand Oaks, CA: Sage.

Austin, James, John Clark, Patricia Hardyman, and D. Alan Henry. 1999. "The Impact of 'Three Strikes and You're Out.'" *Punishment and Society*, 1(1):131-162.

Barak, Gregg. 1994a. "Between the Waves: Mass-Mediated Themes of Crime and Justice." *Social Justice*, 21(3):133-147.

Barak, Gregg. 1994b. "Newsmaking Criminology: Reflections on the Media, Intellectuals, and Crime." Pp. 237-264 in *Media, Process, and the Social Construction of Crime*, edited by G. Barak. New York: Garland.

Barkan, Steven E. and Steven F. Cohn. 1994. "Racial Prejudice and Support for the Death Penalty by Whites." *Journal of Research on Crime and Delinquency*, 31(2):202-209.

Baron, Stephen W. and Timothy F. Hartnagel. 1996. "'Lock 'Em Up': Attitudes Toward Punishing Juvenile Offenders." *Canadian Journal of Criminology*, 38(2):191-212.

Barrile, Leo. 1984. "Television and Attitudes about Crime: Do Heavy Viewers Distort Criminality and Support Retributive Justice?" Pp. 141-158 in *Justice and the Media: Issues and Research*, edited by R. Surette. Springfield, IL: Charles C. Thomas.

Baumer, Terry L. 1978. "Research on Fear of Crime in the United States." *Victimology*, 3(3-4):254-264.

------. 1985. "Testing a General Model of Fear of Crime: Data from a National Sample." *Journal of Research in Crime and Delinquency*, 22(3):239-255.

Beckett, Katherine. 1994. "Setting the Public Agenda: 'Street Crime' and Drug Use in American Politics." *Social Problems*, 41(3):425-447.

------. 1997. *Making Crime Pay: Law and Order in Contemporary American Politics.* New York: Oxford University Press.

Benson, D.E. 1992. "Why Do People Believe in a Just World?: Testing Explanations." *Sociological Spectrum*, 12:73-104.

Best, Joel. 1997. "Victimization and the Victim Industry." *Society*, 34(4)9-17.

Bilsky, Wolfgang and Peter Wetzels. 1997. "On the Relationship between Criminal Victimization and Fear of Crime." *Psychology, Crime & Law,* 3:309-318.

Blumstein, Alfred and Jacqueline Cohen. 1980. "Sentencing of Convicted Offenders: An Analysis of the Public's View." *Law and Society Review*, 14(2):223-261.

Bohm, Robert M. 1991. "American Death Penalty Opinion, 1936-1986: A Critical Examination of the Gallup Polls." Pp. 113-145 in *The Death Penalty in America: Current Research*, edited by R. Bohm. Cincinnati, OH: Anderson.

Borg, Marian J. 1997. "The Southern Subculture of Punitiveness? Regional Variation in Support for Capital Punishment." *Journal of Research in Crime and Delinquency,* 34(1):25-45.

Bortner, M.A. 1984. "Media Images and Public Attitudes toward Crime and Justice." Pp. 15-30 in *Justice and the Media,* edited by R. Surette. Springfield IL: Charles C. Thomas.

Box, Steven, Chris Hale, and Glen Andrews. 1988. "Explaining Fear of Crime." *British Journal of Criminology*, 28(3):340-356.

Boydell, Craig L. and Carl F. Grindstaff. 1974. "Research Notes: Public Opinion toward Legal Sanctions for Crimes of Violence." *The Journal of Criminal Law and Criminology*, 65(1):113-116.

Braungart, Margaret M., Richard G. Braungart, and William J. Hoyer. 1980. "Age, Sex, and Social Factors in Fear of Crime." *Sociological Focus*, 13(1):55-66.

Brillon, Yves. 1988. "Punitiveness, Status and Ideology in Three Canadian Provinces." Pp. 84-110 in *Public Attitudes toward Sentencing: Surveys from Five Countries,* edited by N. Walker and M. Hough. Brooksfield, VT: Gower.

Browning, Sandra Lee, and Liqun Cao. 1992. "The Impact of Race on Criminal Justice Ideology." *Justice Quarterly*, 9(4):687-699.

Brownstein, Henry H. 1995. "The Media and the Construction of Random Drug Violence." Pp. 45-65 in *Cultural Criminology*, edited by J. Ferrell and C. Sanders. Boston: Northeastern University.

Calhoun, Lawrence G. and Arnie Cann. 1994. "Differences in assumptions about a Just World: Ethnicity and Point of View." *Journal of Social Psychology,* 134(6):765-770.

Carlson, James M. 1985. *Prime Time Law Enforcement: Crime Show Viewing and Attitudes toward the Criminal Justice System*. New York: Praeger.

Carlson, James M. and Tricia Williams. 1993. "Perspectives on the Seriousness of Crimes." *Social Science Research*, 22:190-227.

Cavender, Gray and Lisa Bond-Maupin. 1999. "The Construction of Gender in Reality Crime TV." *Gender and Society*, 13(5):643-64.

Cavender, Gray and Mark Fishman. 1998. "Television Reality Crime Programs: Context and History." Pp. 1-15 in *Entertaining Crime: Television Reality Programs*, edited by M. Fishman and G. Cavender. New York: Aldine de Gruyter.

Cesaroni, Carla and Anthony N. Doob. 2003. "The Decline in Support for Penal Welfarism: Evidence of Support among the Elite for Punitive Segregation." *British Journal of Criminology*, 43:434-441.

Chadee, Derek and Jason Ditton. 2003. "Are Older People Most Afraid of Crime?: Revisiting Ferraro and LaGrange in Trinidad." *British Journal of Criminology*, 42(2):417-433.

Chermak, Steven. 1994. "Crime in the News Media: A Refined Understanding of How Crimes Become News." Pp. 95-130 in *Media, Process, and the Social Construction of Crime: Studies in Newsmaking Criminology*, edited by G. Barak. New York: Garland.

------. 1995. *Victims in the News: Crime and the American News Media*. Boulder, CO: Westview Press.

------. 1998. "Predicting Crime Story Salience: The Effects of Crime, Victim, and Defendant Characteristics." *Journal of Criminal Justice*, 26(1):61-70.

Cheurprakobkit, Sutham. 2000. "Police-Citizen Contact and Police Performance: Attitudinal Differences between Hispanics and Non-Hispanics." *Journal of Criminal Justice*, 28:325-336.

Chiricos, Ted and Sarah Eschholz. 2002. "The Racial and Ethnic Typification of Crime and the Criminal Typification of Race and Ethnicity in Local Television News." *Journal of Research in Crime and Delinquency*, 39(4):400-420.

Chiricos, Ted, Sarah Eschholz, and Marc Gertz. 1997. "Crime, News, and Fear of Crime: Toward an Identification of Audience Effects." *Social Problems*, 44(3):342-357.

Chiricos, Ted, Kathy Padgett, and Marc Gertz. 2000. "Fear, TV News, and the Reality of Crime." *Criminology*, 38(3):755-785.

Clear, Todd R. and Dina R. Rose. 1999. "When Neighbors Go to Jail: Impact on Attitudes About Formal and Informal Social Control." *Research in Progress Seminar Series: National Institute of Justice*. Washington, DC: United States Department of Justice.

Clemente, Frank and Michael B. Kleiman. 1977. "Fear of Crime in the United States: A Multivariate Analysis." *Social Forces*, 56:519-531.

Converse, P.M. 1964. "The Nature of Belief Systems in Mass Publics." Pp. 206-261 in *Ideology and Discontent*, edited by D. Apter. New York: Free Press.

Coombs, Clyde H. 1967. "Thurstone's Measurement of Social Values Revisited Forty Years Later." *Journal of Personality and Social Psychology*, 6(1):85-91.

Crew, B. Keith. 1990. "Acting Like Cops: The Social Reality of Crime and Law on TV Police Dramas." Pp. 131-143, in *Marginal Conventions: Popular Culture, Mass Media and Social Deviance*, edited by C. Sanders. Bowling Green, OH: Bowling Green University.

Cullen, Francis T., Gregory A. Clark, John B. Cullen, and Richard A. Mathers. 1985. "Attribution, Salience, and Attitudes toward Criminal Sanctioning." *Criminal Justice and Behavior*, 12(3):305-331.

Cullen, Francis T., Bonnie S. Fisher and Brandon K. Applegate. 2000. "Public Opinion about Punishment and Corrections." *Crime & Justice*, 27:1-79.

Cullen, Francis T., Bruce G. Link, and Craig W. Polanzi. 1982. "The Seriousness of Crime Revisited: Have Attitudes Toward White-Collar Crime Changed?" *Criminology*, 20(1):83-102.

Cullen, Francis T., Sandra Evans Skovron, Joseph E. Scott, and Velmer S. Burton, Jr. 1990. "Public Support for Correctional Treatment: The Tenacity of Rehabilitative Ideology." *Criminal Justice and Behavior*, 17:6-18.

Cullen, Francis T., John Paul Wright, Shayna Brown, Melissa M. Moon, Michael B. Blankenship, and Brandon K. Applegate. 1998. "Public Support for Early Intervention Programs: Implications for a Progressive Policy Agenda." *Crime & Delinquency*, 44(2):187-204.

Davis, F. James. 1952. "Crime News in Colorado Newspapers." *American Journal of Sociology*, 57(4): 325-330.

Davis, J. R. 1990. "A Comparison of Attitudes toward the New York City Police." *Journal of Police Science and Administration*, 17:233-242.

Denkers, Andriaan J. M. and Frans Willem Winkel. 1998. "Crime Victims' Well-Being and Fear in a Prospective and Longitudinal Study." *International Review of Victimology*, 5:141-162.

Ditton, Jason and James Duffy. 1983. "Bias in the Newspaper Reporting of Crime News." *British Journal of Criminology*, 23(2): 159-165.

Dixon, Travis L. and Daniel Linz. 2000. "Race and the Misrepresentation of Victimization on Local Television News." *Communication Research*, 27(5):547-573.

Doble, John. 1987. *Crime and Punishment: The Public's View*. New York: Edna McConnell Clark Foundation.

Dominick, Joseph R. 1973. "Crime and Law Enforcement in Prime-Time Television." *Public Opinion Quarterly*, 37:243-250.

Donnelly, Patrick G. 1988. "Individual and Neighborhood Influences on Fear of Crime." *Sociological Focus*, 22(1):69-85.

Donovan, Pamela. 1998. "Armed With the Power of Television: Reality Crime Programming and the Reconstruction of Law and Order in the United States." Pp. 117-137 in *Entertaining Crime: Television Reality Programs*, edited by M. Fishman and G. Cavender. New York: Aldine de Gruyter.

Doob, Anthony N. and Glenn E. Macdonald. 1979. "Television Viewing and Fear of Victimization: Is the Relationship Causal?" *Journal of Personality and Social Psychology*, 37(2):170-179.

Doob, Anthony N. and Julian V. Roberts. 1984. "Social Psychology, Social Attitudes, and Attitudes toward Sentencing." *Canadian Journal of Behavioral Science*, 16(4):269-280.

------ 1988. "Public Punitiveness and Public Knowledge of the Facts: Some Canadian Surveys." Pp. 111-133 in *Public Attitudes Toward Sentencing: Surveys from Five Countries*, edited by N. Walker and M. Hough. Brookfield, VT: Gower.

Dorfman, Lori and Vincent Schiraldi. 2001. "Off Balance: Youth, Crime, and Race in the News." [Online] (www.buildingblocksforyouth.org/media).

Doyle, Aaron. 1998. "'COPS': Television Policing as Policing Reality." Pp. 95-116 in *Entertaining Crime: Television Reality Programs*, edited by M. Fishman and G. Cavender. New York: Aldine de Gruyter.

Dull, Thomas R. and Arthur V. N. Wint. 1997. "Criminal Victimization and Its Effect on Fear of Crime and Justice Attitudes." *Journal of Interpersonal Violence*, 12(5):748-759.

Durham III, Alexis M. 1989. "Judgments of Appropriate Punishment: The Effects of Question Type." *Journal of Criminal Justice*, 17:75-85.

------. 1993. "Public Opinion Regarding Sentences for Crime: Does It Exist?" *Journal of Criminal Justice*, 21:1-11.

Einstadter, Werner J. 1994. "Crime News in the Old West." Pp. 49-67 in *Media, Process, and the Social Construction of Crime: Studies in Newsmaking Criminology,* edited by G. Barak. New York: Garland.

Ellsworth, Phoebe C. and L. Ross. 1983."Public Opinion and Capital Punishment: A Close Examination of the View of Abolitionists and Retentionists." *Crime and Delinquency*, 29(1):116-169.

Ellsworth, Phoebe C. and Samuel R. Gross. 1994. "Hardening of the Attitudes: Americans' Views on the Death Penalty." *Journal of Social Issues*, 50(2):19-52.

Entman, Robert M. 1989. "How the Media Affects What People Think: An Information Processing Approach." *Journal of Politics,* 51(2):347-370.

------. 1992. "Blacks in the News: Television, Modern Racism, and Cultural Change." *Journalism Quarterly*, 69(2):341-361.

Ericson, Richard V. 1991. "Mass Media, Crime, Law, and Justice: An Institutional Approach." *The British Journal of Criminology,* 31(3): 219-249.

Ericson, Richard, Patricia M. Baranek, and Janet B. L. Chan. 1989. *Negotiating Control: A Study of News Sources.* Toronto, Canada: University of Toronto.

------. 1991. *Representing Order: Crime, Law, and Justice in the News Media.* Toronto, Canada: University of Toronto.

Eschholz, Sarah, Ted Chiricos, and Marc Gertz. 2003. "Television and Fear of Crime: Program Types, Audience Traits, and the Mediating Effect of Perceived Neighborhood Racial Composition." *Social Problems,* 50(3):395-415.

Estep, Rhoda and Patrick T. Macdonald. 1984. "How Prime-Time Crime Evolved on TV, 1976 to 1983." Pp. 110-123 in *Justice and the Media: Issues and Research,* edited by R. Surette. Springfield, IL: Charles C. Thomas.

Evans, Sandra S. and Joseph E. Scott. 1984. "Effects of Item Order on the Perceived Seriousness of Crime: A Reexamination." *Journal of Research in Crime and Delinquency,* 21(2):139-151.

Farrall, Stephen and David Gadd. 2004. "Research Note: The Frequency of the Fear of Crime." *British Journal of Criminology,* 44:127-132.

Ferraro, Kenneth F. 1995. *Fear of Crime: Interpreting Victimization Risk.* Albany, NY: State University of New York.

------. 1996. "Women's Fear of Victimization: Shadow of Sexual Assault?" *Social Forces,* 75(2):667-690.

Ferraro, Kenneth F. and Randy LaGrange. 1987. "The Measurement of Fear of Crime." *Sociological Inquiry,* 57:70-101.

Ferraro, Kenneth F. and Randy LaGrange. 1988. "Are Older People Afraid of Crime?" *Journal of Aging Studies,* 2(3):277-287.

Figlio, Robert M. 1975. "The Seriousness of Offenses: An Evaluation by Offenders and Nonoffenders." *Journal of Criminal Law and Criminology,* 66(2):189-200.

Finamore, Frank and James M. Carlson. 1987. "Religiosity, Belief in a Just World and Crime Control Attitudes." *Psychological Reports,* 61(1): 135-138.

Finkel, Norman J., Stephen T. Maloney, Monique Z. Valbuena, and Jennifer Groscup. 1996. "Recidivism, Proportionalism, and Individualized Punishment." *American Behavioral Scientist,* 39(4):474-487.

Fishman, Mark. 1978. "Crime Waves as Ideology." *Social Problems,* 25(5):531-543.

------. 1980. *Manufacturing the News.* Austin, TX: University of Texas.

------. 1998. "Ratings and Reality: The Persistence of the Reality Crime Genre." Pp. 59-94 in *Entertaining Crime: Television Reality Programs,* edited by M. Fishman and G. Cavender. New York: Aldine de Gruyter.

Flanagan, Timothy J. 1996a. "Public Opinion on Crime and Justice: History, Development, and Trends." Pp. 1-15 in *Americans View Crime and Justice: A National Public Opinion Survey,* edited by T. Flanagan and D. Longmire. Thousand Oaks, CA: Sage.

------. 1996b . "Reform or Punish: Americans' Views of the Correctional System." Pp. 75-92 in *Americans View Crime and Justice: A National Public Opinion Survey,* edited by T. Flanagan and D. Longmire. Thousand Oaks, CA: Sage.

Flanagan, Timothy J. and Sue L. Caulfield. 1984. "Public Opinion and Prison Policy: A Review." *Prison Journal*, 64:39-59.

Forde, David Roberts. 1993, "Perceived Crime, Fear of Crime, and Walking Alone at Night." *Psychological Reports*, 73:403-407.

Fox, Richard L. and Robert W. Van Sickel. 2001. *Tabloid Justice: Criminal Justice in an Age of Media Frenzy*. Boulder, CO: Lynne Rienner.

Furnham, Adrian and Barrie Gunter. 1984. "Just World Beliefs and Attitudes towards the Poor." *British Journal of Social Psychology*, 23:265-269.

Gamson, William A. and Gadi Wolfsfeld. 1993. "Movements and Media as Interacting Systems." *The Annals of the American Academy, 528(July): 114-125.*

Garland, David. 2000. "The Culture of High Crime Societies: Some Preconditions of Recent 'Law and Order' Policies." *British Journal of Criminology*, 40:347-375.

Garland, David and Richard Sparks. 2000. "Criminology, Social Theory and the Challenge of Our Times." *British Journal of Criminology*, 40:189-204.

Garofalo, James. 1979. "Victimization and the Fear of Crime." *Journal of Research in Crime and Delinquency*, 16(1):80-97.

------. 1981. "Crime and the Mass Media." *Journal of Research in Crime and Delinquency*, July:319-349.

Gebotys, Robert J. and Bikram Dasgupta. 1987. "Attribution of Responsibility and Crime Seriousness." *The Journal of Psychology*, 121(6):607-613.

Gebotys, Robert J. and Julian V. Roberts. 1987. "Public Views of Sentencing: The Role of Offender Characteristics." *Canadian Journal of Behavioural Science*, 19(4):479-488.

Gebotys, Robert J., Julian V. Roberts and Bikram Dasgupta. 1988. "News Media Use and Public Perceptions of Crime Seriousness." *Canadian Journal of* Criminology, 30:3-16.

Gerber, Jurg and Simone Engelhardt-Greer. 1996. "Just and Painful: Attitudes toward Sentencing Criminals." Pp. 62-74 in *Americans View Crime and Justice: A National Public Opinion Survey*, edited by T. Flanagan and D. Longmire. Thousand Oaks, CA: Sage.

Gerbner, George. 1996. "TV Violence and What to Do About It." *Nieman Reports,* 50(3):10-16.

Gerbner, George and Larry Gross. 1976. "Living with Television: The Violence Profile." *Journal of Communication*, 26(2):173-199.

Gerbner, George, Larry Gross, Michael Morgan and Nancy Signorelli. 1980. "The 'Mainstreaming' of America: Violence Profile No. 11." *Journal of Communication*, 30(3):10-29.

------. 1986. "Living with Television: The Dynamics of the Cultivation Process." Pp. 17-48 in *Perspectives on Media Effects*, edited by J. Bryant and D. Zimmerman. Hillsdale, NJ: Lawrence Erlbaum Associates.

------. 1994. "Growing Up with Television: The Cultivation Perspective." Pp. 17-42 in *Media Effects: Advances in Theory and Research*, edited by J. Bryant and D. Zimmerman. Hillsdale, NJ: Lawrence Erlbaum Associates.

Gilchrist, Elizabeth, Jon Bannister, Jason Ditton, and Stephen Farrall. 1998. "Women and the Fear of Crime: Challenging the Accepted Stereotype." *British Journal of Criminology*, 38(2):283-298.

Giles-Sims, Jean. 1984. "A Multivariate Analysis of Perceived Likelihood of Victimization and Degree of Worry about Crime among Older People." *Victimology*, 9:222-233.

Gilliam Jr, Franklin D. and Shanto Iyengar. 2000. "Prime Suspects: The Influence of Local Television News on the Viewing Public." *American Journal of Political Science*, 44(3):560-573.

Gomme, Ian M. 1988. "The Role of Experience in the Production of Fear of Crime: A Test of a Causal Model." *Canadian Journal of Criminology*, 30(1):67-76.

Goodey, Jo. 1997. "Boys Don't Cry: Masculinities, Fear of Crime and Fearlessness." *British Journal of Criminology*, 37:401-418.

Gordon, Margaret T. and Linda Heath. 1981. "Reactions to Crime: Institutions React: The News Business, Crime, and Fear." *Sage Criminal Justice System Annals*, 16:227-250.

Gottfredson, Steven D., Barbara D. Warner, and Ralph B. Taylor. 1988. "Conflict and Consensus about Criminal Justice in Maryland." Pp. 16-55 in *Public Attitudes toward Sentencing: Surveys from Five Countries*, edited by N. Walker and M. Hough. Brookfield, VT: Gower.

Graber, Doris A. 1980. *Crime News and the Public.* New York: Praeger.

Greve, Werner. 1998. "Fear of Crime among the Elderly: Foresight, Not Fright." *International Review of Victimology*, 5(3-4):277-309.

Gunter, Barrie. 1987. *Television and the Fear of Crime*. London, England: John Libbey.

Gunter, Barrie and Mallory Wober. 1983. "Television Viewing and Public Trust." *British Journal of Social Psychology*, 22(2):174-176.

Guo, Zhongshi, Jonathan J. H. Zhu, and Huailin Chen. 2001. "Mediated Reality Bites: Comparing Direct and Indirect Experience as Sources of Perceptions across Two Communities in China." *International Journal of Public Opinion Research*, 13(4):398-418.

Haddock, Geoffrey and Mark P. Zanna. 1998. "Assessing the Impact of Affective and Cognitive Information in Predicting Attitudes toward Capital Punishment." *Law and Human Behavior*, 22(3):325-339.

Hagan, John and Celeste Albonetti. 1982. "Race, Class, and Perception of Criminal Injustice in America." *American Journal of Sociology*, 88:329-355.

Haghighi, Bahram and Alma Lopez. 1998. "Gender and Perceptions of Prisons and Prisoners." *Journal of Criminal Justice*, 26(6):453-464.

Hamilton, V. Lee and Steve Rytina. 1980. "Social Consensus on Norms of Justice: Should the Punishment Fit the Crime?" *American Journal of Sociology*, 85(5):1117-1144.

Hans, Valerie P. and Juliet L. Dee. 1991. "Media Coverage of Law: It's Impact on Juries and the Public." *American Behavioral Scientist*, 35(2):136-149.

Hartnagel, Timothy F. 1979. "The Perception of Fear of Crime: Implications For Neighborhood Cohesion, Social Activity, and Community Affect." *Social Forces*, 58(1):176-193.

Haynie, Stacia L. and Ernest A. Dover. 1994. "Prosecutorial Discretion and Press Coverage: The Decision to Try the Case." *American Politics Quarterly*, 22:370-381.

Heath, Linda. 1984. Impact of Newspaper Crime Reports on Fear of Crime: A Multimethodological Investigation." *Journal of Personality and Social Psychology*, 47(2):263-276.

Heath, Linda and John Petraitis. 1987. "Television Viewing and Fear of Crime: Where is the Mean World?" *Basic and Applied Social Psychology*, 8 (1 & 2):97-123.

Hindelang, Michael J. 1973. "Public Opinion Regarding Crime, Criminal Justice, and Delinquency." *Journal for Research in Crime and Delinquency*, 11(2):101-116.

Hindelang, Michael J., Michael R. Gottfredson, and James Garofalo. 1978. *Victims of Personal Crime: An Empirical Foundation for a Theory of Personal Victimization*. Cambridge, MA: Ballinger.

Hirsch, Paul M. 1980. "The 'Scary World' of the Nonviewer and Other Anomalies: A Reanalysis of Gerbner et al.'s Findings on Cultivation Analysis, Part I." *Communications Research*, 7(4):403-456.

------. 1981. "On Not Learning from One's Own Mistakes: A Reanalysis of Gerbner et al.'s Findings on Cultivation Analysis, Part II." *Communications Research*, 8(1):3-37.

Hough, Mike, Helen Lewis, and Nigel Walker. 1988. "Factors Associated with 'Punitiveness' in England and Wales." Pp. 203-217 in *Public Attitudes toward Sentencing: Surveys from Five Countries*, edited by N. Walker and M. Hough. Brookfield, VT: Gower.

Hough, Mike and David Moxon. 1988. "Dealing with Offenders: Popular Opinion and the Views of Victims in England and Wales." Pp. 134-148 in *Public Attitudes toward Sentencing: Surveys from Five Countries*, edited by N. Walker and M. Hough. Brookfield, VT: Gower.

Hough, Mike and Julian V. Roberts. 1999. "Sentencing Trends in Britain: Public Knowledge and Public Opinion." *Punishment and Society*, 1(1): 11-26.

Howitt, Dennis. 1998. *Crime, the Media and the Law*. Chichester, England: John Wiley and Sons.

Hughes, Michael. 1980. "The Fruits of Cultivation Analysis: A Reexamination of Some Effects of Television Watching." *Public Opinion Quarterly*, 44:287-302.

Hunt, Matthew O. 2000. "Status, Religion, and the 'Belief in a Just World': Comparing African Americans, Latinos, and Whites." *Social Science Quarterly*, 81(1):325-343.

Indermaur, David. 1994. "Offenders' Perceptions of Sentencing." *Australian Psychologist*, 29(2):140-144.

Innes, Christopher A. 1993. "Recent Public Opinion in the United States toward Punishment and Corrections." *The Prison Journal,* 73(2):220-236.

Irwin, John, James Austin, and Chris Baird. 1998. "Fanning the Flames of Fear: The Politics of America's Imprisonment Binge." *Crime and Delinquency,* 44(1):32-48.

Iyengar, Shanto. 1989. "How Citizens Think About National Issues: A Matter of Responsibility." *American Journal of Political Science,* 33(4):878-900.

Iyengar, Shanto, Mark D. Peters, and Donald R. Kinder. 1982. "Experimental Demonstrations of the 'Not-So-Minimal' Consequences of Television News Programs." *The American Political Science Review,* 76:848-858.

Jenkins, Philip. 1994. *Using Murder: The Social Construction of Serial Homicide.* New York: Aldine de Gruyter.

Jerin, Robert A. and Charles B. Field. 1994. "Murder and Mayhem in *USA Today*: A Quantitative Analysis of the National Reporting of States' News." Pp. 187-202 in *Media, Process, and the Social Construction of Crime: Studies in Newsmaking Criminology,* edited by G. Barak. New York: Garland.

Johnstone, John W.C., Darnell F. Hawkins, and Arthur Michener. 1994. "Homicide Reporting in Chicago Dailies". *Journalism Quarterly,* 71(4):860-872.

Junger, Marianne. 1987. "Women's Experiences of Sexual Harassment." *British Journal of Criminology,* 27(4):358-383.

Karmen, Andrew. 2001. *Crime Victims: An Introduction to Victimology,* 4$^{th}$ ed. Belmont, CA: Wadsworth/Thompson Learning.

Kasinsky, Renee Goldsmith. 1994. "Patrolling the Facts: Media, Cops, and Crime." Pp. 203-234 in *Media, Process, and the Social Construction of Crime: Studies in Newsmaking Criminology,* edited by G. Barak. New York: Garland.

Keil, Thomas J. and Gennaro F. Vito. 1991. "Fear of Crime and Attitudes toward Capital Punishment: A Structural Equations Model." *Justice Quarterly,* 8:447-464.

Kieso, Douglas William. 2003. "The California Three Strikes Law: The Undemocratic Production of Injustice." Ph.D. Dissertation, Criminology, Law and Society. University of California, Irvine: Irvine, CA.

Killias, Martin. 1990. "Vulnerability: Toward a Better Understanding of a Key Variable in the Genesis of Fear of Crime." *Violence and Victims,* 5(2): 97-108.

Kooistra, Paul G., John S. Mahoney, and Saundra D. Westervelt. 1998. "The World of Crime According to 'COPS'." Pp. 141-158 in *Entertaining Crime: Television Reality Programs,* edited by M. Fishman and G. Cavender . New York: Aldine de Gruyter.

Krisberg, Barry. 1994. "Distorted By Fear: The Make Believe War on Crime." *Social Justice,* 21(3):38-49.

Kury, Helmet and Theodore Ferdinand. 1998. "The Victim's Experience and Fear of Crime." *International Review of Victimology,* 5:93-140.

LaGrange, Randy L., Kenneth F. Ferraro, and Michael Supancic. 1992. "Perceived Risk and Fear of Crime: Role of Social and Physical Incivilities." *Journal of Research in Crime and Delinquency,* 29(3): 311-334.

Langworthy, Robert H. and John T. Whitehead. 1986. "Liberalism and Fear as Explanations of Punitiveness." *Criminology,* 24:575-591.

Lawton, M. Powell and Sylvia Yaffe. 1980. "Victimization and Fear of Crime in Elderly Public Housing Tenants." *Journal of Gerontology,* 35:768-779.

Lee, Gary R. 1983. "Social Integration and Fear of Crime." *Journal of Gerontology,* 38:745-750.

Lerner, Melvin. 1980. *The Belief in a Just World: A Fundamental Delusion.* New York: Plenum.

Lerner, Melvin J. and Dale T. Miller. 1978. "Just World Research and the Attribution Process: Looking Back and Ahead." *Psychological Bulletin,* 85(5):1030-1051.

Lewis, Dan A. and Michael G. Maxfield. 1980. "Fear in the Neighborhoods: An Investigation of the Impact of Crime." Journal of Research in Crime and Delinquency, 17(2):160-189.

Lewis, Dan A. and Greta Salem. 1986. *Fear of Crime: Incivility and the Production of a Social Problem.* New Brunswick, N.J.: Transaction.

Liska, Allen E. and William Baccaglini. 1990. "Feeling Safe by Comparison: Crime in the Newspapers." *Social Problems,* 37:360-374.

Liska, Allen E., Joseph J. Lawrence, and Andrew Sanchirico. 1982. "Fear of Crime as a Social Fact." *Social Forces,* 60(3):760-770.

Liska, Allen E., Andrew Sanchirico, and Mark D. Reed. 1988. "Fear of Crime and Constrained Behavior: Specifying and Estimating a Reciprocal Effects Model." *Social Forces,* 66(3):827-837.

Longmire, Dennis R. 1996. "Americans' Attitudes about the Ultimate Weapon: Capital Punishment." Pp. 93-108 in *Americans View Crime and Justice: A National Public Opinion Survey,* edited by T. Flanagan and D. Longmire. Thousand Oaks, CA: Sage.

MacKuen, Michael Bruce, and Steven Lane Coombs. 1981. *More Than News: Media Power in Public Affairs.* Beverly Hills, CA: Sage.

Macmillan, Ross, Scot Wortley, and John Hagan. 1997."Just Des(s)erts? The Racial Polarization of Perceptions of Criminal Injustice." *Law and Society Review,* 31(4):637-677.

Maguire, Kathleen and Ann L. Pastore, eds. 1995. *Sourcebook of Criminal Justice Statistics - 1994.* Washington, DC: U.S. Government Printing Office.

------. 1996. *Sourcebook of Criminal Justice Statistics - 1995.* Washington, DC: U.S. Government Printing Office.

------. 2000. *Sourcebook of Criminal Justice Statistics.* [Online]. (http://www.albany.edu/sourcebook/).

Mastro, Dana E. and Amanda L. Robinson. 2000. "Cops and Crooks: Images of Minorities on Primetime Television." *Journal of Criminal Justice*, 28(5):385-396.

McCombs, Maxwell E. and Donald L. Shaw. 1972. "The Agenda-Setting Function of Mass Media." *Public Opinion Quarterly*, 36:176-187.

McCorkle, Richard C. 1993. "Research Note: Punish and Rehabilitate? Public Attitudes toward Six Common Crimes." *Crime and Delinquency*, 39(2):240-253.

Mendelberg, Tali. 1997. "Executing Hortons: Racial Crime in the 1988 Presidential Campaign." *Public Opinion Quarterly*, 61:134-157.

Miethe, Terance D. 1982. "Public Consensus on Crime Seriousness: Normative Structure or Methodological Artifact?" *Criminology*, 20(3):515-526.

------. 1984. "Types of Consensus in Public Evaluations of Crime: An Illustration of Strategies for Measuring 'Consensus'." *Journal of Criminal Law and Criminology*, 75(2):459-473.

Miethe, Terance D. and Gary R. Lee. 1984. "Fear of Crime among Older People: A Reassessment of the Predictive Power of Crime-Related Factors." *Sociological Quarterly*, 25:397-415.

Moeller, Gertrude L. 1989. "Fear of Criminal Victimization: The Effects of Neighborhood Racial Composition." *Sociological Inquiry*, 59(2):208-221.

Mohr, Philip B. and Giuseppa Luscri. 1995. "Social Work Orientation and Just World Beliefs." *Journal of Social Psychology*, 135(1):101-103.

Moon, Melissa M., Jody L. Sundt, John Paul Wright, and Francis T. Cullen. 2000. "Is Child Saving Dead? Public Support for Juvenile Rehabilitation." *Crime and Delinquency*, 46:38-60.

Moran, Gary and John Craig Comfort. 1986. "Neither 'Tentative' nor 'Fragmentary': Verdict Preference of Impaneled Felony Jurors as a Function of Attitude toward Capital Punishment." *Journal of Applied Psychology*, 71:146-155.

Nettler, Gynne. 1959. "Cruelty, Dignity, and Determinism." *American Sociological Review*, 24(3):375-384.

Newburn, Tim and Elizabeth A. Stanko. 1994. "When Men Are Victims." in *Just Boys Doing Business? Men, Masculinities and Crime*, edited by T. Newburn and E.A. Stanko. London, England: Routledge.

Newman, Graeme R. and Carol Trilling. 1975. "Public Perceptions of Criminal Behavior: A Review of the Literature." *Criminal Justice and Behavior*, 2(3):217-236.

Norris, Fran H. and Krzysztof Kaniasty. 1994. "Psychological Distress Following Criminal Victimization in the General Population: Cross-Sectional, Longitudinal, and Prospective Analyses." *Journal of Consulting and Clinical Psychology*, 62(1):111-123.

O'Connell, Michael and Anthony Whelan. 1996. "Taking Wrongs Seriously: Public Perceptions of Crime Seriousness." *British Journal of Criminology*, 36(2):299-318.

O'Keefe, Garrett J. and Kathaleen Reid-Nash. 1987. "Crime News and Real-World Blues: The Effects of the Media on Social Reality." *Communication Research,* 14(2):147-168.

Oliver, Mary Beth. 1994. "Portrayals of Crime, Race, and Aggression in 'Reality-Based' Police Shows: A Content Analysis." *Journal of Broadcasting and Electronic Media,* 38:179-192.

Oliver, Mary Beth, and G. Blake Armstrong. 1995. "Predictors of Viewing and Enjoyment of Reality-Based and Fictional Crime Shows." *Journalism & Mass Communication Quarterly,* 72(3):559-570.

------. 1998. "The Color of Crime: Perceptions of Caucasians' and African Americans' Involvement in Crime. Pp. 19-35. in *Entertaining Crime: Television Reality Programs*, edited by M. Fishman and G. Cavender. New York: Aldine de Gruyter.

O'Quin, Karen and Conrad C. Vogler. 1989. "Effects of Just World Beliefs on Perspectives of Crime Perpetrators and Victims." *Social Justice Research,* 3(1):47-56.

Orcutt, James D. and J. Blake Turner. 1993. "Shocking Numbers and Graphic Accounts: Quantified Images of Drug Problems in the Print Media." *Social Problems,* 40(2):190-206.

Ortega, Suzanne T. and Jessie L. Myles. 1987. "Race and Gender Effects on Fear of Crime: An Interactive Model with Age." *Criminology,* 25(1):133-152.

Ouimet, Marc and Edward J. Coyle. 1991. "Fear of Crime and Sentencing Punitiveness: Comparing the General Public and Court Practitioners." *Canadian Journal of Criminology,* 33(2):149-162.

Pain, Rachel H. 1995. "Elderly Women and Fear of Violent Crime: The Least Likely Victims?" *British Journal of Criminology,* 35(4):584-598.

------. 1997. "Whither Women's Fear? Perceptions of Sexual Violence in Public and Private Space." *International Review of Victimology,* 4(4):297-312.

Parisi, Nicolette, Michael Gottfredson, Michael Hindelang, and Timothy Flanagan, eds. 1979. *Sourcebook of Criminal Justice Statistics –1978.* Washington, DC: U.S. Government Printing Office.

Parker, Keith D. and Melvin C. Ray. 1990. "Fear of Crime: An Assessment of Related Factors. *Sociological Spectrum,* 10:29-40.

Potter, W. James. 1986. "Perceived Reality and the Cultivation Hypothesis." *Journal of Broadcasting & Electronic Media,* 30(2):159-174.

Potter, W. James, Misha Vaughn, Ron Warren, Kevin Howley, Art Land, and Jeremy Hagemeyer. 1995. "How Real is the Portrayal of Aggression in Television Entertainment Programming?" *Journal of Broadcast and Electronic Media,* 39:496-516.

Pritchard, David, and Karen D. Hughes. 1997. "Patterns of Deviance in Crime News." *Journal of Communication,* 47(3):49-68.

Rafter, Nicole Hahn. 2000. *Shots in the Mirror.* New York: Oxford University.

Randall, Donna M., Lynette Lee-Simmons, and Paul Hagner. 1988. "Common versus Elite Crime Coverage in Network News." *Social Science Quarterly*, 69:910-929.

Rankin, Joseph. 1979. "Changing Attitudes toward Capital Punishment." *Social Forces*, 58(1):194-211.

Rauma, David. 1991. "The Context of Normative Consensus: An Expansion of the Rossi/Berk Consensus Model, with an Application to Crime Seriousness." *Social Science Research*, 20(1):1-28.

Reeves, Jimmie L. and Richard Campbell. 1994. *Cracked Coverage: Television News, the Anti-Cocaine Crusade, and the Reagan Legacy*. Durham, NC: Duke University.

Reid, Lesley Williams, J. Timmons Roberts, and Heather Monro Hilliard. 1998. "Fear of Crime and Collective Action: An Analysis of Coping Strategies." *Sociological Inquiry*, 68(3):312-328.

Reinarman, Craig and Harry G. Levine. 1997. "The Crack Attack: Politics and Media in the Crack Scare." Pp. 18-51 in *Crack in America: Demon Drugs and Social Justice*, edited by C. Reinarman and H. Levine. Berkeley, CA: University of California.

Reiner, Robert. 1985. *The Politics of the Police*. Brighton, England: Harvester.

------. 1997. "Media Made Criminality: The Representation of Crime in the Mass Media. in *The Oxford Handbook of Criminology, 2nd ed.,* edited by M. Maquire, R. Morgan, & R. Reiner. Oxford, England: Clarendon.

Reith, Margaret. 1999. "Viewing of Crime Drama and Authoritarian Aggression: An Investigation of the Relationship between Crime Viewing, Fear, and Aggression." *Journal of Broadcasting and Electronic Media*, 43(2):211-221.

Rich, Robert F. and Robert J. Sampson. 1990. "Public Perceptions of Criminal Justice Policy: Does Victimization Make a Difference?" *Violence and Victims*, 5(2):109-118.

Riedel, Marc. 1975. "Perceived Circumstances, Inferences of Intent and Judgments of Offense Seriousness." *The Journal of Criminal Law and Criminology*, 66:201-209.

Roberts, Julian V. 1992. "Public Opinion, Crime and Criminal Justice." Pp. 99-180 in *Crime and Justice: A Review of the Research*, vol. 16, edited by M. Tonry. Chicago: University of Chicago.

Roberts, Julian V. and Anthony N. Doob. 1990. "News Media Influences on Public Views of Sentencing." *Law and Human Behavior*, 14(5):451-468.

Roberts, Julian V. and D. Edwards. 1989. "Contextual Effects in Judgments of Crimes, Criminals and the Purposes of Sentencing." *Journal of Applied Social Psychology,* 19:902-917.

Roberts, Julian V. and Robert J. Gebotys. 1989. "The Purposes of Sentencing: Public Support for Competing Aims." *Behavioral Sciences and the Law*, 7(3):387-402.

Roberts, Julian V. and Loretta J. Stalans. 1997. *Public Opinion, Crime and Criminal Justice*. Boulder, CO: Westview Press.

------. 1998. "Crime, Criminal Justice, and Public Opinion. Pp. 31-57 in *The Handbook of Crime & Punishment*, edited by M. Tonry. New York: Oxford University.

Roberts, Julian V., Loretta J. Stalans, David Indermaur, Mike Hough. 2003. *Populism and Public Opinion: Lessons from Five Countries*. New York: Oxford University,

Romer, Daniel, Kathleen H. Jamieson, and Nicole J. de Coteau. 1998. "The Treatment of Persons of Color in Local Television News: Ethnic Blame Discourse or Realistic Group Conflict?" *Communication Research*, 25(3):286-305.

Rossi, Peter H. and Richard A. Berk. 1997. *Just Punishments: Federal Guidelines and Public Views Compared*. New York: Aldine de Gruyter.

Rossi, Peter H., Christine E. Bose, and Richard A. Berk. 1974. "The Seriousness of Crimes: Normative Structure and Individual Differences." *American Sociological Review*, 39:224-237.

Rossi, Peter H., Jon E. Simpson, and JoAnn L. Miller. 1985. "Beyond Crime Seriousness: Fitting the Punishment to the Crime." *Journal of Quantitative Criminology*, 1(1):59-90.

Rotter, Julian B. 1966. "Generalized Expectancies for Internal Versus External Control of Reinforcement." *Psychological Monographs*, 80(1):1-28.

Rountree, Pamela Wilcox, and Kenneth C. Land. 1996. "Perceived Risk versus Fear of Crime: Empirical Evidence of Conceptually Distinct Reactions in Survey Data." *Social Forces*, 74(4):1353-1376.

Rubin, Zick and Anne Peplau. 1973. "Belief in a Just World and Reactions to Another's Lot: A Study of Participation in the National Draft Lottery." *Journal of Social Issues*, 29(4):73-93.

Rubin, Zick and Letitia A. Peplau. 1975. "Who Believes In a Just World?" *Journal of Social Issues*, 31(3):65-89.

Rucker, Robert E. 1990. "Urban Crime: Fear of Victimization and Perceptions of Risk." *Free Inquiry in Creative Sociology*, 18(2):151-160.

Ruiz, Jim and D.F. Treadwell. 2002. "The Perp Walk: Due Process v. Freedom of the Press." *Criminal Justice Ethics*, 21(2):44-56.

Russell, Kathryn K. 1998. *The Color of Crime: Racial Hoaxes, White Fear, Black Protectionism, Police Harassment, and other Macroaggressions*. New York: New York University.

Sacco, Vincent F. 1982. "The Effects of Mass Media on Perceptions of Crime." *Pacific Sociological Review*, 25, 4:475-493.

------. 1995. "Media Constructions of Crime." *The Annals of the American Academy*, 539:141-154.

Samuel, William and Elizabeth Moulds. 1986. "The Effect of Crime Severity on Perceptions of Fair Punishment: A California Case Study." *Journal of Criminal Law and Criminology*, 77:931-948.

Sasson, Theodore. 1995. *Crime Talk: How Citizens Construct a Social Problem*. New York: Aldine de Gruyter.

Scheingold, Stuart A. 1984. *The Politics of Law and Order.* White Plains, NY: Longman.

------. 1995. "The Politics of Street Crime and Criminal Justice." pp. 265-293 in *Crime, Communities, and Public Policy*, edited by L. Joseph. Chicago, IL: University of Chicago.

Schlesinger, Philip and Howard Tumber. 1994. *Reporting Crime: The Media Politics of Criminal Justice.* Oxford, England: Clarendon.

Schlesinger, Philip, Howard Tumber, and Graham Murdock. 1991. "The Media Politics of Crime and Criminal Justice." *British Journal of Sociology*, 42(3):397-420.

Secret, Philip E. and James B. Johnson. 1989. "Racial Differences in Attitudes toward Crime Control." *Journal of Criminal Justice*, 17:361-375.

Sellin, Thorsten and Marvin Wolfgang E. 1964. *The Measurement of Delinquency.* New York: John Wiley.

Seltzer, Rick and Joseph P. McCormick II. 1987. "The Impact of Crime Victimization and Fear of Crime on Attitudes toward Death Penalty Defendants." *Violence and Victims*, 2(2):99-114.

Sheley, Joseph F. and Cindy D. Ashkins. 1981. "Crime News, and Crime Views," *Public Opinion Quarterly*, 45:492-506.

------. 1984 . "Crime, Crime News, and Crime Views." Pp. 124-140 in *Justice and the Media: Issues and Research*, edited by R. Surette. Springfield, IL: Charles C. Thomas.

Sherizen, Sanford. 1978. "Social Creation of Crime News." Pp. 203-224 in *Deviance and Mass Media*, edited by C. Winick. Thousand Oaks, CA: Sage.

Shirlow, Peter and Rachel Pain. 2003. "The Geographies and Politics of Fear." *Capital & Class*, 80:15-26.

Silverman, Robert A. and Leslie W. Kennedy. 1985. "Loneliness, Satisfaction, and Fear of Crime: A Test of Non-Recursive Effects." *Canadian Journal of Criminology*, 27(1):1-13.

Skogan, Wesley G. 1987. "The Impact of Victimization on Fear." *Crime and Delinquency*, 33(1):135-154.

------. 1993. "The Various Meanings of Fear." Pp. 131-140 in *Fear of Crime and Criminal Victimization*, edited by W. Bilsky, C. Pfeiffer and P. Wetzels. Stuttgart, Germany: Ferdinand Enke Verlag.

Skogan, Wesley G. and Michael G. Maxfield. 1981. *Coping with Crime: Individual and Neighborhood Differences.* Beverly Hills, CA: Sage.

Slater, Dan and William R. Elliott. 1982. "Television's Influence on Social Reality." *Quarterly Journal of Speech*, 68:69-79.

Smith, Kevin B. 1985. "Seeing Justice in Poverty: The Belief in a Just World and Ideas about Inequality." *Sociological Spectrum*, 5(1-2):17-29.

Smith, Kevin B. and David N. Green. 1984. "Individual Correlates of the Belief in a Just World." *Psychological Reports*, 52(2):435-438.

Smith, Kevin K., Greg W. Steadman, Todd D. Minton, and Meg Townsend. 1999. "Criminal Victimization and Perceptions of Community Safety in 12 cities [1998]." Bureau of Justice Statistics and the Office of Community Oriented Policing Services, US Department of Justice. NCJ 173940.

Smith, Lynn Newhart and Gary D. Hill. 1991a. "Perceptions of Crime Seriousness and Fear of Crime." *Sociological Focus,* 24(4):315-327.

------. 1991b.:"Victimization and Fear of Crime." *Criminal Justice and Behavior,* 18(2):217-239.

Smith, Michael D. 1988. "Women's Fear of Violent Crime: An Exploratory Test of a Feminist Hypothesis." *Journal of Family Violence,* 3(1):29-38.

Smith, Susan J. 1984. "Crime in the News." *British Journal of Criminology,* 24(3):289-295.

Sorenson, Susan B., Julie G. Peterson Manz, and Richard A. Berk. 1998. "News Media Coverage and the Epidemiology of Homicide." *American Journal of Public Health,* 88(10):1510-1515.

Soss, Joe, Laura Langbein, and Alan R. Metelko. 2003. "Why Do White Americans Support the Death Penalty?" *The Journal of Politics,* 65(2): 397-421.

Sotirovic, Mira. 2001. "Affective and Cognitive Processes as Mediators of Media Influences on Crime-Policy Preferences." *Mass Communication & Society,* 4(3):311-329.

Sparks, Richard. 1992. "Reason and Unreason in 'Left Realism': Some Problems in the Constitution of the Fear of Crime." pp. 119-135 in *Issues in Realist Criminology,* edited by R. Matthews and J. Young. London, England: Sage.

Sprott, Jane B. 1998. "Understanding Public Opposition to a Separate Youth Justice System." *Crime and Delinquency,* 44:399-411.

------. 1999. "Are Members of the Public Tough on Crime?: The Dimensions of Public 'Punitiveness.'" *Journal of Criminal Justice,* 27(5):467-474.

Sprott, Jane B. and Anthony N. Doob. 1997. "Fear, Victimization, and Attitudes to Sentencing, the Courts and the Police." *Canadian Journal of Criminology,* 39(3):275-291.

St. John, Craig and Tamara Heald-Moore. 1995. "Fear of Black Strangers." *Social Science Research,* 24:262-280.

Stafford, Mark C. and Omer P. Galle. 1984. "Victimization Rates, Exposure to Risk, and Fear of Crime." *Criminology,* 22:173-185.

Stalans, Loretta J. and Shari S. Diamond. 1990. "Formation and Change in Lay Evaluations of Criminal Sentencing: Misperceptions and Discontent." *Law and Human Behavior,* 14:199-214.

Stanko, Elizabeth A. 1990. *Everyday Violence.* London, England: Pandora Press.

------. 1995. "Women, Crime, and Fear." *Annals of the American Academy of Political & Social Science,* 539:46-59.

Stark, Steven D. 1987. "Perry Mason Meets Sonny Crockett: The History of Lawyers and the Police as Television Heroes." *University of Miami Law Review*, 42:229-283.

Stinchcombe, Arthur L., Rebecca Adams, Carol A. Heimer, Kim Lane Scheppele, Tom W. Smith, and D. Garth Taylor. 1980. *Crime and Punishment - Changing Attitudes in America.* San Francisco, CA: Jossey-Bass.

Stroman, Carolyn A. and Richard Seltzer. 1985. "Media Use and Perceptions of Crime." *Journalism Quarterly,* 62(2):340-345.

Surette, Ray. 1986. "Television Viewing and Support of Punitive Criminal Justice Policy." *Journalism Quarterly,* 62:373-377.

------. 1992. *Media, Crime, and Criminal Justice: Images and Reality.* Belmont, CA: Wadsworth.

------. 1994. "Predator Criminals as Media Icons." Pp. 131-158 in *Media, Process, and the Social Construction of Crime: Studies of Newsmaking Criminology,* edited by G. Barak. New York: Garland.

------. 1996. "News from Nowhere, Policy to Follow: Media and the Social Construction of 'Three Strikes and You're Out.'" Pp. 177-202 in *Three Strikes and You're Out: Vengeance as Public Policy,* edited by D. Shichor and D. Sechrest. Thousand Oaks, CA: Sage.

------. 1998. *Media, Crime, and Criminal Justice: Images and Reality.* Belmont, CA: Wadsworth.

Taylor, D. Garth, Kim Lane Scheppele, and Arthur L. Stinchcombe. 1979. "Salience of Crime and Support for Harsher Criminal Sanctions." *Social Problems,* 26:413-424.

Taylor, Ralph B. and Jeanette Covington. 1993. "Community Structural Change and Fear of Crime." *Social Problems,* 40:374-395.

Taylor, Ralph B. and Margaret Hale. 1986. "Testing Alternative Models of Fear of Crime." *The Journal of Criminal Law and Criminology,* 77(1):151-189.

Thomas, Charles W., Robin J. Cage, and Samuel C. Foster. 1976. "Public Opinion on Criminal Law and Legal Sanctions: An Examination of Two Conceptual Models." *Journal of Criminal Law and Criminology,* 67: 110-116.

Thomas, Charles W. and Samuel C. Foster. 1975. "A Sociological Perspective on Public Support for Capital Punishment." *American Journal of Orthopsychiatry,* 45(4):641-657.

Thomson, Douglas R. and Anthony J. Ragona. 1987. "Popular Moderation versus Governmental Authoritarianism: An Interactionist View of Public Sentiments Toward Criminal Sanctions." *Crime and Delinquency,* 33: 337-357.

Thompson, Carol Y., William B. Bankston, and Robert L. St. Pierre. 1992. "Parity and Disparity among Three Measure of Fear of Crime: A Research Note." *Deviant Behavior,* 13(4):373-389.

Thompson, Martie P. and Fran H. Norris. 1992. "Crime, Social Status, and Alienation. *American Journal of Community Psychology,* 20(1):970-119.

Tonry, Michael. 1998. "Crime and Punishment in America." Pp. 3-27 in *The Handbook of Crime & Punishment,* edited by M. Tonry. New York: Oxford University.

Tygart, C.E. 1996. "Do Fear of Crime Victimization and/or Ideological Orientation Increase Support For Increased Punishment?" *International Journal of Group Tensions,* 26(4):215-224.

Tyler, Tom R. 1980. "Impact of Directly and Indirectly Experienced Events: The Origin of Crime-Related Judgements and Behavior." *Journal of Personality and Social Psychology,* 47:693-708.

------. 1984. "Assessing the Risk of Crime Victimization: The Integration of Personal Victimization Experience and Socially Transmitted Information." *Journal of Social Issues,* 40:27-38.

Tyler, Tom R. and Robert J. Boeckmann. 1997. "Three Strikes and You Are Out, But Why? The Psychology of Public Support for Punishing Rule Breakers." *Law and Society Review,* 31(2):237-265.

Tyler, Tom R. and Fay Lomax Cook. 1984. "The Mass Media and Judgments of Risk: Distinguishing Impact on Personal and Societal Level Judgments." *Journal of Personality and Social Psychology,* 47(4):693-708.

Tyler, Tom R. and Renee Weber. 1982. "Support for the Death Penalty: Instrumental Response to Crime, or Symbolic Attitude?" *Law and Society Review,* 17(1):21-45.

Van Der Wurff, Adri and Peter Stringer. 1989. "Postvictimization Fear of Crime: Differences in the Perceptions of People and Places." *Journal of Interpersonal Violence,* 4(4):469-481.

Van Dijk, Teun Adrianus. 1993. "Stories and Racism." Pp. 121-142 in *Narrative and Social Control: Critical Perspectives,* edited by D. Mumby. Newbury Park, CA: Sage.

Vidmar, Neil. 1974. "Retributive and Utilitarian Motives and Other Correlates of Canadian Attitudes toward the Death Penalty." *Canadian Psychologist,* 15(4):337-356.

Viney, Wayne, David A. Waldman, and Jacqueline Barchilon. 1982. "Attitudes toward Punishment in Relation to Beliefs in Free Will and Determinism." *Human Relations,* 35(11):939-950.

Vitelli, Romeo and Normal S. Endler. 1993. "Psychological Determinants of Fear of Crime: A Comparison of General and Situational Prediction Models." *Personality and Individual Differences,* 14(1):77-85.

Walker, Monica A. "Measuring Concern about Crime: Some Inter-Racial Comparisons." *British Journal of Criminology,* 34(3):366-378.

Walklate, Sandra. 1997. "Risk and Criminal Victimization: A Modernist Dilemma?" *British Journal of Criminologist,* 37(1):35-45.

------. 1998. "Excavating the Fear of Crime: Fear, Anxiety or Trust?" *Theoretical Criminology,* 2(4):403-418.

Warr, Mark. 1981. "Which Norms of Justice? A Commentary on Hamilton and Rytina." *American Journal of Sociology*, 87(2):433-435.

------. 1982. "The Accuracy of Public Beliefs about Crime." *Criminology*, 20(2):185-204.

------. 1984. "Fear of Victimization: Why Are Women and the Elderly More Afraid?" *Social Science Quarterly*, 65(4):681-702.

------. 1987. "Fear of Victimization and Sensitivity to Risk." *Journal of Quantitative Criminology*, 3(1):29-46.

------. 1989. "What is the Perceived Seriousness of Crimes?" *Criminology*, 27(4):795-821.

------. 1992. "Altruistic Fear of Victimization in Households." *Social Science Quarterly*, 73(4):723-736.

------. 1994. "Public Perceptions and Reactions to Violent Offending and Victimization." Pp. 1-66 in *Understanding and Preventing Violence. Vol. 4: Consequences and Control*, edited by A. J. Reiss, Jr. and J. A. Roth. Washington, D.C.: National Academy Press.

------. 1995. "The Polls-Poll Trends: Public Opinion on Crime and Punishment." *Public Opinion Quarterly*, 59:296-310.

Warr, Mark, Robert F. Meier, and Maynard L. Erickson. 1983. "Norms, Theories of Punishment, and Publicly Preferred Punishments For Crimes." *Sociological Quarterly*, 24(1):75-91.

Weaver, James and Jacob Wakshlag. 1986. "Perceived Vulnerability to Crime, Criminal Victimization Experience, and Television Viewing." *Journal of Broadcasting and Electronic Media*, 30(2):141-158.

Weinrath, Michael and John Gartrell. 1996. "Victimization and Fear of Crime." *Violence and Victims,* 11(3):187-197.

Weisberg, Herbert, John A. Krosnick, and Bruce D. Brown. 1989. *An Introduction to Survey Research and Data Analysis, 2^{nd} Edition.* Glenview, IL: Scott, Foresman and Co.

Welch, Michael, Melissa Fenwick and Meredith Roberts. 1997. "Primary Definitions of Crime and Moral Panic: A Content Analysis of Experts' Quotes in Feature Newspaper Articles on Crime." *Journal of Research in Crime and Delinquency*, 34, 4:474-494.

Whatley, Mark A. 1993. "Belief in a Just World Scale: Unidimensional or Multidimensional?" *Journal of Social Psychology*, 133(4):547-551.

Whitehead, John T., Michael B. Blankenship, and John Paul Wright. 1999. "Elite versus Citizen Attitudes on Capital Punishment: Incongruity between the Public and Policymakers." *Journal of Criminal Justice*, (27)3:249-258.

Williams, Frank P., Marilyn D. McShane, and Ronald L. Akers. 2000. "Worry About Victimization: An Alternative and Reliable Measure for Fear of Crime." *Western Criminal Review*, 2(2). [Online]. (http://wcr.sonoma.edu/v2n2/williams.html)

Williams, Paul and Julie Dickinson. 1993. "Fear of Crime: Read All About It? The Relationship between Newspaper Crime Reporting and Fear of Crime." *British Journal of Criminology*, 33(1):33-56.

Winkel, Frans Willem, and Aldert Vrij. 1990. "Fear of Crime and Mass Media Crime Reports Testing Similarity Hypotheses." *International Review of Victimology*, 1:251-265.

Wortley, Scot. 1996. "Justice For All? Race and Perceptions of Bias in the Ontario Criminal Justice System - A Toronto Survey." *Canadian Journal of Criminology*, 38(4):439-467.

Zatz, Marjorie S. 1987. "Youth Gangs and Crime: The Creation of a Moral Panic." *Contemporary Crises*, 11(2):129-158.

Ziegler, Raphael and David B. Mitchell. 2003. "Aging and Fear of Crime: An Experimental Approach to an Apparent Paradox." *Experimental Aging Research*, 29:173-187.

Zillman, Dolf and Jacob Wakshlag. 1985. "Fear of Victimization and the Appeal of Crime Drama." Pp. 141-155 in *Selective Exposure to Communication*, edited by D. Zillman and J. Bryant. Hillsdale, NJ: Lawrence Erlbaum Associates.

Zimmerman, Sherwood, David J. Van Alstyne, and Christopher S. Dunn. 1988. "The National Punishment Survey and Public Policy Consequences." *Journal of Research in Crime and Delinquency*, 25:120-149.

*1*

# Index